DATA MINING WITH DECISION TREES
Theory and Applications

2nd Edition

SERIES IN MACHINE PERCEPTION AND ARTIFICIAL INTELLIGENCE*

Editors: **H. Bunke** (Univ. Bern, Switzerland)
P. S. P. Wang (Northeastern Univ., USA)

---

*The complete list of the published volumes in the series can be found at
http://www.worldscientific.com/series/smpai

Series in Machine Perception and Artificial Intelligence – Vol. 81

DATA MINING WITH DECISION TREES

Theory and Applications

2nd Edition

Lior Rokach

Ben-Gurion University of the Negev, Israel

Oded Maimon

Tel-Aviv University, Israel

 World Scientific

NEW JERSEY · LONDON · SINGAPORE · BEIJING · SHANGHAI · HONG KONG · TAIPEI · CHENNAI

Published by

World Scientific Publishing Co. Pte. Ltd.

5 Toh Tuck Link, Singapore 596224

USA office: 27 Warren Street, Suite 401-402, Hackensack, NJ 07601

UK office: 57 Shelton Street, Covent Garden, London WC2H 9HE

Library of Congress Cataloging-in-Publication Data
Rokach, Lior.
 Data mining with decision trees : theory and applications / by Lior Rokach (Ben-Gurion
University of the Negev, Israel), Oded Maimon (Tel-Aviv University, Israel). -- 2nd edition.
  pages cm
  Includes bibliographical references and index.
  ISBN 978-9814590075 (hardback : alk. paper) -- ISBN 978-9814590082 (ebook)
  1. Data mining. 2. Decision trees. 3. Machine learning. 4. Decision support systems.
I. Maimon, Oded. II. Title.
  QA76.9.D343R654 2014
  006.3'12--dc23
                                                                2014029799

British Library Cataloguing-in-Publication Data
A catalogue record for this book is available from the British Library.

In-house Editor: Amanda Yun

Typeset by Stallion Press
Email: enquiries@stallionpress.com

Printed in Singapore

Dedicated to our families
in appreciation for their patience and support
during the preparation of this book.

L.R.
O.M.

About the Authors

Lior Rokach is an Associate Professor of Information Systems and Software Engineering at Ben-Gurion University of the Negev. Dr. Rokach is a recognized expert in intelligent information systems and has held several leading positions in this field. His main areas of interest are Machine Learning, Information Security, Recommender Systems and Information Retrieval. Dr. Rokach is the author of over 100 peer reviewed papers in leading journals conference proceedings, patents, and book chapters. In addition, he has also authored six books in the field of data mining.

Professor **Oded Maimon** from Tel Aviv University, previously at MIT, is also the Oracle chair professor. His research interests are in data mining and knowledge discovery and robotics. He has published over 300 papers and ten books. Currently he is exploring new concepts of core data mining methods, as well as investigating artificial and biological data.

Preface for the Second Edition

The first edition of the book, which was published six years ago, was extremely well received by the data mining research and development communities. The positive reception, along with the fast pace of research in the data mining, motivated us to update our book. We received many requests to include the new advances in the field as well as the new applications and software tools that have become available in the second edition of the book. This second edition aims to refresh the previously presented material in the fundamental areas, and to present new findings in the field; nearly quarter of this edition is comprised of new materials.

We have added four new chapters and updated some of the existing ones. Because many readers are already familiar with the layout of the first edition, we have tried to change it as little as possible. Below is the summary of the main alterations:

- The first edition has mainly focused on using decision trees for classification tasks (i.e. classification trees). In this edition we describe how decision trees can be used for other data mining tasks, such as regression, clustering and survival analysis.
- The new addition includes a walk-through-guide for using decision trees software. Specifically, we focus on open-source solutions that are freely available.
- We added a chapter on cost-sensitive active and proactive learning of decision trees since the cost aspect is very important in many domain applications such as medicine and marketing.
- Chapter 16 is dedicated entirely to the field of recommender systems which is a popular research area. Recommender Systems help customers

to choose an item from a potentially overwhelming number of alternative items.

We apologize for the errors that have been found in the first edition and we are grateful to the many readers who have found those. We have done our best to avoid errors in this new edition. Many graduate students have read parts of the manuscript and offered helpful suggestions and we thank them for that.

Many thanks are owed to Elizaveta Futerman. She has been the most helpful assistant in proofreading the new chapters and improving the manuscript. The authors would like to thank Amanda Yun and staff members of World Scientific Publishing for their kind cooperation in writing this book. Moreover, we are thankful to Prof. H. Bunke and Prof. P.S.P. Wang for including our book in their fascinating series on machine perception and artificial intelligence.

Finally, we would like to thank our families for their love and support.

Beer-Sheva, Israel   *Lior Rokach*
Tel-Aviv, Israel   *Oded Maimon*

April 2014

Preface for the First Edition

Data mining is the science, art and technology of exploring large and complex bodies of data in order to discover useful patterns. Theoreticians and practitioners are continually seeking improved techniques to make the process more efficient, cost-effective and accurate. One of the most promising and popular approaches is the use of decision trees. Decision trees are simple yet successful techniques for predicting and explaining the relationship between some measurements about an item and its target value. In addition to their use in data mining, decision trees, which originally derived from logic, management and statistics, are today highly effective tools in other areas such as text mining, information extraction, machine learning, and pattern recognition.

Decision trees offer many benefits:

- Versatility for a wide variety of data mining tasks, such as classification, regression, clustering and feature selection
- Self-explanatory and easy to follow (when compacted)
- Flexibility in handling a variety of input data: nominal, numeric and textual
- Adaptability in processing datasets that may have errors or missing values
- High predictive performance for a relatively small computational effort
- Available in many data mining packages over a variety of platforms
- Useful for large datasets (in an ensemble framework)

This is the first comprehensive book about decision trees. Devoted entirely to the field, it covers almost all aspects of this very important technique.

The book has three main parts:

- Part I presents the data mining and decision tree foundations (including basic rationale, theoretical formulation, and detailed evaluation).
- Part II introduces the basic and advanced algorithms for automatically growing decision trees (including splitting and pruning, decision forests, and incremental learning).
- Part III presents important extensions for improving decision tree performance and for accommodating it to certain circumstances. This part also discusses advanced topics such as feature selection, fuzzy decision trees and hybrid framework.

We have tried to make as complete a presentation of decision trees in data mining as possible. However, new applications are always being introduced. For example, we are now researching the important issue of data mining privacy, where we use a hybrid method of genetic process with decision trees to generate the optimal privacy-protecting method. Using the fundamental techniques presented in this book, we are also extensively involved in researching language-independent text mining (including ontology generation and automatic taxonomy).

Although we discuss in this book the broad range of decision trees and their importance, we are certainly aware of related methods, some with overlapping capabilities. For this reason, we recently published a complementary book "Soft Computing for Knowledge Discovery and Data Mining", which addresses other approaches and methods in data mining, such as artificial neural networks, fuzzy logic, evolutionary algorithms, agent technology, swarm intelligence and diffusion methods.

An important principle that guided us while writing this book was the extensive use of illustrative examples. Accordingly, in addition to decision tree theory and algorithms, we provide the reader with many applications from the real-world as well as examples that we have formulated for explaining the theory and algorithms. The applications cover a variety of fields, such as marketing, manufacturing, and bio-medicine. The data referred to in this book, as well as most of the Java implementations of the pseudo-algorithms and programs that we present and discuss, may be obtained via the Web.

We believe that this book will serve as a vital source of decision tree techniques for researchers in information systems, engineering, computer science, statistics and management. In addition, this book is highly useful to researchers in the social sciences, psychology, medicine, genetics, business intelligence, and other fields characterized by complex data-processing problems of underlying models.

Since the material in this book formed the basis of undergraduate and graduates courses at Ben-Gurion University of the Negev and Tel-Aviv University and it can also serve as a reference source for graduate/ advanced undergraduate level courses in knowledge discovery, data mining and machine learning. Practitioners among the readers may be particularly interested in the descriptions of real-world data mining projects performed with decision trees methods.

We would like to acknowledge the contribution to our research and to the book to many students, but in particular to Dr. Barak Chizi, Dr. Shahar Cohen, Roni Romano and Reuven Arbel. Many thanks are owed to Arthur Kemelman. He has been a most helpful assistant in proofreading and improving the manuscript.

The authors would like to thank Mr. Ian Seldrup, Senior Editor, and staff members of World Scientific Publishing for their kind cooperation in connection with writing this book. Thanks also to Prof. H. Bunke and Prof P.S.P. Wang for including our book in their fascinating series in machine perception and artificial intelligence.

Last, but not least, we owe our special gratitude to our partners, families, and friends for their patience, time, support, and encouragement.

Beer-Sheva, Israel   *Lior Rokach*
Tel-Aviv, Israel   *Oded Maimon*

October 2007

Contents

Chapter 1

Introduction to Decision Trees

1.1 Data Science

Data Science is the discipline of processing and analyzing data for the purpose of extracting valuable knowledge. The term "Data Science" was coined in the 1960's. However, it really took shape only recently when technology has become sufficiently mature.

Various domains such as commerce, medicine and research are applying data-driven discovery and prediction in order to gain some new insights. Google is an excellent example of a company that applies data science on a regular basis. It is well-known that Google tracks user clicks in an attempt to improve the relevance of its search engine results and its ad campaign management.

One of the ultimate goals of data mining is the ability to make predictions about certain phenomena. Obviously, prediction is not an easy task. As the famous quote says, "It is difficult to make predictions, especially about the future" (attributed to Mark Twain and others). Still, we use prediction successfully all the time. For example, the popular YouTube website (also owned by Google) analyzes our watching habits in order to predict which other videos we might like. Based on this prediction, YouTube service can present us with a personalized recommendation which is mostly very effective. In order to roughly estimate the service's efficiency you could simply ask yourself how often watching a video on YouTube lead you to watch a number of similar videos that were recommended to you by the system? Similarly, online social networks (OSN), such as Facebook and LinkedIn, automatically suggest friends and acquaintances that we might want to connect with.

Google Trends enables anyone to view search trends for a topic across regions of the world, including comparative trends of two or more topics.

This service can help in epidemiological studies by aggregating certain search terms that are found to be good indicators of the investigated disease. For example, Ginsberg *et al.* (2008) used search engine query data to detect influenza epidemics. However, a pattern forms when all the flu-related phrases are accumulated. An analysis of these various searches reveals that many search terms associated with flu tend to be popular exactly when flu season is happening.

Many people struggle with the question: What differentiates data science from statistics and consequently, what distinguishes data scientist from statistician? Data science is a holistic approach in the sense that it supports the entire process including data sensing and collection, data storing, data processing and feature extraction, data mining and knowledge discovery. As such, the field of data science incorporates theories and methods from various fields including statistics, mathematics, computer science and particularly, its sub-domains: Artificial Intelligence and information technology.

1.2 Data Mining

Data mining is a term coined to describe the process of shifting through large databases in search of interesting and previously unknown patterns. The accessibility and abundance of data today makes data mining a matter of considerable importance and necessity. The field of data mining provides the techniques and tools by which large quantities of data can be automatically analyzed. Data mining is a part of the overall process of Knowledge Discovery in Databases (KDD) defined below. Some of the researchers consider the term "Data Mining" as misleading, and prefer the term "Knowledge Mining" as it provides a better analogy to gold mining [Klosgen and Zytkow (2002)].

Most of the data mining techniques are based on inductive learning [Mitchell (1997)], where a model is constructed explicitly or implicitly by generalizing from a sufficient number of training examples. The underlying assumption of the inductive approach is that the trained model is applicable to future unseen examples. Strictly speaking, any form of inference in which the conclusions are not deductively implied by the premises can be thought of as an induction.

Traditionally, data collection was regarded as one of the most important stages in data analysis. An analyst (e.g. a statistician or data scientist) would use the available domain knowledge to select the variables that were to be collected. The number of selected variables was usually limited and the collection of their values could be done manually (e.g. utilizing hand-written records or oral interviews). In the case of computer-aided analysis, the analyst had to enter the collected data into a statistical computer package or an electronic spreadsheet. Due to the high cost of data collection, people learned to make decisions based on limited information.

Since the dawn of the Information Age, accumulating and storing data has become easier and inexpensive. It has been estimated that the amount of stored information doubles every 20 months [Frawley *et al.* (1991)]. Unfortunately, as the amount of machine-readable information increases, the ability to understand and make use of it does not keep pace with its growth.

1.3 The Four-Layer Model

It is useful to arrange the data mining domain into four layers. Figure 1.1 presents this model. The first layer represents the target application. Data mining can benefit many applications, such as:

(1) Credit Scoring — The aim of this application is to evaluate the credit worthiness of a potential consumer. Banks and other companies use credit scores to estimate the risk posed by doing a business transaction (such as lending money) with this consumer.

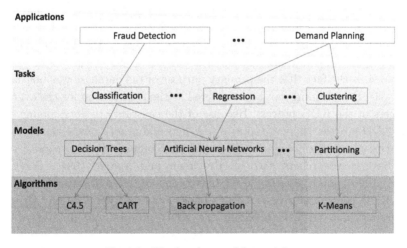

Fig. 1.1   The four layers of data mining.

(2) Fraud Detection — Oxford English Dictionary defines fraud as "An act or instance of deception, an artifice by which the right or interest of another is injured, a dishonest trick or stratagem." Fraud detection aims to identify fraud as quickly as possible once it has been perpetrated.

(3) Churn Detection — This application helps sellers to identify customers with a higher probability of leavingand potentially moving to a competitor. By identifying these customers in advance, the company can act to prevent churning (for example, offering a better deal to the consumer).

Each application is built by accomplishing one or more machine learning tasks. The second layer in our four layers model is dedicated to the machine learning tasks, such as: Classification, Clustering, Anomaly Detection, Regression etc. Each machine learning task can be accomplished by various machine learning models as indicated in the third layer. For example, the classification task can be accomplished by the following two models: Decision Trees or Artificial Neural Networks. In turn, each model can be induced from the training data using various learning algorithms. For example, a decision tree can be built using either C4.5 algorithm or CART algorithm that will be described in the following chapters.

1.4   Knowledge Discovery in Databases (KDD)

KDD process was defined by [Fayyad *et al.* (1996)] as "the nontrivial process of identifying valid, novel, potentially useful, and ultimately understandable patterns in data." Friedman (1997a) considers the KDD process as an automatic exploratory data analysis of large databases. Hand (1998) views it as a secondary data analysis of large databases. The term "Secondary" emphasizes the fact that the primary purpose of the database was not data analysis. Data Mining can be considered as the central step for the overall process of the KDD process. Because of the centrality of data mining for the KDD process, there are some researchers and practitioners who use the term "data mining" as synonymous with the complete KDD process.

Several researchers, such as [Brachman and Anand (1994)], [Fayyad *et al.* (1996)] and [Reinartz (2002)] have proposed different ways of dividing the KDD process into phases. This book adopts a hybridization of these proposals and suggests breaking the KDD process into nine steps as presented in Figure 1.2. Note that the process is iterative at each step, which means that going back to adjust previous steps may be necessary. The

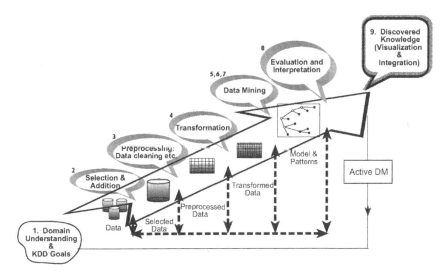

Fig. 1.2   The process of KDD.

process has many "creative" aspects in the sense that one cannot present one formula or make a complete taxonomy for the right choices for each step and application type. Thus, it is necessary to properly understand the process and the different needs and possibilities in each step.

The process starts with determining the goals and "ends" with the implementation of the discovered knowledge. As a result, changes would have to be made in the application domain (such as offering different features to mobile phone users in order to reduce churning). This closes the loop and the effects are then measured on the new data repositories, after which the process is launched again. In what follows is a brief description of the nine-step process, starting with a managerial step:

1. **Developing an understanding of the application domain.** This
   is the initial preparatory step that aims to understand what should
   be done with the many decisions (about transformation, algorithms,
   representation, etc.). The people who are in charge of a data mining
   project need to understand and define the goals of the end-user and the
   environment in which the knowledge discovery process will take place
   (including relevant prior knowledge). As the process proceeds, there
   may be even revisions and tuning of this step. Having understood the
   goals, the preprocessing of the data starts as defined in the next three

steps (note that some of the methods here are similar to Data Mining algorithms, but these are used in the preprocessing context).

2. **Creating a dataset on which discovery will be performed.**
Having defined the goals, the data that will be used for the knowledge discovery should be determined. This step includes finding out what data is available, obtaining additional necessary data and then integrating all the data for the knowledge discovery into one dataset, including the attributes that will be considered for the process. This process is very important because the Data Mining learns and discovers new patterns from the available data. This is the evidence base for constructing the models. If some important attributes are missing, then the entire study may fail. For a successful process it is good to consider as many as possible attributes at this stage. However, collecting, organizing and operating complex data repositories is expensive.

3. **Preprocessing and cleansing.** At this stage, data reliability is enhanced. It includes data clearing, such as handling missing values and removing noise or outliers. It may involve complex statistical methods, or using specific Data Mining algorithm in this context. For example, if one suspects that a certain attribute is not reliable enough or has too much missing data, then this attribute could become the goal of a data mining supervised algorithm. A prediction model for this attribute will be developed and then, the missing value can be replaced with the predicted value. The extent to which one pays attention to this level depends on many factors. Regardless, studying these aspects is important and is often insightful about enterprise information systems.

4. **Data transformation.** At this stage, the generation of better data for the data mining is prepared and developed. One of the methods that can be used here is dimension reduction, such as feature selection and extraction as well as record sampling. Another method that one could use at this stage is attribute transformation, such as discretization of numerical attributes and functional transformation. This step is often crucial for the success of the entire project, but it is usually very project-specific. For example, in medical examinations, it is not the individual aspects/characteristics that make the difference rather, it is the quotient of attributes that often is considered to be the most important factor. In marketing, we may need to consider effects beyond our control as well as efforts and temporal issues such as, studying the effect of advertising accumulation. However, even if we do not use the

right transformation at the beginning, we may obtain a surprising effect that hints to us about the transformation needed. Thus, the process reflects upon itself and leads to an understanding of the transformation needed. Having completed the above four steps, the following four steps are related to the Data Mining part where the focus is on the algorithmic aspects employed for each project.

5. **Choosing the appropriate Data Mining task.** We are now ready to decide which task of Data Mining would fit best our needs, i.e. classification, regression, or clustering. This mostly depends on the goals and the previous steps. There are two major goals in Data Mining: prediction and description. Prediction is often referred to as supervised Data Mining, while descriptive Data Mining includes the unsupervised classification and visualization aspects of Data Mining. Most data mining techniques are based on inductive learning where a model is constructed explicitly or implicitly by generalizing from a sufficient number of training examples. The underlying assumption of the inductive approach is that the trained model is applicable to future cases. The strategy also takes into account the level of meta-learning for the particular set of available data.

6. **Choosing the Data Mining algorithm.** Having mastered the strategy, we are able to decide on the tactics. This stage includes selecting the specific method to be used for searching patterns. For example, in considering precision versus understandability, the former is better with neural networks, while the latter is better with decision trees. Meta-learning focuses on explaining what causes a Data Mining algorithm to be successful or unsuccessful when facing a particular problem. Thus, this approach attempts to understand the conditions under which a Data Mining algorithm is most appropriate.

7. **Employing the Data Mining algorithm.** In this step, we might need to employ the algorithm several times until a satisfied result is obtained. In particular, we may have to tune the algorithm's control parameters such as the minimum number of instances in a single leaf of a decision tree.

8. **Evaluation.** In this stage, we evaluate and interpret the extracted patterns (rules, reliability, etc.) with respect to the goals defined in the first step. This step focuses on the comprehensibility and usefulness of the induced model. At this point, we document the discovered knowledge for further usage.

9. **Using the discovered knowledge.** We are now ready to incorporate
   the knowledge into another system for further action. The knowledge
   becomes active in the sense that we can make changes to the system
   and measure the effects. In fact, the success of this step determines
   the effectiveness of the entire process. There are many challenges in
   this step, such as losing the "laboratory conditions" under which we
   have been operating. For instance, the knowledge was discovered from a
   certain static snapshot (usually a sample) of the data, but now the data
   becomes dynamic. Data structures may change as certain attributes
   become unavailable and the data domain may be modified (e.g. an
   attribute may have a value that has not been assumed before).

1.5 Taxonomy of Data Mining Methods

It is useful to distinguish between two main types of data mining: verification-oriented (the system verifies the user's hypothesis) and
discovery-oriented (the system finds new rules and patterns autonomously).
Figure 1.3 illustrates this taxonomy. Each type has its own methodology.

Discovery methods, which automatically identify patterns in the data,
involve both prediction and description methods. Description methods

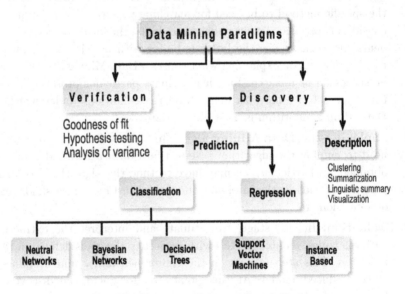

Fig. 1.3   Taxonomy of data mining methods.

focus on understanding the way the underlying data operates while prediction-oriented methods aim to build a behavioral model for obtaining new and unseen samples and for predicting values of one or more variables related to the sample. Some prediction-oriented methods, however, can also contribute to the understanding of the data.

While most of the discovery-oriented techniques use inductive learning as discussed above, verification methods evaluate a hypothesis proposed by an external source, such as expert. These techniques include the most common methods of traditional statistics, like the goodness-of-fit test, the *t*-test of means and analysis of variance. These methods are not as much related to data mining as are their discovery-oriented counterparts because most data mining problems are concerned with selecting a hypothesis (out of a set of hypotheses) rather than testing a known one. While one of the main objectives of data mining is model identification, statistical methods usually focus on model estimation [Elder and Pregibon (1996)].

1.6 Supervised Methods

1.6.1 *Overview*

In the machine learning community, prediction methods are commonly referred to as supervised learning. Supervised learning stands in opposition to unsupervised learning which refers to modeling the distribution of instances in a typical, high-dimensional input space.

According to Kohavi and Provost (1998), the term "unsupervised learning" refers to "learning techniques that group instances without a prespecified dependent attribute". Thus, the term "unsupervised learning" covers only a portion of the description methods presented in Figure 1.3. For instance, the term covers clustering methods but not visualization methods.

Supervised methods are methods that attempt to discover the relationship between input attributes (sometimes called independent variables) and a target attribute (sometimes referred to as a dependent variable). The relationship that is discovered is represented in a structure referred to as a *Model*. Usually, models describe and explain phenomena which are hidden in the dataset and which can be used for predicting the value of the target attribute whenever the values of the input attributes are known. The supervised methods can be implemented in a variety of domains such as marketing, finance and manufacturing.

It is useful to distinguish between two main supervised models: *Classification Models* (*Classifiers*) and *Regression Models*. Regression models map the input space into a real-valued domain. For instance, a regressor can predict the demand for a certain product given its characteristics. Classifiers map the input space into predefined classes. For example, classifiers can be used to classify mortgage consumers as good (full mortgage pay back on time) and bad (delayed pay back). Among the many alternatives for representing classifiers, there are for example, support vector machines, decision trees, probabilistic summaries, algebraic function, etc.

This book deals mainly with classification problems. Along with regression and probability estimation, classification is one of the most studied approaches, possibly one with the greatest practical relevance. The potential benefits of progress in classification are immense since the technique has great impact on other areas, both within data mining and in its applications.

1.7   Classification Trees

While in data mining a decision tree is a predictive model which can be used to represent both classifiers and regression models, in operations research decision trees refer to a hierarchical model of decisions and their consequences. The decision maker employs decision trees to identify the strategy which will most likely reach its goal.

When a decision tree is used for classification tasks, it is most commonly referred to as a classification tree. When it is used for regression tasks, it is called a regression tree.

In this book, we concentrate mainly on classification trees. Classification trees are used to classify an object or an instance (such as insurant) into a predefined set of classes (such as risky/non-risky) based on their attributes values (such as age or gender). Classification trees are frequently used in applied fields such as finance, marketing, engineering and medicine. The classification tree is useful as an exploratory technique. However, it does not attempt to replace existing traditional statistical methods and there are many other techniques that can be used to classify or predict the affiliation of instances with a predefined set of classes, such as artificial neural networks or support vector machines.

Figure 1.4 presents a typical decision tree classifier. This decision tree is used to facilitate the underwriting process of mortgage applications of a certain bank. As part of this process the applicant fills in an application form that includes the following data: number of dependents (DEPEND), loan-to-value ratio (LTV), marital status (MARST), payment-to-income ratio

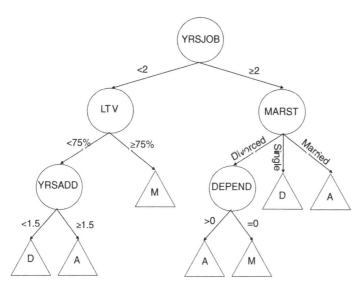

Fig. 1.4   Underwriting decision tree.

(PAYINC), interest rate (RATE), years at current address (YRSADD), and years at current job (YRSJOB).

Based on the above information, the underwriter will decide if the application should be approved for a mortgage. More specifically, this decision tree classifies mortgage applications into one of the following two classes:

- Approved (denoted as "A") — The application should be approved.
- Denied (denoted as "D") — The application should be denied.
- Manual underwriting (denoted as "M") — An underwriter should manually examine the application and decide if it should be approved (in some cases after requesting additional information from the applicant). The decision tree is based on the fields that appear in the mortgage application forms.

The above example illustrates how a decision tree can be used to represent a classification model. In fact, it can be seen as an expert system which partially automates the underwriting process. Moreover, the decision tree can be regarded as an expert system which has been built manually by a knowledge engineer after interrogating an experienced underwriter at the company. This sort of expert interrogation is called knowledge elicitation namely, obtaining knowledge from a human expert (or human experts) to be used by an intelligent system. Knowledge elicitation is usually difficult because it is challenging to find an available expert who would be willing to provide the knowledge engineer with the information he or she needs to create a reliable expert system. In fact, the difficulty inherent in the process is one of the main reasons why companies avoid intelligent systems. This phenomenon constitutes the knowledge elicitation bottleneck.

A decision tree can be also used in order to analyze the payment ethics of customers who received a mortgage. In this case there are two classes:

- Paid (denoted as "P") — The recipient has fully paid off his or her mortgage.
- Not Paid (denoted as "N") — The recipient has not fully paid off his or her mortgage.

This new decision tree can be used to improve the underwriting decision model presented in Figure 16.1. It shows that there are relatively many customers who pass the underwriting process but that they have not yet fully paid back the loan. Note that as opposed to the decision tree presented in Figure 16.1, this decision tree is constructed according to data that was accumulated in the database. Thus, there is no need to manually elicit knowledge. In fact, the tree can be built automatically. This type of knowledge acquisition is referred to as knowledge discovery from databases.

The employment of a decision tree is a very popular technique in data mining. Many researchers argue that decision trees are popular due to their simplicity and transparency. Decision trees are self-explanatory; there is no need to be a data mining expert in order to follow a certain decision tree. Usually, classification trees are graphically represented as hierarchical structures, which renders them easier to interpret than other techniques. If the classification tree becomes complicated (i.e. has many nodes) then its straightforward graphical representation become useless. For complex trees, other graphical procedures should be developed to simplify interpretation.

1.8 Characteristics of Classification Trees

A decision tree is a classifier expressed as a recursive partition of the instance space. The decision tree consists of nodes that form a Rooted Tree, namely, it is a Directed Tree with a node called a "root" that has no incoming edges. All other nodes have exactly one incoming edge. A node with outgoing edges is referred to as an "internal" node or a "test" node. All other nodes are called "leaves" (also known as "terminal" nodes or

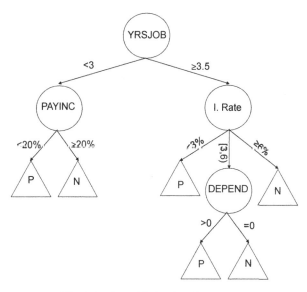

Fig. 1.5   Actual behavior of customer.

"decision" nodes). In a decision tree, each internal node splits the instance space into two or more sub-spaces according to a certain discrete function of the input attributes values. In the simplest and most frequent case, each test considers a single attribute, such that the instance space is partitioned according to the attributes value. In the case of numeric attributes, the condition refers to a range.

Each leaf is assigned to one class representing the most appropriate target value. Alternatively, the leaf may hold a probability vector (affinity vector) indicating the probability of the target attribute having a certain value. Figure 1.6 describes another example of a decision tree that predicts whether or not a potential customer will respond to a direct mailing. Internal nodes are represented as circles, whereas leaves are denoted as triangles. Two or more branches may grow out from each internal node. Each node corresponds with a certain characteristic and the branches correspond with a range of values. These ranges of values must be mutually exclusive and complete. These two properties of *disjointness* and *completeness* are important since they ensure that each data instance is mapped to one instance.

Instances are classified by navigating them from the root of the tree down to a leaf according to the outcome of the tests along the path. We start with a root of a tree; we consider the characteristic that corresponds

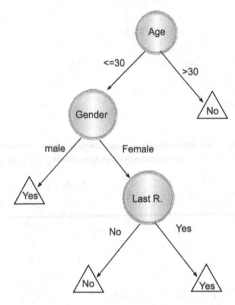

Fig. 1.6   Decision tree presenting response to direct mailing.

to the root and we define to which branch the observed value of the given characteristic corresponds. Then, we consider the node in which the given branch appears. We repeat the same operations for this node until we reach a leaf. Note that this decision tree incorporates both nominal and numeric attributes. Given this classifier the analyst can predict the response of a potential customer (by sorting it down the tree) and understand the behavioral characteristics of the entire population of potential customers regarding direct mailing. Each node is labeled with the attribute it tests, and its branches are labeled with its corresponding values.

In case of numeric attributes, decision trees can be geometrically interpreted as a collection of hyperplanes, each orthogonal to one of the axes.

1.8.1   *Tree Size*

Naturally, decision makers prefer a decision tree that is not complex since it is apt to be more comprehensible. Furthermore, tree complexity has a crucial effect on its accuracy [Breiman *et al.* (1984)]. Typically, the tree complexity is measured by one of the following metrics: the total number of nodes, total number of leaves, tree depth and number of attributes used.

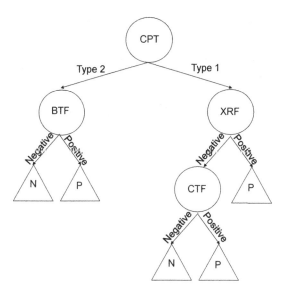

Fig. 1.7 Decision tree for medical applications.

Tree complexity is explicitly controlled by the stopping criteria and the pruning method that are employed.

1.8.2 *The Hierarchical Nature of Decision Trees*

Another characteristic of decision trees is their hierarchical nature. Imagine that you want to develop a medical system for diagnosing patients according to the results of several medical tests. Based on the result of one test, the physician can perform or order additional laboratory tests. Specifically, Figure 1.7 illustrates the diagnosis process using decision trees of patients who suffer from a certain respiratory problem. The decision tree employs the following attributes: CT findings (CTF), X-ray findings (XRF), chest pain type (CPT) and blood test findings (BTF). The physician will order an X-ray if chest pain type is "1". However, if chest pain type is "2", then the physician will not order an X-ray but rather, he or she will order a blood test. Thus, medical tests are performed just when needed and the total cost of medical tests is reduced.

1.9 Relation to Rule Induction

Decision tree induction is closely related to rule induction. Each path from the root of a decision tree to one of its leaves can be transformed into a rule simply by conjoining the tests along the path to form the antecedent part and taking the leaf's class prediction as the class value. For example, one of the paths in Figure 1.6 can be transformed into the rule: "If customer age is less than or equal to 30, and the gender of the customer is male — then the customer will respond to the mail". The resulting rule set can then be simplified to improve its comprehensibility to a human user, and possibly its accuracy [Quinlan (1987)].

Chapter 2

Training Decision Trees

2.1 What is Learning?

The aim of this chapter is to provide an intuitive description of training in decision trees. The main goal of learning is to improve at some task with experience. This goal requires the definition of three components:

(1) Task T that we would like to improve with learning.
(2) Experience E to be used for learning.
(3) Performance measure P that is used to measure the improvement.

In order to better understand the above components, consider the problem of email spam. We all suffer from email spam in which spammers exploit the electronic mail systems to send unsolicited bulk messages. A spam message is any message that the user does not want to receive and did not ask to receive. Machine learning techniques can be used to automatically filter such spam messages. Applying machine learning in this case requires the definition of the above-mentioned components, as follows:

(1) The task T is to identify spam emails.
(2) The experience E is a set of emails that were labeled by users as spams and non-spam (ham).
(3) The performance measure P is the percentage of spam emails that were correctly filtered and the percentage of ham (non-spam) emails that were incorrectly filtered-out.

2.2 Preparing the Training Set

In order to automatically filter spam messages, we need to train a classification model. Obviously, data is very crucial for training the classifier or as Prof. Deming puts it: "In God we trust; all others must bring data".

The data that is used to train the model is called the "training set". In the spam filtering example, a training set, that is represented as a database of previous emails, can be extracted from the past experience. Possible attributes that can be used as indicators for spam activity are: Number of recipients, Size of message, Number of attachments, Number of times the string "re" appears in the subject line, the country from which the email is sent, etc.

The training set is usually represented as a table. Each row represents a single email instance that was delivered via the mail server. Each column corresponds to an attribute that characterizes the email instance (such as the Number of recipients). In any supervised learning task and particularly in classification tasks, one column corresponds to the target attribute that we try to predict. In our example, the target attribute indicates if the email is spam or ham (non-spam). All other columns hold the input attributes that are used for making the predicted classification. There are three main types of input attributes:

(1) Numeric — such as in the case of the attribute "Number of recipients".
(2) Ordinal (or categorical) — that provides an order by which the data can be sorted, but unlike the numeric type there is no notion of distance. For example, the three classes of medal (Gold, Silver and Bronze) can suit an ordinal attribute.
(3) Nominal — in which the values are merely distinct names or labels with no meaningful order by which one can sort the data. For example, the Gender attribute can be referred as a nominal value.

Since in many machine learning algorithms, the training set size and the predictive performance are positively correlated, usually we will prefer to use the largest possible training set. In practice, however, we might want to limit the training set due to resource constraints. Having a large training set implies that the training time will be long as well, therefore we might select a sample of our data to fit our computational resources. Moreover, data collection and particularly labeling the instances may come with a price tag in terms of human effort. In our email filtering example, labeling the training emails as either "spam" or "ham" is done manually by the users and therefore it might be too expensive to label all the emails.

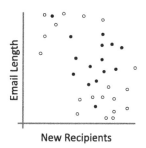

Fig. 2.1   The training set projected onto a two-dimensional graph.

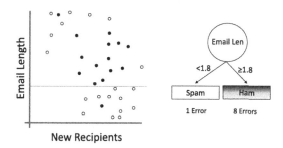

Fig. 2.2   A decision tree (decision stump) based on a horizontal split.

2.3   Training the Decision Tree

For the sake of simplicity, let us simplify the spam filtering task and assume that there are only two numeric input attributes. This allows us to project the training set onto a two-dimensional graph as illustrated in Figure 2.1. The x-axis corresponds to the "New Recipients" attribute and the y-axis corresponds to the "Email Length". Each email instance is represented as a circle. More specifically, spam emails are indicated by a filled circle; ham emails are marked by an empty circle.

A decision tree divides the space into axis-parallel boxes and associates each box with the most frequent label in it. It begins by finding the best horizontal split and the best vertical split (best in the sense of yielding the lowest misclassification rate). Figure 2.2 presents the best horizontal split and its corresponding decision tree. Similarly, Figure 2.3 presents the best vertical split and its corresponding decision tree. A single node decision tree as presented in Figures 2.2 and 2.3 is sometimes called a Decision Stump.

Data Mining with Decision Trees

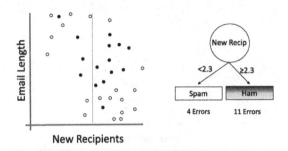

Fig. 2.3 A decision tree (decision stump) based on a vertical split.

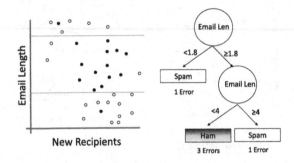

Fig. 2.4 A decision tree obtained after two splits.

Comparing the two trees reveals that the horizontal split leads to 9 misclassification errors (1 misclassification in the left leaf and 8 misclassifications in the right leaf), while the vertical split yields 15 misclassifications. Therefore, by adopting a greedy strategy, we select the former tree and move on to develop the tree's branches. The procedure is recursively applied to each of the resulting branches. Namely, for each branch we try to split the corresponding sub-sample even further as illustrated in Figure 2.4.

Note that the number of classification regions in the graph is equal to the number of leaves in the tree. Moreover, since we are dealing with a binary tree, the amount of internal nodes (i.e. non-leaf nodes) equals the number of leaves minus 1.

Each node continues to branch out until we reach a sub-sample that contains only instances from the same label, or until no further splitting is possible. In the above spam filtering example, the process continues until the graph in Figure 2.5 is reached. Note that there are nine regions in this graph. Each region consists of instances of only one label. Namely, there are no misclassification errors in regard to the training set. However, the

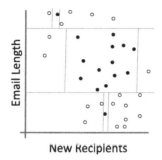

Fig. 2.5 A graph splited to regions with a single label.

corresponding tree is relatively bushy with nine leaves and eight internal nodes.

Complicated decision trees might have a limited generalization capabilities, i.e. although it seems to correctly classify all training instances, it fails to do so in new and unseen instances. As we will see later in Section 4.9, in many cases we should prefer simple trees over complicated ones even if the latter seems to outperform the former in the training set.

In the following chapters, we will provide formal definitions and detailed description of the decision tree learning algorithms.

Chapter 3

A Generic Algorithm for Top-Down Induction of Decision Trees

3.1 Training Set

Before presenting the pseudo code for top-down inducing algorithm of a decision tree, we present several definitions and notations that will be used.

In a typical supervised learning scenario, a training set is given and the goal is to form a description that can be used to predict previously unseen examples.

In many machine learning algorithms, the training set size and the classification accuracy are positively correlated. In particular, the predictive performance of a decision tree is expected to be poor if the training set used to train the model is too small. Moreover, the size of a classification tree is strongly correlated to the training set size. This phenomenon can be explained by the fact that in most decision trees algorithms (such as CART and C4.5) the number of leaves is bounded by the number of instances (as you can't split a node if you don't have enough instances).

The training set can be described in a variety of ways. Most frequently, it is described as a bag instance of a certain bag schema. A bag instance is a collection of tuples (also known as records, rows or instances) that may contain duplicates. Each tuple is described by a vector of attribute values. The bag schema provides the description of the attributes and their domains. In this book, a bag schema is denoted as $B(A \cup y)$ where A denotes the set of input attributes containing n attributes: $A = \{a_1, \ldots, a_i, \ldots, a_n\}$ and y represents the class variable or the target attribute.

Attributes (sometimes called field, variable or feature) are typically one of two types: nominal (values are members of an unordered set), or numeric (values are real numbers). In attribute a_i, it is useful to denote its domain values by $dom(a_i) = \{v_{i,1}, v_{i,2}, \ldots, v_{i,|dom(a_i)|}\}$, where

$|dom(a_i)|$ stands for its finite cardinality. In a similar way, $dom(y) = \{c_1, \ldots, c_{|dom(y)|}\}$ represents the domain of the target attribute. Numeric attributes have infinite cardinalities.

The instance space (the set of all possible examples) is defined as a Cartesian product of all the input attributes domains: $X = dom(a_1) \times dom(a_2) \times \ldots \times dom(a_n)$. The universal instance space (or the *labeled instance space*) U is defined as a Cartesian product of all input attribute domains and the target attribute domain, i.e.: $U = X \times dom(y)$.

The training set is a bag instance consisting of a set of m tuples. Formally, the training set is denoted as $S(B) = (\langle x_1, y_1 \rangle, \ldots, \langle x_m, y_m \rangle)$ where $x_q \in X$ and $y_q \in dom(y)$.

Usually, it is assumed that the training set tuples are generated randomly and independently according to some fixed and unknown joint probability distribution D over U. Note that this is a generalization of the deterministic case when a supervisor classifies a tuple using a function $y = f(x)$.

This book uses the common notation of bag algebra to present projection (π) and selection (σ) of tuples. For example, given the dataset S presented in Table 3.1, the expression $\pi_{a_2, a_3} \sigma_{a_1 = \text{``}Yes\text{''}\ AND\ a_4 > 6} S$ corresponds with the dataset presented in Table 3.2.

Table 3.1 Illustration of a dataset S with five attributes.

a_1	a_2	a_3	a_4	y
Yes	17	4	7	0
No	81	1	9	1
Yes	17	4	9	0
No	671	5	2	0
Yes	1	123	2	0
Yes	1	5	22	1
No	6	62	1	1
No	6	58	54	0
No	16	6	3	0

Table 3.2 The result of the expression $\pi_{a_2, a_3} \sigma_{a_1 = \text{``}Yes\text{''}\ AND_{a_4 > 6}} S$ based on Table 3.1.

a_2	a_3
17	4
17	4
1	5

3.2 Definition of the Classification Problem

The machine learning community was among the first to introduce the problem of *concept learning*. Concepts are mental categories for objects, events, or ideas that have a common set of features. According to Mitchell (1997): "each concept can be viewed as describing some subset of objects or events defined over a larger set" (e.g. the subset of a vehicle that constitutes trucks). To learn a concept is to infer its general definition from a set of examples. This definition may be either explicitly formulated or left implicit, but either way it assigns each possible example to the concept or not. Thus, a concept can be regarded as a function from the instance space to the Boolean set, namely: $c : X \to \{-1, 1\}$. Alternatively, one can refer a concept c as a subset of X, namely: $\{x \in X : c(x) = 1\}$. A *concept class C* is a set of concepts.

To learn a concept is to infer its general definition from a set of examples. This definition may be either explicitly formulated or left implicit, but either way it assigns each possible example to the concept or not. Thus, a concept can be formally regarded as a function from the set of all possible examples to the Boolean set {True, False}.

Other communities, such as the KDD community, prefer to deal with a straightforward extension of *concept learning*, known as the *classification task*. In this case, we search for a function that maps the set of all possible examples into a predefined set of class labels which are not limited to the Boolean set. Most frequently, the goal of the classifiers inducers is formally defined as:

Given a training set S with input attributes set $A = \{a_1, a_2, \ldots, a_n\}$ and a nominal target attribute y from an unknown fixed distribution D over the labeled instance space, the goal is to induce an optimal classifier with minimum generalization error.

The generalization error is defined as the misclassification rate over the distribution D. In case of the nominal attributes, it can be expressed as:

$$\varepsilon(DT(S), D) = \sum_{\langle x, y \rangle \in U} D(x, y) \cdot L(y, DT(S)(x)), \qquad (3.1)$$

where $L(y, DT(S)(x))$ is the zero one loss function defined as:

$$L(y, DT(S)(x)) = \begin{cases} 0 & \text{if } y = DT(S)(x) \\ 1 & \text{if } y \neq DT(S)(x) \end{cases}. \qquad (3.2)$$

In case of numeric attributes the sum operator is replaced with the integration operator.

Table 3.3   An illustration of direct mailing dataset.

Age	Gender	Last Reaction	Buy
35	Male	Yes	No
26	Female	No	No
22	Male	Yes	Yes
63	Male	No	Yes
47	Female	No	No
54	Male	No	No
27	Female	Yes	Yes
38	Female	No	Yes
42	Female	Yes	Yes
19	Male	No	No

Consider the training set in Table 3.3 containing data about 10 customers. Each customer is characterized by three attributes: Age, Gender and Last Reaction (an indication whether the customer has positively responded to the last previous direct mailing campaign). The last attribute ("Buy") describes whether that customer was willing to purchase a product in the current campaign. The goal is to induce a classifier that most accurately classifies a potential customer to "Buyers" and "Non-Buyers" in the current campaign, given the attributes: Age, Gender, Last Reaction.

3.3   Induction Algorithms

An *induction algorithm*, or more concisely an *inducer* (also known as learner), is an entity that obtains a training set and forms a model that generalizes the relationship between the input attributes and the target attribute. For example, an inducer may take as an input specific training tuples with the corresponding class label, and produce a *classifier*.

The notation DT represents a decision tree inducer and $DT(S)$ represents a classification tree which was induced by performing DT on a training set S. Using $DT(S)$, it is possible to predict the target value of a tuple x_q. This prediction is denoted as $DT(S)(x_q)$.

Given the long history and recent growth of the machine learning field, it is not surprising that several mature approaches to induction are now available to the practitioner.

3.4   Probability Estimation in Decision Trees

The classifier generated by the inducer can be used to classify an unseen tuple either by explicitly assigning it to a certain class (crisp classifier) or by providing a vector of probabilities representing the conditional probability of the given instance to belong to each class (probabilistic classifier). Inducers that can construct probabilistic classifiers are known as probabilistic inducers. In decision trees, it is possible to estimate the conditional probability $\hat{P}_{DT(S)}(y = c_j | a_i = x_{q,i} ; i = 1, \ldots, n)$ of an observation x_q. Note the addition of the "hat" — ^ — to the conditional probability estimation is used for distinguishing it from the actual conditional probability.

In classification trees, the probability is estimated for each leaf separately by calculating the frequency of the class among the training instances that belong to the leaf.

Using the frequency vector as is, will typically over-estimate the probability. This can be problematic especially when a given class never occurs in a certain leaf. In such cases we are left with a zero probability. There are two known corrections for the simple probability estimation which avoid this phenomenon. The following sections describe these corrections.

3.4.1 *Laplace Correction*

According to Laplace's law of succession [Niblett (1987)], the probability of the event $y = c_i$ where y is a random variable and c_i is a possible outcome of y which has been observed m_i times out of m observations is:

$$\frac{m_i + k p_a}{m + k}, \tag{3.3}$$

where p_a is an *a priori* probability estimation of the event and k is the equivalent sample size that determines the weight of the *a priori* estimation relative to the observed data. According to [Mitchell (1997)], k is called "equivalent sample size" because it represents an augmentation of the m actual observations by additional k virtual samples distributed according to p_a. The above ratio can be rewritten as the weighted average of the *a priori* probability and *a posteriori* probability (denoted as p_p):

$$\begin{aligned}
&\frac{m_i + k \cdot p_a}{m + k} \\
&= \frac{m_i}{m} \cdot \frac{m}{m + k} + p_a \cdot \frac{k}{m + k} \\
&= p_p \cdot \frac{m}{m + k} + p_a \cdot \frac{k}{m + k} \\
&= p_p \cdot w_1 + p_a \cdot w_2.
\end{aligned} \tag{3.4}$$

In the case discussed here, the following correction is used:

$$\hat{P}_{Laplace}(a_i = x_{q,i} \,|\, y = c_j) = \frac{|\sigma_{y=c_j \, AND \, a_i = x_{q,i}} S| + k \cdot p}{|\sigma_{y=c_j} S| + k}. \tag{3.5}$$

In order to use the above correction, the values of p and k should be selected. It is possible to use $p = 1/ |dom(y)|$ and $k = |dom(y)|$. Some are using $k = 2$ and $p = 1/2$ in any case even if $|dom(y)| > 2$ in order to emphasize the fact that the estimated event is always compared to the opposite event, while others are using $k = |dom(y)| / |S|$ and $p = 1/ |dom(y)|$.

3.4.2   *No Match*

According to Clark and Niblett (1989), only zero probabilities are corrected and replaced by the following value: $p_a/|S|$. Kohavi *et al.* (1997) suggest using $p_a = 0.5$. They also empirically compared the Laplace correction and the no-match correction and indicate that there is no significant difference between them. However, both of them are significantly better than not performing any correction at all.

3.5   Algorithmic Framework for Decision Trees

Decision tree inducers are algorithms that automatically construct a decision tree from a given dataset. Typically, the goal is to find the optimal decision tree by minimizing the generalization error. However, other target functions can be also defined, for instance, minimizing the number of nodes or minimizing the average depth of the tree.

Induction of an optimal decision tree from a given data is considered to be a difficult task. Hancock *et al.* (1996) have shown that finding a minimal decision tree consistent with the training set is NP-hard while Hyafil and Rivest (1976) have demonstrated that constructing a minimal binary tree with respect to the expected number of tests required for classifying an unseen instance is NP-complete. Even finding the minimal equivalent decision tree for a given decision tree [Zantema and Bodlaender (2000)] or building the optimal decision tree from decision tables is known to be NP-hard [Naumov (1991)].

These results indicate that using optimal decision tree algorithms is feasible only in small problems. Consequently, heuristics methods are required for solving the problem. Roughly speaking, these methods can be divided into two groups: top-down and bottom-up with clear preference in the literature to the first group.

There are various top-down decision trees inducers such as ID3 [Quinlan (1986)], C4.5 [Quinlan (1993)], CART [Breiman *et al.* (1984)]. Some inducers consist of two conceptual phases: Growing and Pruning (C4.5 and CART). Other inducers perform only the growing phase.

Figure 3.1 presents a typical pseudo code for a top-down inducing algorithm of a decision tree using growing and pruning. Note that these

---

TreeGrowing $(S, A, y, SplitCriterion, StoppingCriterion)$

Where:

S - Training Set

A - Input Feature Set

y - Target Feature

$SplitCriterion$ — the method for evaluating a certain split

$StoppingCriterion$ — the criteria to stop the growing process

Create a new tree T with a single root node.

IF $StoppingCriterion(S)$ THEN

    Mark T as a leaf with the most

    common value of y in S as a label.

ELSE

    $\forall a_i \in A$ find a that obtain the best $SplitCriterion(a_i, S)$.

    Label t with a

    FOR each outcome v_i of a:

        Set $Subtree_i$ ■ TreeGrowing $(\sigma_{a=v_i} S, A, y)$.

        Connect the root node of t_T to $Subtree_i$ with

                an edge that is labeled as v_i

    END FOR

END IF

RETURN TreePruning (S, T, y)

TreePruning (S, T, y)

Where:

S - Training Set

y - Target Feature

T - The tree to be pruned

DO

    Select a node t in T such that pruning it

        maximally improve some evaluation criteria

    IF $t \neq \emptyset$ THEN $T = pruned(T, t)$

UNTIL $t = \emptyset$

RETURN T

Fig. 3.1   Top-down algorithmic framework for decision trees induction.

algorithms are greedy by nature and construct the decision tree in a top-down, recursive manner (also known as divide and conquer). In each iteration, the algorithm considers the partition of the training set using the outcome of discrete input attributes. The selection of the most appropriate attribute is made according to some splitting measures. After the selection of an appropriate split, each node further subdivides the training set into smaller subsets, until a stopping criterion is satisfied.

3.6   Stopping Criteria

The growing phase continues until a stopping criterion is triggered. The following conditions are common stopping rules:

(1) All instances in the training set belong to a single value of y.
(2) The maximum tree depth has been reached.
(3) The number of cases in the terminal node is less than the minimum number of cases for parent nodes.
(4) If the node were split, the number of cases in one or more child nodes would be less than the minimum number of cases for child nodes.
(5) The best splitting criterion is not greater than a certain threshold.

Chapter 4

Evaluation of Classification Trees

4.1 Overview

An important problem in the KDD process is the development of efficient indicators for assessing the quality of the analysis results. In this chapter, we introduce the main concepts and quality criteria in decision trees evaluation.

Evaluating the performance of a classification tree is a fundamental aspect of machine learning. As stated above, the decision tree inducer receives a training set as input and constructs a classification tree that can classify an unseen instance. Both the classification tree and the inducer can be evaluated using evaluation criteria. The evaluation is important for understanding the quality of the classification tree and for refining parameters in the KDD iterative process.

While there are several criteria for evaluating the predictive performance of classification trees, other criteria such as the computational complexity or the comprehensibility of the generated classifier can be important as well.

4.2 Generalization Error

Let $DT(S)$ represent a classification tree trained on dataset S. The generalization error of $DT(S)$ is its probability to misclassify an instance selected according to the distribution D of the labeled instance space. The *classification accuracy* of a classification tree is one minus the generalization error. The *training error* is defined as the percentage of examples in the training set correctly classified by the classification tree, formally:

$$\hat{\varepsilon}(DT(S), S) = \sum_{\langle x,y \rangle \in S} L(y, DT(S)(x)), \qquad (4.1)$$

where $L(y, DT(S)(x))$ is the zero-one loss function defined in Equation (3.2).

In this book, classification accuracy is the primary evaluation criterion for experiments.

Although generalization error is a natural criterion, its actual value is known only in rare cases (mainly synthetic cases). The reason for that is that the distribution D of the labeled instance space is not known.

One can take the training error as an estimation of the generalization error. However, using the training error as is will typically provide an optimistically biased estimate, especially if the inducer *overfits* the training data. There are two main approaches for estimating the generalization error: Theoretical and Empirical. In this book, we utilize both approaches.

4.2.1   *Theoretical Estimation of Generalization Error*

A low training error does not guarantee low generalization error. There is often a trade-off between the training error and the confidence assigned to the training error as a predictor for the generalization error, measured by the difference between the generalization and training errors. The capacity of the inducer is a major factor in determining the degree of confidence in the training error. In general, the capacity of an inducer indicates the variety of classifiers it can induce. The VC-dimension presented below can be used as a measure of the inducers capacity.

Decision trees with many nodes, relative to the size of the training set, are likely to obtain a low training error. On the other hand, they might just be memorizing or overfitting the patterns and hence exhibit a poor generalization ability. In such cases, the low error is likely to be a poor predictor of the higher generalization error. When the opposite occurs, that is to say, when capacity is too small for the given number of examples, inducers may underfit the data, and exhibit both poor training and generalization error.

In "Mathematics of Generalization", Wolpert (1995) discusses four theoretical frameworks for estimating the generalization error: PAC, VC, Bayesian, and statistical physics. All these frameworks combine the training error (which can be easily calculated) with some penalty function expressing the capacity of the inducers.

4.2.2   *Empirical Estimation of Generalization Error*

Another approach for estimating the generalization error is the holdout method in which the given dataset is randomly partitioned into two sets:

training and test sets. Usually, two-thirds of the data is considered for the training set and the remaining data are allocated to the test set. First, the training set is used by the inducer to construct a suitable classifier and then we measure the misclassification rate of this classifier on the test set. This test set error usually provides a better estimation of the generalization error than the training error. The reason for this is the fact that the training error usually under-estimates the generalization error (due to the overfitting phenomena). Nevertheless, since only a proportion of the data is used to derive the model, the estimate of accuracy tends to be pessimistic.

A variation of the holdout method can be used when data is limited. It is common practice to resample the data, that is, partition the data into training and test sets in different ways. An inducer is trained and tested for each partition and the accuracies averaged. By doing this, a more reliable estimate of the true generalization error of the inducer is provided.

Random subsampling and n-fold cross-validation are two common methods of resampling. In random subsampling, the data is randomly partitioned several times into disjoint training and test sets. Errors obtained from each partition are averaged. In n-fold cross validation, the data is randomly split into n mutually exclusive subsets of approximately equal size. An inducer is trained and tested n times; each time it is tested on one of the k folds and trained using the remaining $n - 1$ folds.

The cross-validation estimate of the generalization error is the overall number of misclassifications divided by the number of examples in the data. The random subsampling method has the advantage that it can be repeated an indefinite number of times. However, a disadvantage is that the test sets are not independently drawn with respect to the underlying distribution of examples. Because of this, using a t-test for paired differences with random subsampling can lead to an increased chance of type I error, i.e. identifying a significant difference when one does not actually exist. Using a t-test on the generalization error produced on each fold lowers the chances of type I error but may not give a stable estimate of the generalization error. It is common practice to repeat n-fold cross-validation n times in order to provide a stable estimate. However, this, of course, renders the test sets non-independent and increases the chance of type I error. Unfortunately, there is no satisfactory solution to this problem. Alternative tests suggested by Dietterich (1998) have a low probability of type I error but a higher chance of type II error, that is, failing to identify a significant difference when one does actually exist.

Stratification is a process often applied during random subsampling and n-fold cross-validation. Stratification ensures that the class distribution from the whole dataset is preserved in the training and test sets. Stratification has been shown to help reduce the variance of the estimated error especially for datasets with many classes.

Another cross-validation variation is the bootstraping method which is a n-fold cross-validation, with n set to the number of initial samples. It samples the training instances uniformly with replacement and leave-one-out. In each iteration, the classifier is trained on the set of $n-1$ samples that is randomly selected from the set of initial samples, S. The testing is performed using the remaining subset.

4.2.3 *Alternatives to the Accuracy Measure*

Accuracy is not a sufficient measure for evaluating a model with an imbalanced distribution of the class. There are cases where the estimation of an accuracy rate may mislead one about the quality of a derived classifier. In such circumstances, where the dataset contains significantly more majority class than minority class instances, one can always select the majority class and obtain good accuracy performance. Therefore, in these cases, the sensitivity and specificity measures can be used as an alternative to the accuracy measures [Han and Kamber (2001)].

Sensitivity (also known as recall) assesses how well the classifier can recognize positive samples and is defined as

$$Sensitivity = \frac{true\_positive}{positive}, \qquad (4.2)$$

where *true_positive* corresponds to the number of the true positive samples and positive is the number of positive samples.

Specificity measures how well the classifier can recognize negative samples. It is defined as

$$Specificity = \frac{true\_negative}{negative}, \qquad (4.3)$$

where *true_negative* corresponds to the number of the true negative examples and negative the number of samples that is negative.

Another well-known performance measure is precision. Precision measures how many examples classified as "positive" class are indeed "positive". This measure is useful for evaluating crisp classifiers that are used to classify an entire dataset. Formally:

$$Precision = \frac{true\_positive}{true\_positive + false\_positive}. \qquad (4.4)$$

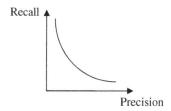

Fig. 4.1   A typical precision-recall diagram.

Based on the above definitions, the *accuracy* can be defined as a function of *sensitivity* and *specificity*:

$$Accuracy = Sensitivity \cdot \frac{positive}{positive+negative} + Specificity \cdot \frac{negative}{positive+negative}. \qquad (4.5)$$

4.2.4   *The F-Measure*

Usually, there is a tradeoff between the precision and recall measures. Trying to improve one measure often results in a deterioration of the second measure. Figure 4.1 illustrates a typical precision-recall graph. This two-dimensional graph is closely related to the well-known receiver operating characteristics (ROC) graphs in which the true positive rate (recall) is plotted on the Y-axis and the false positive rate is plotted on the X-axis [Ferri *et al.* (2002)]. However, unlike the precision-recall graph, the ROC diagram is always convex.

Given a probabilistic classifier, this trade-off graph may be obtained by setting different threshold values. In a binary classification problem, the classifier prefers the class "not pass" over the class "pass" if the probability for "not pass" is at least 0.5. However, by setting a different threshold value other than 0.5, the trade-off graph can be obtained.

The problem here can be described as multi-criteria decision-making (MCDM). The simplest and the most commonly used method to solve MCDM is the weighted sum model. This technique combines the criteria into a single value by using appropriate weighting. The basic principle behind this technique is the additive utility assumption. The criteria measures must be numerical, comparable and expressed in the same unit. Nevertheless, in the case discussed here, the arithmetic mean can mislead. Instead, the harmonic mean provides a better notion of "average". More specifically, this measure is defined as [Van Rijsbergen (1979)]:

$$F = \frac{2 \cdot P \cdot R}{P + R}. \qquad (4.6)$$

Actual

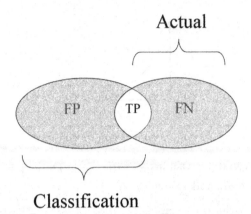

Classification

Fig. 4.2   A graphic explanation of the F-measure.

The intuition behind the F-measure can be explained using Figure 4.2. Figure 4.2 presents a diagram of a common situation in which the right ellipsoid represents the set of all defective batches and the left ellipsoid represents the set of all batches that were classified as defective by a certain classifier. The intersection of these sets represents the true positive (TP), while the remaining parts represent false negative (FN) and false positive (FP). An intuitive way of measuring the adequacy of a certain classifier is to measure to what extent the two sets match, namely, to measure the size of the unshaded area. Since the absolute size is not meaningful, it should be normalized by calculating the proportional area. This value is the F-measure:

$$\text{Proportion of unshaded area} = \frac{2 \cdot (True\ Positive)}{False\ Positive + False\ Negative + 2 \cdot (True\ Positve)} = F. \qquad (4.7)$$

The F-measure can have values between 0 to 1. It obtains its highest value when the two sets presented in Figure 4.2 are identical and it obtains its lowest value when the two sets are mutually exclusive. Note that each point on the precision-recall curve may have a different F-measure. Furthermore, different classifiers have different precision-recall graphs.

4.2.5 *Confusion Matrix*

The confusion matrix is used as an indication of the properties of a classification (discriminant) rule. It contains the number of elements that have been correctly or incorrectly classified for each class. We can see on its main diagonal the number of observations that have been correctly classified

Table 4.1   A confusion matrix.

	Predicted negative	Predicted positive
Negative Examples	A	B
Positive Examples	C	D

for each class; the off-diagonal elements indicate the number of observations that have been incorrectly classified. One benefit of a confusion matrix is that it is easy to see if the system is confusing two classes (i.e. commonly mislabeling one as an other).

For every instance in the test set, we compare the actual class to the class that was assigned by the trained classifier. A positive (negative) example that is correctly classified by the classifier is called a TP (true negative); a positive (negative) example that is incorrectly classified is called a false negative (false positive). These numbers can be organized in a confusion matrix shown in Table 4.1.

Based on the values in Table 4.1, one can calculate all the measures defined above:

- Accuracy is: $(a + d)/(a + b + c + d)$
- Misclassification rate is: $(b + c)/(a + b + c + d)$
- Precision is: $d/(b + d)$
- True positive rate (Recall) is: $d/(c + d)$
- False positive rate is: $b/(a + b)$
- True negative rate (Specificity) is: $a/(a + b)$
- False negative rate is: $c/(c + d)$

4.2.6 *Classifier Evaluation under Limited Resources*

The above-mentioned evaluation measures are insufficient when probabilistic classifiers are used for choosing objects to be included in a limited quota. This is a common situation that arises in real-life applications due to resource limitations that require cost-benefit considerations. Resource limitations prevent the organization from choosing all the instances. For example, in direct marketing applications, instead of mailing everybody on the list, the marketing efforts must implement a limited quota, i.e. target the mailing audience with the highest probability of positively responding to the marketing offer without exceeding the marketing budget.

Another example deals with a security officer in an air terminal. Following September 11, the security officer needs to search all passengers who may be carrying dangerous instruments (such as scissors, penknives and shaving blades). For this purpose the officer is using a classifier that is capable of classifying each passenger either as class A, which means, "Carry dangerous instruments" or as class B, "Safe".

Suppose that searching a passenger is a time-consuming task and that the security officer is capable of checking only 20 passengers prior to each flight. If the classifier has labeled exactly 20 passengers as class A, then the officer will check all these passengers. However, if the classifier has labeled more than 20 passengers as class A, then the officer is required to decide which class A passenger should be ignored. On the other hand, if less than 20 people were classified as A, the officer, who must work constantly, has to decide who to check from those classified as B after he has finished with the class A passengers.

There are also cases in which a quota limitation is known to exist but its size is not known in advance. Nevertheless, the decision maker would like to evaluate the expected performance of the classifier. Such cases occur, for example, in some countries regarding the number of undergraduate students that can be accepted to a certain department in a state university. The actual quota for a given year is set according to different parameters including governmental budget. In this case, the decision maker would like to evaluate several classifiers for selecting the applicants while not knowing the actual quota size. Finding the most appropriate classifier in advance is important because the chosen classifier can dictate what the important attributes are, i.e. the information that the applicant should provide the registration and admission unit.

In probabilistic classifiers, the above-mentioned definitions of precision and recall can be extended and defined as a function of a probability threshold τ. If we evaluate a classifier based on a given test set which consists of n instances denoted as $(<x_1, y_1>, \ldots, <x_n, y_n>)$ such that x_i represents the input features vector of instance i and y_i represents its true class ("positive" or "negative"), then:

$$\text{Precision } (\tau) = \frac{|\{<x_i, y_i>: \hat{P}_{DT}(pos|x_i) > \tau, y_i = pos\}|}{|\{<x_i, y_i>: \hat{P}_{DT}(pos|x_i) > \tau|}, \quad (4.8)$$

$$\text{Recall } (\tau) = \frac{|\{<x_i, y_i>: \hat{P}_{DT}(pos|x_i) > \tau, y_i = pos\}|}{|\{<x_i, y_i>: y_i = pos\}|}, \quad (4.9)$$

where DT represents a probabilistic classifier that is used to estimate the conditional likelihood of an observation x_i to "positive" which is denoted as

$\hat{P}_{DT}(pos|x_i)$. The typical threshold value of 0.5 means that the predicted probability of "positive" must be higher than 0.5 for the instance to be predicted as "positive". By changing the value of τ, one can control the number of instances that are classified as "positive". Thus, the τ value can be tuned to the required quota size. Nevertheless, because there might be several instances with the same conditional probability, the quota size is not necessarily incremented by one.

The above discussion is based on the assumption that the classification problem is binary. In cases where there are more than two classes, adaptation could be easily made by comparing one class to all the others.

4.2.6.1 *ROC Curves*

Another measure is the ROC curves which illustrate the tradeoff between true positive to false positive rates [Provost and Fawcett (1998)]. Figure 4.3 illustrates a ROC curve in which the X-axis represents a false positive rate and the Y-axis represents a true positive rate. The ideal point on the ROC curve would be (0,100), that is, all positive examples are classified correctly and no negative examples are misclassified as positive.

The ROC convex hull can also be used as a robust method of identifying potentially optimal classifiers [Provost and Fawcett (2001)]. Given a family of ROC curves, the ROC convex hull can include points that are more towards the north-west frontier of the ROC space. If a line passes through a point on the convex hull, then there is no other line with the same slope passing through another point with a larger TP intercept. Thus, the classifier at that point is optimal under any distribution assumptions in tandem with that slope.

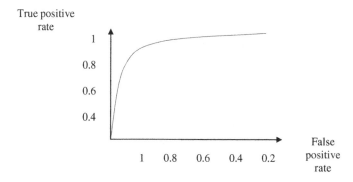

Fig. 4.3   A typical ROC curve.

4.2.6.2   *Hit-Rate Curve*

The hit-rate curve presents the hit ratio as a function of the quota size. *Hit-rate* is calculated by counting the actual positive labeled instances inside a determined quota [An and Wang (2001)]. More precisely, for a quota of size j and a ranked set of instances, *hit-rate* is defined as:

$$\text{Hit-Rate}(j) = \frac{\sum_{k=1}^{j} t^{[k]}}{j}, \qquad (4.10)$$

where $t^{[k]}$ represents the truly expected outcome of the instance located in the k'th position when the instances are sorted according to their conditional probability for "positive" by descending order. Note that if the k'th position can be uniquely defined (i.e. there is exactly one instance that can be located in this position) then $t^{[k]}$ is either 0 or 1 depending on the actual outcome of this specific instance. Nevertheless, if the k'th position is not uniquely defined and there are $m_{k,1}$ instances that can be located in this position, and $m_{k,2}$ of which are truly positive, then:

$$t^{[k]} = m_{k,2} / m_{k,1}. \qquad (4.11)$$

The sum of $t^{[k]}$ over the entire test set is equal to the number of instances that are labeled "positive". Moreover, $Hit\text{-}Rate(j) \approx Precision(p^{[j]})$ where $p^{[j]}$ denotes the j'th order of $\hat{P}_I(pos|x_1), \ldots, \hat{P}_I(pos|x_m)$. The values are strictly equal when the value of j'th is uniquely defined.

It should be noted that the hit-rate measure was originally defined without any reference to the uniqueness of a certain position. However, there are some classifiers that tend to provide the same conditional probability to several different instances. For instance, in a decision tree, any instances in the test set that belongs to the same leaf get the same conditional probability. Thus, the proposed correction is required in those cases. Figure 4.4 illustrates a hit-curve.

4.2.6.3   *Qrecall (Quota Recall)*

The hit-rate measure, presented above, is the "precision" equivalent for quota-limited problems. Similarly, we suggest the Qrecall (for quota recall) to be the "recall" equivalent for quota-limited problems. The Qrecall for a certain position in a ranked list is calculated by dividing the number of positive instances, from the head of the list until that position, by the total

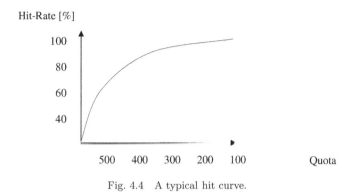

Fig. 4.4 A typical hit curve.

positive instances in the entire dataset. Thus, the Qrecall for a quota of j is defined as:

$$\text{Qrecall}(j) = \frac{\sum_{k=1}^{j} t^{[k]}}{n^+}. \qquad (4.12)$$

The denominator stands for the total number of instances that are classified as positive in the entire dataset. Formally, it can be calculated as:

$$n^+ = |\{< x_i, y_i >: y_i = pos\}|. \qquad (4.13)$$

4.2.6.4 *Lift Curve*

A popular method of evaluating probabilistic models is *lift*. After a ranked test set is divided into several portions (usually deciles), lift is calculated as follows [Coppock (2002)]: the ratio of really positive instances in a specific decile is divided by the average ratio of really positive instances in the population. Regardless of how the test set is divided, a good model is achieved if the lift decreases when proceeding to the bottom of the scoring list. A good model would present a lift greater than 1 in the top deciles and a lift smaller than 1 in the last deciles. Figure 4.5 illustrates a lift chart for a typical model prediction. A comparison between models can be done by comparing the lift of the top portions, depending on the resources available and cost/benefit considerations.

4.2.6.5 *Pearson Correlation Coefficient*

There are also some statistical measures that may be used as performance evaluators of models. These measures are well known and can be found in many statistical books. In this section, we examine the Pearson correlation

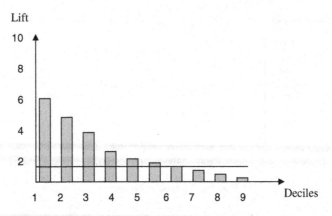

Fig. 4.5   A typical lift chart.

coefficient. This measure can be used to find the correlation between the ordered estimated conditional probability $(p^{[k]})$ and the ordered actual expected outcome $(t^{[k]})$. A Pearson correlation coefficient can have any value between -1 and 1 where the value 1 represents the strongest positive correlation. It should be noticed that this measure take into account not only the ordinal place of an instance but also its value (i.e. the estimated probability attached to it). The *Pearson* correlation coefficient for two random variables is calculated by dividing the co-variance by the product of both standard deviations. In this case, the standard deviations of the two variables assuming a quota size of j are:

$$\sigma_p(j) = \sqrt{\frac{1}{j}\sum_{i=1}^{j}\left(p^{[i]} - \bar{p}(j)\right)}; \quad \sigma_t(j) = \sqrt{\frac{1}{j}\sum_{i=1}^{j}\left(t^{[i]} - \bar{t}(j)\right)}, \quad (4.14)$$

where $\bar{p}(j), \bar{t}(j)$ represent the average of $p^{[i]}$'s and $t^{[i]}$'s respectively:

$$\bar{p}(j) = \frac{\sum_{i=1}^{j} p^{[i]}}{j}; \quad \bar{t}(j) = \frac{\sum_{i=1}^{j} t^{[i]}}{j} = Hit\text{-}Rate(j). \quad (4.15)$$

The co-variance is calculated as follows:

$$Cov_{p,t}(j) = \frac{1}{j}\sum_{i-1}^{j}\left(p^{[i]} - \bar{p}(j)\right)(t^{[i]} - \bar{t}(j)). \quad (4.16)$$

Thus, the Pearson correlation coefficient for a quota j, is:

$$\rho_{p,t}(j) = \frac{Cov_{p,t}(j)}{\sigma_p(j) \cdot \sigma_t(j)}. \quad (4.17)$$

4.2.6.6 *Area Under Curve (AUC)*

Evaluating a probabilistic model without using a specific fixed quota is not a trivial task. Using continuous measures like hit curves, ROC curves and lift charts, mentioned previously, is problematic. Such measures can give a definite answer to the question "Which is the best model?" only if one model dominates in the curve space, meaning that the curves of all the other models are beneath it or equal to it over the entire chart space. If a dominating model does not exist, then there is no answer to that question, using only the continuous measures mentioned above. Complete order demands no intersections of the curves. Of course, in practice there is almost never one dominating model. The best answer that can be obtained is in regard to which areas one model outperforms the others. As shown in Figure 4.6, every model gets different values in different areas. If a complete order of model performance is needed, another measure should be used.

Area under the ROC curve (AUC) is a useful metric for classifier performance since it is independent of the decision criterion selected and prior probabilities. The AUC comparison can establish a dominance relationship between classifiers. If the ROC curves are intersecting, the total AUC is an average comparison between models [Lee (2000)]. The bigger it is, the better the model is. As opposed to other measures, the area under the ROC curve (AUC) does not depend on the imbalance of the training set [Kolcz (2003)]. Thus, the comparison of the AUC of two classifiers is fairer and more informative than comparing their misclassification rates.

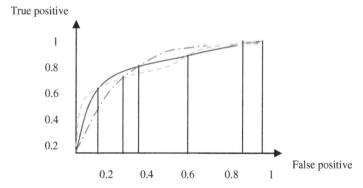

Fig. 4.6 Areas of dominancy. A ROC curve is an example of a measure that gives areas of dominancy and not a complete order of the models. In this example, the equally dashed line model is the best for f.p < 0.2. The full line model is the best for 0.2 < f.p < 0.4. The dotted line model is best for 0.4 < f.p < 0.9 and from 0.9 to 1 again the dashed line model is the best.

4.2.6.7 *Average Hit-Rate*

The average hit-rate is a weighted average of all hit-rate values. If the model is optimal, then all the really positive instances are located in the head of the ranked list, and the value of the average hit-rate is 1. The use of this measure fits an organization that needs to minimize type II statistical error (namely, to include a certain object in the quota although in fact this object will be labeled as "negative"). Formally, the Average Hit-Rate for binary classification problems is defined as:

$$Average\ Hit\text{-}Rate = \frac{\sum\limits_{j=1}^{n} t^{[j]} \cdot Hit\text{-}Rate(j)}{n^+}, \tag{4.18}$$

where $t^{[j]}$ is defined as in Equation (4) and is used as a weighting factor. Note that the average hit-rate ignores all hit-rate values on unique positions that are actually labeled as "negative" class (because $t^{[j]}=0$ in these cases).

4.2.6.8 *Average Qrecall*

Average Qrecall is the average of all the Qrecalls which extends from the position that is equal to the number of positive instances in the test set to the bottom of the list. Average Qrecall fits an organization that needs to minimize type I statistical error (namely, not including a certain object in the quota although in fact this object will be labeled as "positive"). Formally, average Qrecall is defined as:

$$\frac{\sum\limits_{j=n^+}^{n} Qrecall(j)}{n - (n^+ - 1)}, \tag{4.19}$$

where n is the total number of instances and n^+ is defined in Equation (4.13).

Table 4.2 illustrates the calculation of average Qrecall and average hit-rate for a dataset of 10 instances. The table presents a list of instances in descending order according to their predicted conditional probability to be classified as "positive". Because all probabilities are unique, the third column ($t^{[k]}$) indicates the actual class ("1" represent "positive" and "0" represents "negative"). The average values are simple algebraic averages of the highlighted cells.

Note that both *average Qrecall* and *average hit-rate* get the value 1 in an optimum classification, where all the positive instances are located at

Table 4.2   An example for calculating average Qrecall and average hit-rate.

Place in list (j)	Positive probability	$t^{[k]}$	Qrecall	Hit-rate
1	0.45	1	0.25	1
2	0.34	0	0.25	0.5
3	0.32	1	0.5	0.667
4	0.26	1	0.75	0.75
5	0.15	0	0.75	0.6
6	0.14	0	0.75	0.5
7	0.09	1	1	0.571
8	0.07	0	1	0.5
9	0.06	0	1	0.444
10	0.03	0	1	0.4
		Average:	0.893	0.747

Table 4.3   Qrecall and Hit-rate in an optimum prediction.

Place in list (j)	Positive probability	$t^{[k]}$	Qrecall	Hit-rate
1	0.45	1	0.25	1
2	0.34	1	0.5	1
3	0.32	1	0.75	1
4	0.26	1	1	1
5	0.15	0	1	0.8
6	0.14	0	1	0.667
7	0.09	0	1	0.571
8	0.07	0	1	0.5
9	0.06	0	1	0.444
10	0.03	0	1	0.4
		Average:	1	1

the head of the list. This case is illustrated in Table 4.3. A summary of the key differences are provided in Table 4.4.

4.2.6.9   Potential Extract Measure (PEM)

To better understand the behavior of Qrecall curves, consider the cases of random prediction and optimum prediction.

Suppose no learning process was applied on the data and the list produced as a prediction would be the test set in its original (random) order. On the assumption that positive instances are distributed uniformly in the population, then a quota of random size contains a number of positive instances that are proportional to the *a priori* proportion of positive instances in the population. Thus, a Qrecall curve that describes a uniform distribution (which can be considered as a model that predicts as well as a

Table 4.4   Characteristics of Qrecall and Hit-rate.

Parameter	Hit-rate	Qrecall
Function increasing/decreasing	Non-monotonic	Monotonically increasing
End point	Proportion of positive samples in the set	1
Sensitivity of the measures value to positive instances	Very sensitive to positive instances at the top of the list. Less sensitive on going down to the bottom of the list.	Same sensitivity to positive instances in all places in the list.
Effect of negative class on the measure	A negative instance affects the measure and cause its value to decrease.	A negative instance does not affect the measure.
Range	$0 \leq$ Hit-rate ≤ 1	$0 \leq$ Qrecall ≤ 1

random guess, without any learning) is a linear line (or semi-linear because values are discrete) which starts at 0 (for zero quota size) and ends in 1.

Suppose now that a model gave an optimum prediction, meaning that all positive instances are located at the head of the list and below them, all the negative instances. In this case, the Qrecall curve climbs linearly until a value of 1 is achieved at point, n^+ (n^+ = number of positive samples). From that point, any quota that has a size bigger than n^+, fully extracts test set potential and the value 1 is kept until the end of the list.

Note that a "good model", which outperforms random classification, though not an optimum one, will fall "on average" between these two curves. It may drop sometimes below the random curve but generally, more area is delineated between the "good model" curve and the random curve, above the latter than below it. If the opposite is true then the model is a "bad model" that does worse than a random guess.

The last observation leads us to consider a measure that evaluates the performance of a model by summing the areas delineated between the Qrecall curve of the examined model and the Qrecall curve of a random model (which is linear). Areas above the linear curve are added and areas below the linear curve are subtracted. The areas themselves are calculated by subtracting the Qrecall of a random classification from the Qrecall of the model's classification in every point as shown in Figure 4.7. The areas where the model performed better than a random guess increase the measure's value while the areas where the model performed worse than a random guess decrease it. If the last total computed area is divided in the area delineated

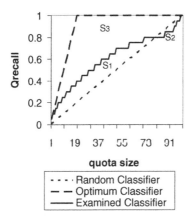

Fig. 4.7   A qualitative representation of PEM.

between the optimum model Qrecall curve and the random model (linear) Qrecall curve, then it reaches the extent to which the potential is extracted, independently of the number of instances in the dataset.

Formally, the PEM measure is calculated as:

$$PEM = \frac{S_1 - S_2}{S_3}, \tag{4.20}$$

where S_1 is the area delimited by the Qrecall curve of the examined model above the Qrecall curve of a random model; S_2 is the area delimited by the Qrecall curve of the examined model under the Qrecall curve of a random model; and S_3 is the area delimited by the optimal Qrecall curve and the curve of the random model. The division in S_3 is required in order to normalize the measure, thus datasets of different size can be compared. In this way, if the model is optimal, then PEM gets the value 1. If the model is as good as a random choice, then the PEM gets the value 0. If it gives the worst possible result (that is to say, it puts the positive samples at the bottom of the list), then its PEM is -1. Based on the notations defined above, the PEM can be formulated as:

$$PEM = \frac{S_1 - S_2}{S_3} = \frac{\sum\limits_{j=1}^{n} \left(Qrecall(j) - \frac{j}{n} \right)}{\sum\limits_{j=1}^{n^+} \left(\frac{j}{n^+} \right) + n^- - \sum\limits_{j=1}^{n} \left(\frac{j}{n} \right)} \tag{4.21}$$

$$= \frac{\sum\limits_{j=1}^{n} \left(Qrecall(j) \right) - \frac{(n+1)}{2}}{\frac{(n^+ +1)}{2} + n^- - \frac{(n+1)}{2}} = \frac{\sum\limits_{j=1}^{n} \left(Qrecall(j) \right) - \frac{(n+1)}{2}}{\frac{n^-}{2}}, \tag{4.22}$$

Table 4.5   An example for calculating PEM for instances of Table 4.2.

Place in list	Success probability	$t^{[k]}$	Model Qrecall	Random Qrecall	Optimal Qrecall	S1	S2	S3
1	0.45	1	0.25	0.1	0.25	0.15	0	0.15
2	0.34	0	0.25	0.2	0.5	0.05	0	0.3
3	0.32	1	0.5	0.3	0.75	0.2	0	0.45
4	0.26	1	0.75	0.4	1	0.35	0	0.6
5	0.15	0	0.75	0.5	1	0.25	0	0.5
6	0.14	0	0.75	0.6	1	0.15	0	0.4
7	0.09	1	1	0.7	1	0.3	0	0.3
8	0.07	0	1	0.8	1	0.2	0	0.2
9	0.06	0	1	0.9	1	0.1	0	0.1
10	0.03	0	1	1	1	0	0	0
					Total	**1.75**	**0**	**3**

where n^- denotes the number of instances that are actually classified as "negative". Table 4.5 illustrates the calculation of PEM for the instances in Table 4.2. Note that the random Qrecall does not represent a certain realization but the expected values. The optimal qrecall is calculated as if the "positive" instances have been located in the top of the list.

Note that the PEM somewhat resembles the Gini index produced from Lorentz curves which appear in economics when dealing with the distribution of income. Indeed, this measure indicates the difference between the distribution of positive samples in a prediction and the uniform distribution. Note also that this measure gives an indication of the total lift of the model at every point. In every quota size, the difference between the Qrecall of the model and the Qrecall of a random model expresses the lift in extracting the potential of the test set due to the use in the model (for good or for bad).

4.2.7   *Which Decision Tree Classifier is Better?*

Below we discuss some of the most common statistical methods proposed [Dietterich (1998)] for answering the following question: *Given two inducers A and B and a dataset S, which inducer will produce more accurate classifiers when trained on datasets of the same size?*

4.2.7.1   *McNemar's Test*

Let S be the available set of data, which is divided into a training set R and a test set T. Then we consider two inducers A and B trained on the

Table 4.6   McNemar's test: contingency table.

Number of examples misclassified by both classifiers (n_{00})	Number of examples misclassified by $\hat{f}_A$ but not by $\hat{f}_B(n_{01})$
Number of examples misclassified by $\hat{f}_B$ but not by $\hat{f}_A(n_{10})$	Number of examples misclassified neither by $\hat{f}_A$ nor by $\hat{f}_B(n_{11})$

Table 4.7   Expected counts under H_0.

n_{00}	$(n_{01} + n_{10})/2$
$(n_{01} + n_{10})/2$	$n_{11})$

training set and the result is two classifiers. These classifiers are tested on T and for each example $x \in T$ we record how it was classified. Thus, the contingency table presented in Table 4.6 is constructed.

The two inducers should have the same error rate under the null hypothesis H_0. McNemar's test is based on a χ^2 test for goodness-of-fit that compares the distribution of counts expected under null hypothesis to the observed counts. The expected counts under H_0 are presented in Table 4.7.

The following statistic, s, is distributed as χ^2 with 1 degree of freedom. It incorporates a "continuity correction" term (of -1 in the numerator) to account for the fact that the statistic is discrete while the χ^2 distribution is continuous:

$$s = \frac{(|n_{10} - n_{01}| - 1)^2}{n_{10} + n_{01}}. \tag{4.23}$$

According to the probabilistic theory [Athanasopoulos, 1991], if the null hypothesis is correct, the probability that the value of the statistic, s, is greater than $\chi^2_{1,0.95}$ is less than 0.05, i.e. $P(|s| > \chi^2_{1,0.95}) < 0.05$. Then, to compare the inducers A and B, the induced classifiers $\hat{f}_A$ and $\hat{f}_B$ are tested on T and the value of s is estimated as described above. Then if $|s| > \chi^2_{1,0.95}$, the null hypothesis could be rejected in favor of the hypothesis that the two inducers have different performance when trained on the particular training set R.

The shortcomings of this test are:

(1) It does not directly measure variability due to the choice of the training set or the internal randomness of the inducer. The inducers are compared using a single training set R. Thus McNemar's test should be only applied if we consider that the sources of variability are small.

(2) It compares the performance of the inducers on training sets, which are substantially smaller than the size of the whole dataset. Hence, we must assume that the relative difference observed on training sets will still hold for training sets of size equal to the whole dataset.

4.2.7.2 *A Test for the Difference of Two Proportions*

This statistical test is based on measuring the difference between the error rates of algorithms A and B [Snedecor and Cochran (1989)]. More specifically, let $p_A = (n_{00} + n_{01})/n$ be the proportion of test examples incorrectly classified by algorithm A and let $p_B = (n_{00} + n_{10})/n$ be the proportion of test examples incorrectly classified by algorithm B. The assumption underlying this statistical test is that when algorithm A classifies an example x from the test set T, the probability of misclassification is p_A. Then the number of misclassifications of n test examples is a binomial random variable with mean np_A and variance $p_A(1 - p_A)n$.

The binomial distribution can be well approximated by a normal distribution for reasonable values of n. The difference between two independent normally distributed random variables is itself normally distributed. Thus, the quantity $p_A - p_B$ can be viewed as normally distributed if we assume that the measured error rates p_A and p_B are independent. Under the null hypothesis, H_0, the quantity $p_A - p_B$ has a mean of zero and a standard deviation error of

$$se = \sqrt{2p \cdot \left(1 - \frac{p_A + p_B}{2}\right) \Big/ n}, \qquad (4.24)$$

where n is the number of test examples.

Based on the above analysis, we obtain the statistic:

$$z = \frac{p_A - p_B}{\sqrt{2p(1-p)/n}}, \qquad (4.25)$$

which has a standard normal distribution. According to the probabilistic theory, if the z value is greater than $Z_{0.975}$, the probability of incorrectly rejecting the null hypothesis is less than 0.05. Thus, if $|z| > Z_{0.975} = 1.96$, the null hypothesis could be rejected in favor of the hypothesis that the two algorithms have different performances. Two of the most important problems with this statistic are:

(1) The probabilities p_A and p_B are measured on the same test set and thus they are not independent.

(2) The test does not measure variation due to the choice of the training set or the internal variation of the learning algorithm. Also it measures the performance of the algorithms on training sets of a size significantly smaller than the whole dataset.

4.2.7.3 *The Resampled Paired t Test*

The resampled paired t test is the most popular in machine learning. Usually, there are a series of 30 trials in the test. In each trial, the available sample S is randomly divided into a training set R (it is typically two thirds of the data) and a test set T. The algorithms A and B are both trained on R and the resulting classifiers are tested on T. Let $p_A^{(i)}$ and $p_B^{(i)}$ be the observed proportions of test examples misclassified by algorithm A and B respectively during the ith trial. If we assume that the 30 differences $p^{(i)} = p_A^{(i)} - p_B^{(i)}$ were drawn independently from a normal distribution, then we can apply Student's t test by computing the statistic:

$$t = \frac{\bar{p} \cdot \sqrt{n}}{\sqrt{\frac{\sum_{i=1}^n (p^{(i)} - \bar{p})^2}{n-1}}}, \tag{4.26}$$

where $\bar{p} = \frac{1}{n} \cdot \sum_{i=1}^n p^{(i)}$. Under the null hypothesis, this statistic has a t distribution with $n - 1$ degrees of freedom. Then for 30 trials, the null hypothesis could be rejected if $|t| > t_{29,0.975} = 2.045$. The main drawbacks of this approach are:

(1) Since $p_A^{(i)}$ and $p_B^{(i)}$ are not independent, the difference $p^{(i)}$ will not have a normal distribution.
(2) The $p^{(i)}$'s are not independent, because the test and training sets in the trials overlap.

4.2.7.4 *The k-fold Cross-validated Paired t Test*

This approach is similar to the resampled paired t test except that instead of constructing each pair of training and test sets by randomly dividing S, the dataset is randomly divided into k disjoint sets of equal size, $T_1, T_2, \ldots, T_k$. Then k trials are conducted. In each trial, the test set is T_i and the training set is the union of all of the others T_j, $j \neq i$. The t statistic is computed as described in Section 4.2.7.3. The advantage of this approach is that each test set is independent of the others. However, there is the problem that the training sets overlap. This overlap may prevent this statistical test from obtaining a good estimation of the amount of variation that would be observed if each training set were completely independent of the others training sets.

4.3 Computational Complexity

Another useful criterion for comparing inducers and classifiers is their computational complexity. Strictly speaking computational complexity is the amount of CPU consumed by each inducer. It is convenient to differentiate between three metrics of computational complexity:

- Computational complexity for generating a new classifier: This is the most important metric, especially when there is a need to scale the data mining algorithm to massive datasets. Because most of the algorithms have computational complexity, which is worse than linear in the numbers of tuples, mining massive datasets might be prohibitively expensive.
- Computational complexity for updating a classifier: Given new data, what is the computational complexity required for updating the current classifier such that the new classifier reflects the new data?
- Computational complexity for classifying a new instance: Generally this type of metric is neglected because it is relatively small. However, in certain methods (like k-nearest neighborhood) or in certain real-time applications (like anti-missiles applications), this type can be critical.

4.4 Comprehensibility

Comprehensibility criterion (also known as interpretability) refers to how well humans grasp the induced classifier. While the generalization error measures how the classifier fits the data, comprehensibility measures the "mental fit" of that classifier.

Many techniques, like neural networks or support vector machines, are designed solely to achieve accuracy. However, as their classifiers are represented using large assemblages of real valued parameters, they are also difficult to understand and are referred to as black-box models.

However, it is often important for the researcher to be able to inspect an induced classifier. For such domains as medical diagnosis, users must understand how the system makes its decisions in order to be confident of the outcome. Since data mining can also play an important role in the process of scientific discovery, a system may discover salient features in the input data whose importance was not previously recognized. If the representations formed by the inducer are comprehensible, then these discoveries can be made accessible to human review [Hunter and Klein (1993)].

Comprehensibility can vary between different classifiers created by the same inducer. For instance, in the case of decision trees, the size (number of nodes) of the induced trees is also important. Smaller trees are preferred because they are easier to interpret. There are also other reasons for preferring smaller decision trees. According to a fundamental principle in science, known as the Occam's razor, when searching for the explanation of any phenomenon, one should make as few assumptions as possible, and eliminating those that make no difference in the observable predictions of the explanatory hypothesis. The implication in regard to decision trees is that the tree which can be defined as the smallest decision tree that is consistent with the training set is the one that is most likely to classify unseen instances correctly. However, this is only a rule of thumb; in some pathologic cases a large and unbalanced tree can still be easily interpreted [Buja and Lee (2001)]. Moreover, the problem of finding the smallest consistent tree is known to be NP-complete [Murphy and McCraw (1991)].

As the reader can see, the accuracy and complexity factors can be quantitatively estimated; the comprehensibility is more subjective.

4.5 Scalability to Large Datasets

Scalability refers to the ability of the method to construct the classification model efficiently given large amounts of data. Classical induction algorithms have been applied with practical success in many relatively simple and small-scale problems. However, trying to discover knowledge in real life and large databases introduces time and memory problems.

As large databases have become the norm in many fields (including astronomy, molecular biology, finance, marketing, health care, and many others), the use of data mining to discover patterns in them has become a potentially very productive enterprise. Many companies are staking a large part of their future on these "data mining" applications, and looking to the research community for solutions to the fundamental problems they encounter.

While a very large amount of available data used to be a dream of any data analyst, nowadays the synonym for "very large" has become "terabyte", a hardly imaginable volume of information. Information-intensive organizations (like telecom companies and banks) are supposed to accumulate several terabytes of raw data every one to two years.

However, the availability of an electronic data repository (in its enhanced form known as a "data warehouse") has caused a number of previously unknown problems, which, if ignored, may turn the task of efficient data mining into mission impossible. Managing and analyzing huge data warehouses requires special and very expensive hardware and software, which often causes a company to exploit only a small part of the stored data.

According to Fayyad *et al.* (1996), the explicit challenges for the data mining research community is to develop methods that facilitate the use of data mining algorithms for real-world databases. One of the characteristics of a real-world databases is high volume data.

Huge databases pose several challenges:

- Computing complexity: Since most induction algorithms have a computational complexity that is greater than linear in the number of attributes or tuples, the execution time needed to process such databases might become an important issue.
- Poor classification accuracy due to difficulties in finding the correct classifier. Large databases increase the size of the search space, and thus it increases the chance that the inducer will select an over fitted classifier that is not valid in general.
- Storage problems: In most machine learning algorithms, the entire training set should be read from the secondary storage (such as magnetic storage) into the computer's primary storage (main memory) before the induction process begins. This causes problems since the main memory's capability is much smaller than the capability of magnetic disks.

The difficulties in implementing classification algorithms as-is on high volume databases derives from the increase in the number of records/instances in the database and from the increase in the number of attributes/features in each instance (high dimensionality).

Approaches for dealing with a high number of records include:

- Sampling methods — statisticians are selecting records from a population by different sampling techniques.
- Aggregation — reduces the number of records either by treating a group of records as one, or by ignoring subsets of "unimportant" records.
- Massively parallel processing — exploiting parallel technology — to simultaneously solve various aspects of the problem.

- Efficient storage methods — enabling the algorithm to handle many records. For instance, Shafer *et al.* (1996) presented the SPRINT which constructs an attribute list data structure.
- Reducing the algorithm's search space — For instance, the PUBLIC algorithm [Rastogi and Shim (2000)] integrates the growing and pruning of decision trees by using Minimum Description Length (MDL) approach in order to reduce the computational complexity.

4.6 Robustness

The ability of the model to handle noise or data with missing values and make correct predictions is called robustness. Different decision trees algorithms have different robustness levels. In order to estimate the robustness of a classification tree, it is common to train the tree on a clean training set and then train a different tree on a noisy training set. The noisy training set is usually the clean training set to which some artificial noisy instances have been added. The robustness level is measured as the difference in the accuracy of these two situations.

4.7 Stability

Formally, stability of a classification algorithm is defined as the degree to which an algorithm generates repeatable results, given different batches of data from the same process. In mathematical terms, stability is the expected agreement between two models on a random sample of the original data, where agreement on a specific example means that both models assign it to the same class. The instability problem raises questions about the validity of a particular tree provided as an output of a decision-tree algorithm. The users view the learning algorithm as an oracle. Obviously, it is difficult to trust an oracle that says something radically different each time you make a slight change in the data.

Existing methods of constructing decision trees from data suffer from a major problem of instability. The symptoms of instability include variations in the predictive accuracy of the model and in the model's topology. Instability can be revealed not only by using disjoint sets of data, but even by replacing a small portion of training cases, like in the cross-validation procedure. If an algorithm is unstable, the cross-validation results become estimators with high variance which means that an algorithm fails to make a clear distinction between persistent and random patterns in the data. As we will see below, certain type of decision trees can be used to solve the instability problem.

4.8   Interestingness Measures

The number of classification patterns generated could be very large and it is possible that different approaches result in different sets of patterns. The patterns extracted during the classification process could be represented in the form of rules, known as classification rules. It is important to evaluate the discovered patterns identifying the ones that are valid and provide new knowledge. Techniques that aim at this goal are broadly referred to as interestingness measures and the interestingness of the patterns that are discovered by a classification approach may also be considered as another quality criterion. Some representative measures [Hilderman and Hamilton, 1999] for ranking the usefulness and utility of discovered classification patterns (each path from the root to the leaf represents a different pattern) are:

- *Rule-Interest Function.* Piatetsky-Shapiro introduced the rule-interest [Piatetsky-Shapiro, (1991)] that is used to quantify the correlation between attributes in a classification rule. It is suitable only for single classification rules, i.e. rules where both the left- and right-hand sides correspond to a single attribute.
- *Smyth and Goodman's J-Measure.* The J-measure is a measure for probabilistic classification rules and is used to find the best rules relating discrete-valued attributes [Smyth and Goodman (1991)]. A probabilistic classification rule is a logical implication, $X \rightarrow Y$, satisfied with some probability p. The left- and right-hand sides of this implication correspond to a single attribute. The right-hand side is restricted to simple single-valued assignment expressions while the left-hand side may be a conjunction of simple expressions.
- *General Impressions.* In Liu *et al.* (1997), general impression is proposed as an approach for evaluating the importance of classification rules. It compares discovered rules to an approximate or vague description of what is considered to be interesting. Thus a general impression can be considered as a kind of specification language.
- *Gago and Bento's Distance Metric.* The distance metric measures the distance between classification rules and is used to determine the rules that provide the highest coverage for the given data. The rules with the

highest average distance to the other rules are considered to be most interesting [Gago and Bentos, 1998].

4.9 Overfitting and Underfitting

The concept of overfitting is very important in data mining. It refers to the situation in which the induction algorithm generates a classifier which perfectly fits the training data but has lost the capability of generalizing to instances not presented during training. In other words, instead of learning, the classifier just memorizes the training instances. Overfitting is generally recognized to be a violation of the principle of Occams razor presented in Section 4.4.

In decision trees, overfitting usually occurs when the tree has too many nodes relative to the amount of training data available. By increasing the number of nodes, the training error usually decreases while at some point the generalization error becomes worse.

Figure 4.8 illustrates the overfitting process. The figure presents the training error and the generalization error of a decision tree as a function of the number of nodes for a fixed training set. The training error continues to decline as the tree become bigger. On the other hand, the generalization error declines at first then at some point starts to increase due to overfitting. The optimal point for the generalization error is obtained for a tree with 130 nodes. In bigger trees, the classifier is overfitted. In smaller trees, the classifier is underfitted.

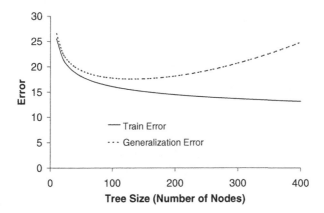

Fig. 4.8 Overfitting in decision trees.

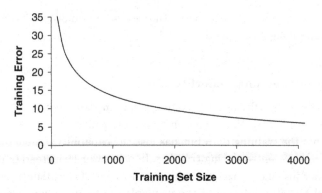

Fig. 4.9   Overfitting in decision trees.

Another aspect of overfitting is presented in Figure 4.9. This graph presents the generalization error for increasing training set sizes. The generalization error decreases with the training set size. This can be explained by the fact that for a small training set, it is relatively hard to generalize, and the classifier memorizes all instances.

It was found that overfitting decreases prediction accuracy in decision trees either in the presence of significant noise or when the input attributes are irrelevant to the classification problem [Schaffer (1991)].

In order to avoid overfitting, it is necessary to estimate when further training will not result in a better generalization. In decision trees there are two mechanisms that help to avoid overfitting. The first is to avoid splitting the tree if the split is not useful (for instance by approving only statistically significant splits). The second approach is to use pruning; after growing the tree, we prune unnecessary nodes.

4.10   "No Free Lunch" Theorem

Empirical comparison of the performance of different approaches and their variants in a wide range of application domains has shown that each performs best in some, but not all, domains. This has been termed the selective superiority problem [Brodley (1995)].

It is well known that no induction algorithm can be the best in all possible domains; each algorithm contains an explicit or implicit bias that leads it to prefer certain generalizations over others [Mitchell (1980)]. The algorithm will be successful only insofar as this bias matches the characteristics of the application domain [Brazdil *et al.* (1994)]. Furthermore, other results have demonstrated the existence and correctness of the "conservation law" [Schaffer (1994)] or "no free lunch theorem" [Wolpert (1996)]: if one inducer is better than another in some domains, then there are necessarily other domains in which this relationship is reversed.

The "no free lunch theorem" implies that for a given problem, a certain approach can yield more information from the same data than other approaches.

A distinction should be made between all the mathematically possible domains, which are simply a product of the representation languages used, and the domains that occur in the real world, and are therefore the ones of primary interest [Rao *et al.* (1995)]. Without doubt there are many domains in the former set that are not in the latter, and average accuracy in the realworld domains can be increased at the expense of accuracy in the domains that never occur in practice. Indeed, achieving this is the goal of inductive learning research. It is still true that some algorithms will match certain classes of naturally occurring domains better than other algorithms, and so achieve higher accuracy than these algorithms. While this may be reversed in other realworld domains, it does not preclude an improved algorithm from being as accurate as the best in each of the domain classes.

Indeed, in many application domains, the generalization error of even the best methods is far above 0%, and the question of whether it can be improved, and if so how, is an open and important one. One aspect in answering this question is determining the minimum error achievable by any classifier in the application domain (known as the optimal Bayes error). If existing classifiers do not reach this level, new approaches are needed. Although this problem has received considerable attention (see for instance [Tumer and Ghosh (1996)]), no generally reliable method has so far been demonstrated.

The "no free lunch" concept presents a dilemma to the analyst approaching a new task: Which inducer should be used?

If the analyst is looking for accuracy only, one solution is to try each one in turn, and by estimating the generalization error, to choose the one that appears to perform best [Schaffer (1994)]. Another approach, known as *multistrategy learning* [Michalski and Tecuci (1994)], attempts to combine two or more different paradigms in a single algorithm. Most research in this area has been concerned with combining empirical approaches with analytical methods (see for instance [Towell and Shavlik (1994)]. Ideally, a multistrategy learning algorithm would always perform as well as the best of its "parents" obviating the need to try each one and simplifying the knowledge acquisition task. Even more ambitiously, there is hope that this combination of paradigms might produce synergistic effects (for instance, by allowing different types of frontiers between classes in different regions of the example space), leading to levels of accuracy that neither atomic approach by itself would be able to achieve.

Unfortunately, this approach has often been used with only moderate success. Although it is true that in some industrial applications (like in the case of demand planning) this strategy proved to boost the error performance, in many other cases the resulting algorithms are prone to be cumbersome, and often achieve an error that lies between those of their parents, instead of matching the lowest.

The dilemma of which method to choose becomes even greater, if other factors such as comprehensibility are taken into consideration. For instance, for a specific domain, a neural network may outperform decision trees in accuracy. However, from the comprehensibility aspect, decision trees are considered better. In other words, even if the researcher knows that neural network is more accurate, he still has a dilemma regarding which method to use.

Chapter 5

Splitting Criteria

5.1 Univariate Splitting Criteria

5.1.1 *Overview*

In most decision trees inducers, discrete splitting functions are univariate, i.e. an internal node is split according to the value of a single attribute. Consequently, the inducer searches for the best attribute upon which to perform the split. There are various univariate criteria which can be characterized in different ways, such as:

- according to the origin of the measure: Information Theory, Dependence, and Distance.
- according to the measure structure: Impurity-based criteria, Normalized Impurity-based criteria and Binary criteria.

    The following section describes the most common criteria appearing in the literature.

5.1.2 *Impurity-based Criteria*

Given a random variable x with k discrete values, distributed according to $P = (p_1, p_2, \ldots, p_k)$, an impurity measure is a function $\phi : [0, 1]^k \to R$ that satisfies the following conditions:

- $\phi(P) \geq 0$.
- $\phi(P)$ is minimum if $\exists i$ such that component $p_i = 1$.
- $\phi(P)$ is maximum if $\forall i, 1 \leq i \leq k, p_i = 1/k$.
- $\phi(P)$ is symmetric with respect to components of P.
- $\phi(P)$ is smooth (differentiable everywhere) in its range.

It should be noted that if the probability vector has a component of 1 (the variable x gets only one value), then the variable is defined as pure. On the other hand, if all components are equal the level of impurity reaches maximum.

Given a training set S the probability vector of the target attribute y is defined as:

$$P_y(S) = \left(\frac{|\sigma_{y=c_1}S|}{|S|}, \ldots, \frac{|\sigma_{y=c_{|dom(y)|}}S|}{|S|} \right). \tag{5.1}$$

The goodness-of-split due to discrete attribute a_i is defined as reduction in impurity of the target attribute after partitioning S according to the values $v_{i,j} \in dom(a_i)$:

$$\Delta\Phi(a_i, S) = \phi(P_y(S)) - \sum_{j=1}^{|dom(a_i)|} \frac{|\sigma_{a_i=v_{i,j}}S|}{|S|} \cdot \phi(P_y(\sigma_{a_i=v_{i,j}}S)). \tag{5.2}$$

5.1.3   *Information Gain*

Information Gain is an impurity-based criteria that uses the entropy measure (originating from information theory) as the impurity measure.

Information Gain$(a_i, S) =$
$$Entropy(y, S) - \sum_{v_{i,j} \in dom(a_i)} \frac{|\sigma_{a_i=v_{i,j}}S|}{|S|} \cdot Entropy(y, \sigma_{a_i=v_{i,j}}S), \tag{5.3}$$

where:

$$Entropy(y, S) = \sum_{c_j \in dom(y)} -\frac{|\sigma_{y=c_j}S|}{|S|} \cdot \log_2 \frac{|\sigma_{y=c_j}S|}{|S|}. \tag{5.4}$$

Information gain is closely related to the maximum likelihood estimation (MLE), which is a popular statistical method used to make inferences about parameters of the underlying probability distribution from a given dataset.

5.1.4   *Gini Index*

The Gini index is an impurity-based criteria that measures the divergences between the probability distributions of the target attributes values. The

Gini index has been used in various works such as [Breiman *et al.* (1984)] and [Gelfand *et al.* (1991)] and it is defined as:

$$Gini(y, S) = 1 - \sum_{c_j \in dom(y)} \left(\frac{|\sigma_{y=c_j}S|}{|S|} \right)^2. \tag{5.5}$$

Consequently, the evaluation criterion for selecting the attribute a_i is defined as:

$$GiniGain(a_i, S) = Gini(y, S)$$
$$- \sum_{v_{i,j} \in dom(a_i)} \frac{|\sigma_{a_i=v_{i,j}}S|}{|S|} \cdot Gini(y, \sigma_{a_i=v_{i,j}}S). \tag{5.6}$$

5.1.5 *Likelihood Ratio Chi-squared Statistics*

The likelihood-ratio is defined as [Attneave (1959)]

$$G^2(a_i, S) = 2 \cdot \ln(2) \cdot |S| \cdot \text{InformationGain}(a_i, S). \tag{5.7}$$

This ratio is useful for measuring the statistical significance of the information gain criterion. The zero hypothesis (H_0) is that both the input and target attributes are conditionally independent. If H_0 holds, the test statistic is distributed as χ^2 with degrees of freedom equal to: $(dom(a_i) - 1) \cdot (dom(y) - 1)$.

5.1.6 *DKM Criterion*

The DKM criterion is an impurity-based splitting criteria designed for binary class attributes [Kearns and Mansour (1999)]. The impurity-based function is defined as:

$$DKM(y, S) = 2 \cdot \sqrt{\left(\frac{|\sigma_{y=c_1}S|}{|S|} \right) \cdot \left(\frac{|\sigma_{y=c_2}S|}{|S|} \right)}. \tag{5.8}$$

It has been theoretically proved that this criterion requires smaller trees for obtaining a certain error than other impurity-based criteria (information gain and Gini index).

5.1.7 *Normalized Impurity-based Criteria*

The impurity-based criterion described above is biased towards attributes with larger domain values. Namely, it prefers input attributes with many values over those with less values [Quinlan (1986)]. For instance, an input attribute that represents the national security number will probably get the highest information gain. However, adding this attribute to a decision tree will result in a poor generalized accuracy. For that reason, it is useful to "normalize" the impurity-based measures, as described in the following sections.

5.1.8 Gain Ratio

The gain ratio normalizes the information gain as follows [Quinlan (1993)]:

$$Gain\ Ratio|(a_i, S) = \frac{Information\ Gain(a_i, S)}{Entropy(a_i, S)}. \tag{5.9}$$

Note that this ratio is not defined when the denominator is zero. Furthermore, the ratio may tend to favor attributes for which the denominator is very small. Accordingly, it is suggested that the ratio be carried out in two stages. First, the information gain is calculated for all attributes. As a consequence of considering only attributes that have performed at least as well as the average information gain, the attribute that has obtained the best ratio gain is selected. Quinlan (1988) has shown that the gain ratio tends to outperform simple information gain criteria, both in accuracy and in terms of classifier complexity. A penalty is assessed for the information gain of a continuous attribute with many potential splits.

5.1.9 Distance Measure

The Distance Measure, like the Gain Ratio, normalizes the impurity measure. However, it is performed differently [Lopez de Mantras (1991)]:

$$\frac{\Delta\Phi(a_i, S)}{-\sum_{v_{i,j} \in dom(a_i)} \sum_{c_k \in dom(y)} \frac{|\sigma_{a_i=v_{i,j}\ AND\ y=c_k} S|}{|S|} \cdot \log_2 \frac{|\sigma_{a_i=v_{i,j}\ AND\ y=c_k} S|}{|S|}}. \tag{5.10}$$

5.1.10 Binary Criteria

The binary criteria are used for creating binary decision trees. These measures are based on division of the input attribute domain into two subdomains.

Let $\beta(a_i, dom_1(a_i), dom_2(a_i), S)$ denote the binary criterion value for attribute a_i over sample S when $dom_1(a_i)$ and $dom_2(a_i)$ are its corresponding subdomains. The value obtained for the optimal division of the attribute domain into two mutually exclusive and exhaustive subdomains is used for comparing attributes, namely:

$$\beta^*(a_i, S) = \max_{\forall dom_1(a_i); \, dom_2(a_i)} \beta(a_i, dom_1(a_i), dom_2(a_i), S). \qquad (5.11)$$

5.1.11 Twoing Criterion

The Gini index may encounter problems when the domain of the target attribute is relatively wide [Breiman *et al.* (1984)]. In such cases, it is possible to employ binary criterion called twoing criterion. This criterion is defined as:

$$twoing(a_i, dom_1(a_i), dom_2(a_i), S)$$

$$= 0.25 \cdot \frac{\left| \sigma_{a_i \in dom_1(a_i)} S \right|}{|S|} \cdot \frac{\left| \sigma_{a_i \in dom_2(a_i)} S \right|}{|S|} \cdot$$

$$\left(\sum_{c_i \in dom(y)} \left| \frac{\left| \sigma_{a_i \in dom_1(a_i) \; AND \; y=c_i} S \right|}{\left| \sigma_{a_i \in dom_1(a_i)} S \right|} - \frac{\left| \sigma_{a_i \in dom_2(a_i) \; AND \; y=c_i} S \right|}{\left| \sigma_{a_i \in dom_2(a_i)} S \right|} \right| \right)^2$$

$$(5.12)$$

When the target attribute is binary, the Gini and twoing criteria are equivalent. For multi-class problems, the twoing criteria prefers attributes with evenly divided splits.

5.1.12 Orthogonal Criterion

The ORT criterion was presented by [Fayyad and Irani (1992)]. This binary criterion is defined as:

$$ORT(a_i, dom_1(a_i), dom_2(a_i), S) = 1 - cos\theta(P_{y,1}, P_{y,2}), \qquad (5.13)$$

where $\theta(P_{y,1}, P_{y,2})$ is the angle between two vectors $P_{y,1}$ and $P_{y,2}$. These vectors represent the probability distribution of the target attribute in the partitions $\sigma_{a_i \in dom_1(a_i)} S$ and $\sigma_{a_i \in dom_2(a_i)} S$, respectively.

It has been shown that this criterion performs better than the information gain and the Gini index for specific constellations of problems.

5.1.13 *Kolmogorov–Smirnov Criterion*

A binary criterion that uses Kolmogorov–Smirnov distance has been proposed by [Friedman (1977)] and [Rounds (1980)]. Assuming a binary target attribute, namely $dom(y) = \{c_1, c_2\}$, the criterion is defined as:

$$KS(a_i, dom_1(a_i), dom_2(a_i), S)$$

$$= \left| \frac{\left| \sigma_{a_i \in dom_1(a_i) \ AND \ y=c_1} S \right|}{\left| \sigma_{y=c_1} S \right|} - \frac{\left| \sigma_{a_i \in dom_1(a_i) \ AND \ y=c_2} S \right|}{\left| \sigma_{y=c_2} S \right|} \right|. \qquad (5.14)$$

This measure was extended by [Utgoff and Clouse (1996)] to handle target attribute with multiple classes and missing data values. Their results indicate that the suggested method outperforms the gain ratio criteria.

5.1.14 *AUC Splitting Criteria*

In Section 4.2.6.6, we have shown that the AUC metric can be used for evaluating the predictive performance of classifiers. The AUC metric can be also used as a splitting criterion [Ferri *et al.* (2002)]. The attribute that obtains the maximal area under the convex hull of the ROC curve is selected. It has been shown that the AUC-based splitting criterion outperforms other splitting criteria both with respect to classification accuracy and area under the ROC curve. It is important to note that unlike impurity criteria, this criterion does not perform a comparison between the impurity of the parent node with the weighted impurity of the children after splitting.

5.1.15 *Other Univariate Splitting Criteria*

Additional univariate splitting criteria can be found in the literature, such as permutation statistic [Li and Dubes (1986)]; mean posterior improvement [Taylor and Silverman (1993)]; and hypergeometric distribution measure [Martin (1997)].

5.1.16 *Comparison of Univariate Splitting Criteria*

Over the past 30 years, several researchers have conducted comparative studies of splitting criteria both those described above and others. Among these researchers are: [Breiman (1996)]; [Baker and Jain (1976)]; [Mingers (1989)]; [Fayyad and Irani (1992)]; [Buntine and Niblett (1992)]; [Loh and Shih (1997)]; [Loh and Shih (1999)]; and [Lim *et al.* (2000)]. The majority of the comparisons are based on empirical results, although there are some theoretical conclusions.

Most of the researchers point out that in nearly all of the cases the choice of splitting criteria will not make much difference on the tree performance. As the no-free lunch theorem suggests, each criterion is superior in some cases and inferior in others.

5.2 Handling Missing Values

Missing values are a common experience in real-world datasets. This situation can complicate both induction (a training set where some of its values are missing) as well as classification of a new instance that is missing certain values.

The problem of missing values has been addressed by several researchers such as [Friedman (1977)], [Breiman *et al.* (1984)] and [Quinlan (1989)]. Friedman (1977) suggests handling missing values in the training set in the following way. Let $\sigma_{a_i=?}S$ indicate the subset of instances in S whose a_i values are missing. When calculating the splitting criteria using attribute a_i, simply ignore all instances whose values in attribute a_i are unknown. Instead of using the splitting criteria $\Delta\Phi(a_i, S)$ we use $\Delta\Phi(a_i, S - \sigma_{a_i=?}S)$.

On the other hand, Quinlan (1989) argues that in case of missing values, the splitting criteria should be reduced proportionally as nothing has been learned from these instances. In other words, instead of using the splitting criteria $\Delta\Phi(a_i, S)$, we use the following correction:

$$\frac{|S - \sigma_{a_i=?}S|}{|S|}\Delta\Phi(a_i, S - \sigma_{a_i=?}S).$$ (5.15)

In cases where the criterion value is normalized (as in the case of gain ratio), the denominator should be calculated as if the missing values represent an additional value in the attribute domain. For instance, the gain ratio with missing values should be calculated as follows:

$$GainRatio(a_i, S) = \frac{\frac{|S-\sigma_{a_i=?}S|}{|S|}InformationGain(a_i, S-\sigma_{a_i=?}S)}{-\frac{|\sigma_{a_i=?}S|}{|S|}\log(\frac{|\sigma_{a_i=?}S|}{|S|}) - \sum_{v_{i,j}\in dom(a_i)}\frac{|\sigma_{a_i=v_{i,j}}S|}{|S|}\log(\frac{|\sigma_{a_i=v_{i,j}}S|}{|S|})}.$$ (5.16)

Once a node is split, Quinlan (1989) suggests adding $\sigma_{a_i=?}S$ to each one of the outgoing edges with the following corresponding weight:

$$|\sigma_{a_i=v_{i,j}}S|/|S - \sigma_{a_i=?}S|.$$ (5.17)

The same idea is used for classifying a new instance with missing attribute values. When an instance encounters a node where its splitting criteria can be evaluated due to a missing value, it is passed through to all outgoing edges. The predicted class will be the class with the highest probability in the weighted union of all the leaf nodes at which this instance ends up.

Another approach known as *surrogate splits* is implemented in the CART algorithm. The idea is to find for each split in the tree a surrogate split which uses a different input attribute and which most resembles the original split. If the value of the input attribute used in the original split is missing, then it is possible to use the surrogate split. The resemblance between two binary splits over sample S is formally defined as:

$$res(a_i, dom_1(a_i), dom_2(a_i), a_j, dom_1(a_j), dom_2(a_j), S)$$

$$= \frac{\left|\sigma_{a_i \in dom_1(a_i) \ AND \ a_j \in dom_1(a_j)} S\right|}{|S|} + \frac{\left|\sigma_{a_i \in dom_2(a_i) \ AND \ a_j \in dom_2(a_j)} S\right|}{|S|},$$

$$(5.18)$$

where the first split refers to attribute a_i and it splits $dom(a_i)$ into $dom_1(a_i)$ and $dom_2(a_i)$. The alternative split refers to attribute a_j and splits its domain to $dom_1(a_j)$ and $dom_2(a_j)$.

The missing value can be estimated based on other instances. On the learning phase, if the value of a nominal attribute a_i in tuple q is missing, then it is estimated by its mode over all instances having the same target attribute value. Formally,

$$estimate(a_i, y_q, S) = \underset{v_{i,j} \in dom(a_i)}{\mathrm{argmax}} \left|\sigma_{a_i = v_{i,j} \ AND \ y = y_q} S\right|, \qquad (5.19)$$

where y_q denotes the value of the target attribute in the tuple q. If the missing attribute a_i is numeric, then, instead of using mode of a_i, it is more appropriate to use its mean.

Chapter 6

Pruning Trees

6.1 Stopping Criteria

The growing phase continues until a stopping criterion is triggered. The following conditions are common stopping rules:

(1) All instances in the training set belong to a single value of y.
(2) The maximum tree depth has been reached.
(3) The number of cases in the terminal node is less than the minimum number of cases for parent nodes.
(4) If the node were split, the number of cases in one or more child nodes would be less than the minimum number of cases for child nodes.
(5) The best splitting criteria is not greater than a certain threshold.

6.2 Heuristic Pruning

6.2.1 *Overview*

Employing tight stopping criteria tends to create small and underfitted decision trees. On the other hand, using loose stopping criteria tends to generate large decision trees that are overfitted to the training set. To solve this dilemma, Breiman *et al.* (1984) developed a pruning methodology based on a loose stopping criterion and allowing the decision tree to overfit the training set. Then the overfitted tree is cut back into a smaller tree by removing sub-branches that are not contributing to the generalization accuracy. It has been shown in various studies that pruning methods can improve the generalization performance of a decision tree, especially in noisy domains.

Another key motivation of pruning is "trading accuracy for simplicity" as presented by Bratko and Bohanec (1994). When the goal is to produce a sufficiently accurate, compact concept description, pruning is highly useful. Since within this process the initial decision tree is seen as a completely accurate one, the accuracy of a pruned decision tree indicates how close it is to the initial tree.

There are various techniques for pruning decision trees. Most perform top-down or bottom-up traversal of the nodes. A node is pruned if this operation improves a certain criteria. The following subsections describe the most popular techniques.

6.2.2 Cost Complexity Pruning

Cost complexity pruning (also known as weakest link pruning or error complexity pruning) proceeds in two stages [Breiman *et al.* (1984)]. In the first stage, a sequence of trees $T_0, T_1, \ldots, T_k$ is built on the training data where T_0 is the original tree before pruning and T_k is the root tree.

In the second stage, one of these trees is chosen as the pruned tree, based on its generalization error estimation.

The tree T_{i+1} is obtained by replacing one or more of the sub-trees in the predecessor tree T_i with suitable leaves. The sub-trees that are pruned are those that obtain the lowest increase in apparent error rate per pruned leaf:

$$\alpha = \frac{\varepsilon(pruned(T,t), S) - \varepsilon(T,S)}{|leaves(T)| - |leaves(pruned(T,t))|}, \qquad (6.1)$$

where $\varepsilon(T,S)$ indicates the error rate of the tree T over the sample S and $|leaves(T)|$ denotes the number of leaves in T. $pruned(T,t)$ denotes the tree obtained by replacing the node t in T with a suitable leaf.

In the second phase, the generalization error of each pruned tree is estimated. The best pruned tree is then selected. If the given dataset is large enough, the authors suggest breaking it into a training set and a pruning set. The trees are constructed using the training set and evaluated on the pruning set. On the other hand, if the given dataset is not large enough, they propose using cross-validation methodology, despite the computational complexity implications.

6.2.3 Reduced Error Pruning

A simple procedure for pruning decision trees, known as Reduced Error Pruning, has been suggested by Quinlan (1987). While traversing over the internal nodes from the bottom to the top, the procedure checks each internal node to determine whether replacing it with the most frequent class does not reduce the trees accuracy. The node is pruned if accuracy is not reduced. The procedure continues until any further pruning would decrease the accuracy.

In order to estimate the accuracy, Quinlan (1987) proposes the usage of a pruning set. It can be shown that this procedure ends with the smallest accurate sub-tree with respect to a given pruning set.

6.2.4 *Minimum Error Pruning (MEP)*

MEP, proposed by Niblett and Bratko (1986), involves bottom-up traversal of the internal nodes. This technique compares, in each node, the l probability error rate estimation with and without pruning.

The l-probability error rate estimation is a correction to the simple probability estimation using frequencies. If S_t denotes the instances that have reached a leaf t, then the expected error rate in this leaf is:

$$\varepsilon'(t) = 1 - \max_{c_i \in dom(y)} \frac{|\sigma_{y=c_i} S_t| + l \cdot p_{apr}(y = c_i)}{|S_t| + l}, \qquad (6.2)$$

where $p_{apr}(y = c_i)$ is the *a priori* probability of y getting the value c_i, and l denotes the weight given to the *a priori* probability.

The error rate of an internal node is the weighted average of the error rate of its branches. The weight is determined according to the proportion of instances along each branch. The calculation is performed recursively up to the leaves.

If an internal node is pruned, then it becomes a leaf and its error rate is calculated directly using the last equation. Consequently, we can compare the error rate before and after pruning a certain internal node. If pruning this node does not increase the error rate, the pruning should be accepted.

6.2.5 *Pessimistic Pruning*

Pessimistic pruning avoids the need of a pruning set or cross-validation and uses the pessimistic statistical correlation test instead [Quinlan (1993)].

The basic idea is that the error ratio that was estimated using the training set is not reliable enough. Instead, a more realistic measure, known as the continuity correction for binomial distribution, should be used:

$$\varepsilon'(T, S) = \varepsilon(T, S) + \frac{|leaves(T)|}{2 \cdot |S|}. \qquad (6.3)$$

However, this correction still produces an optimistic error rate. Consequently, Quinlan (1993) suggests pruning an internal node t if its error rate is within one standard error from a reference tree, namely:

$$\varepsilon'(pruned(T,t),S) \leq \varepsilon'(T,S) + \sqrt{\frac{\varepsilon'(T,S) \cdot (1 - \varepsilon'(T,S))}{|S|}}. \qquad (6.4)$$

The last condition is based on the statistical confidence interval for proportions. Usually, the last condition is used such that T refers to a subtree whose root is the internal node t and S denotes the portion of the training set that refers to the node t.

The pessimistic pruning procedure performs top-down traversal over the internal nodes. If an internal node is pruned, then all its descendants are removed from the pruning process, resulting in a relatively fast pruning.

6.2.6 *Error-Based Pruning (EBP)*

EBP is an evolution of the pessimistic pruning. It is implemented in the well-known C4.5 algorithm.

As in pessimistic pruning, the error rate is estimated using the upper bound of the statistical confidence interval for proportions.

$$\varepsilon_{UB}(T,S) = \varepsilon(T,S) + Z_\alpha \cdot \sqrt{\frac{\varepsilon(T,S) \cdot (1 - \varepsilon(T,S))}{|S|}}, \qquad (6.5)$$

where $\varepsilon(T,S)$ denotes the misclassification rate of the tree T on the training set S; Z is the inverse of the standard normal cumulative distribution; and α is the desired significance level.

Let $subtree(T,t)$ denote the subtree rooted by the node t. Let $maxchild(T,t)$ denote the most frequent child node of t (namely most of the instances in S reach this particular child) and let S_t denote all instances in S that reach the node t. The procedure traverses bottom-up all nodes and compares the following values:

(1) $\varepsilon_{UB}(subtree(T,t), S_t)$
(2) $\varepsilon_{UB}(pruned(subtree(T,t),t), S_t)$
(3) $\varepsilon_{UB}(subtree(T, maxchild(T,t)), S_{maxchild(T,t)})$.

According to the lowest value, the procedure either leaves the tree as is; prune the node t; or replaces the node t with the subtree rooted by $maxchild(T,t)$.

6.2.7 *Minimum Description Length (MDL) Pruning*

MDL can be used for evaluating the generalized accuracy of a node ([Rissanen (1989)], [Quinlan and Rivest (1989)] and [Mehta *et al.* (1995)]). This method measures the size of a decision tree by means of the number of bits required to encode the tree. The MDL method prefers decision trees that can be encoded with fewer bits. Mehta *et al.* (1995) indicate that the cost of a split at a leaf t can be estimated as:

$$\text{Cost(t)} = \sum_{c_i \in dom(y)} |\sigma_{y=c_i} S_t| \cdot \ln \frac{|S_t|}{|\sigma_{y=c_i} S_t|} + \frac{|dom(y)| - 1}{2} \ln \frac{|S_t|}{2}$$
$$+ \ln \frac{\pi^{\frac{|dom(y)|}{2}}}{\Gamma(\frac{|dom(y)|}{2})}, \tag{6.6}$$

where S_t denotes the instances that have reached node t. The splitting cost of an internal node is calculated based on the cost aggregation of its children.

6.2.8 *Other Pruning Methods*

There are other pruning methods reported in the literature. Wallaces and Patrick (1993) proposed a Minimum Message Length (MML) pruning method while Kearns and Mansour (1998) provide a theoretically-justified pruning algorithm. Mingers (1989) proposed the Critical Value Pruning (CVP). This method, which prunes an internal node if its splitting criterion is not greater than a certain threshold, is similar to a stopping criterion. However, contrary to a stopping criterion, a node is not pruned if at least one of its children does not fulfill the pruning criterion.

6.2.9 *Comparison of Pruning Methods*

Several studies compare the performance of different pruning techniques: ([Quinlan (1987)], [Mingers (1989)] and [Esposito *et al.* (1997)]). The results indicate that some methods (such as Cost-Complexity Pruning, Reduced Error Pruning) tend to over-pruning, i.e. creating smaller but less accurate decision trees. Other methods (like error-based pruning, pessimistic error pruning and minimum error pruning) bias toward under-pruning. Most of the comparisons concluded that the no free lunch theorem also applies to pruning, namely, there is no pruning method that outperforms other pruning methods.

6.3   Optimal Pruning

The issue of finding the optimal pruning method has been studied by Bratko and Bohanec (1994) and Almuallim (1996). The Optimal Pruning Technique (OPT) algorithm guarantees optimality based on dynamic programming, with the complexity of $\Theta(|leaves(T)|^2)$, where T is the initial decision tree. Almuallim (1996) introduced an improvement of OPT called OPT-2, which also performs optimal pruning using dynamic programming. However, the time and space complexities of OPT-2 are both $\Theta(|leaves(T^*)| \cdot |internal(T)|)$, where T^* is the target (pruned) decision tree and T is the initial decision tree.

Since the pruned tree is habitually much smaller than the initial tree and the number of internal nodes is smaller than the number of leaves, OPT-2 is usually more efficient than OPT in terms of computational complexity.

According to Almuallim, when pruning a given decision tree (DT) with s leaves, it is common to progressively replace various sub-trees of DT by leaves, thus leading to a sequence of pruned DT, DT_{s-1}, $DT_{s-2}, \ldots, DT_i, \ldots, DT_1$, such that each DT_i has at most i leaves. When seeing the error as the difference from the original tree (DT), the trees in the sequence are of increasing error. The goal in choosing the best tree from the above sequence of pruned trees, according to some appropriate criteria, is to achieve a good balance between the trees size and accuracy.

In their paper, Bratko and Bohanec (1994) address the following problem: "Given a completely accurate but complex definition of a concept, simplify the definition, possibly at the expanse of accuracy, so that the simplified definition still corresponds to the concept 'sufficiently' well". In this context, "concepts" are represented by decision trees and the method of simplification is tree pruning. Therefore, the problem can be stated as: "Given a decision tree that accurately specifies a concept, the problem is to find the smallest pruned tree that still represents the concept within some specified accuracy."

In a new algorithm [Almuallim (1996)], OPT-2, which also performs optimal pruning, is introduced. The problem of optimal pruning is formally presented in this paper as follows: "Given a DT and a positive integer C, find a pruned DT' from DT such that $s(DT') \leq C$ and error(DT') is minimized." where $s(DT')$ is the size of DT' (number of leaves in DT') and error(DT') is the proportion of cases that are incorrectly handled by DT'.

The OPT-2 algorithm is based on dynamic programming. In its most basic form, the time and space complexities of OPT-2 are both $\Theta(nC)$, where n is the number of internal nodes in the initial decision tree and C is the number of leaves in the target (pruned) decision tree. This is an improvement of the OPT algorithm presented by Bohanec and Bratko (1994). One important characteristic of the OPT-2 algorithm is its significant flexibility. The OPT-2 works sequentially, generating the trees of the sequence one after the other in increasing order of the number of leaves (that is in the order $DT_1, DT_2, DT_3, \ldots$). This differs from OPT which simultaneously generates the whole sequence of pruned trees. Sequence generation in OPT-2 can be terminated once a tree with adequate predetermined criteria is found.

Given that trees $DT_1, DT_2, \ldots, DT_{i-1}$ have already been generated, OPT-2 finds DT_i in time $\Theta(n)$, where n is the number of the internal nodes of the initial decision tree. Thus, if the number of leaves of the target tree is C, the total running time of OPT-2 will be $\Theta(nC)$. Since the goal is to prune the tree, C is habitually much smaller then s. Additionally, n is smaller than s, specifically in the case of attributes with many values. Hence, OPT-2 is usually more efficient than OPT in terms of execution time.

Although both OPT and OPT-2 are based on dynamic programming the two algorithms differ substantially in the way the problem is divided into sub-problems. The approach adopted in OPT is usually viewed as a "bottom-up" approach, where the idea is to compute solutions for the sub-trees rooted at the lowest level of the tree. These solutions are then used to compute the nodes of the next upper level. This process is repeated until the root of the initial tree is reached. A basic characteristic of this "bottom-up" approach is that the trees DT_i of the pruning sequence are simultaneously computed as we advance towards the root. These pruned trees are not final unless we reach the root. However, once it is reached, the whole sequence becomes available at once.

The OPT-2 produces the pruned trees one after the other using an algorithm derivative of a dynamic programming method given by Johnson and Niemi (1983). Unlike the bottom-up approach of OPT, processing in OPT-2 is done in a left to right fashion: Given that we have already computed trees $DT_1, DT_2, \ldots, DT_{i-1}$ and that necessary intermediate results for these computations are kept in memory the OPT-2 algorithm finds DT_i from these through a linear 'left to right' pass over the tree.

In optimal pruning the error of each DT_i in the sequence should be a minimum over all pruned trees of i (or less) leaves. To date, the only two works that address optimal pruning are Bohanec and Bratko's paper (1994) and Almuallim's paper (1996).

Chapter 7

Popular Decision Trees Induction Algorithms

7.1 Overview

In this chapter, we shortly review some of the popular decision trees induction algorithms, including: ID3, C4.5, and CART. All of these algorithms are using splitting criterion and pruning methods that were already described in previous chapters. Therefore, the aim of this chapter is merely to indicate which setting each algorithm is using and what are the advantages and disadvantages of each algorithm.

7.2 ID3

The ID3 algorithm is considered to be a very simple decision tree algorithm [Quinlan (1986)]. Using information gain as a splitting criterion, the ID3 algorithm ceases to grow when all instances belong to a single value of a target feature or when best information gain is not greater than zero. ID3 does not apply any pruning procedure nor does it handle numeric attributes or missing values.

The main advantage of ID3 is its simplicity. Due to this reason, ID3 algorithm is frequently used for teaching purposes. However, ID3 has several disadvantages:

(1) ID3 does not guarantee an optimal solution, it can get stuck in local optimums because it uses a greedy strategy. To avoid local optimum, backtracking can be used during the search.
(2) ID3 can overfit to the training data. To avoid overfitting, smaller decision trees should be preferred over larger ones. This algorithm

usually produces small trees, but it does not always produce the smallest possible tree.

(3) ID3 is designed for nominal attributes. Therefore, continuous data can be used only after converting them to nominal bins.

Due to the above drawbacks, most of the practitioners prefer the C4.5 algorithm over ID3 mainly because C4.5 is an evolution of the ID3 algorithm that tries to tackle its drawbacks.

7.3 C4.5

C4.5, an evolution of ID3, presented by the same author [Quinlan (1993)], uses gain ratio as splitting criteria. The splitting ceases when the number of instances to be split is below a certain threshold. Error-based pruning is performed after the growing phase. C4.5 can handle numeric attributes. It can also induce from a training set that incorporates missing values by using corrected gain ratio criteria as described in Section 5.1.8.

C4.5 algorithm provides several improvements to ID3. The most important improvements are:

(1) C4.5 uses a pruning procedure which removes branches that do not contribute to the accuracy and replace them with leaf nodes.
(2) C4.5 allows attribute values to be missing (marked as ?).
(3) C4.5 handles continuous attributes by splitting the attribute's value range into two subsets (binary split). Specifically, it searches for the best threshold that maximizes the gain ratio criterion. All values above the threshold constitute the first subset and all other values constitute the second subset.

C5.0 is an updated, commercial version of C4.5 that offers a number of improvements: it is claimed that C5.0 is much more efficient than C4.5 in terms of memory and computation time. In certain cases, it provides an impressive speedup from hour and a half (that it took to C4.5 algorithm) to only 3.5 seconds. Moreover, it supports the boosting procedure that can improve predictive performance and is described in Section 9.4.1.

J48 is an open source Java implementation of the C4.5 algorithm in the Weka data mining tool (see Section 10.2 for additional information). Because J48 algorithm is merely a reimplementation of C4.5, it is expected to perform similarly to C4.5. Nevertheless, a recent comparative study that compares C4.5 with J48 and C5.0 [Moore *et al.* (2009)] indicates that C4.5 performs consistently better (in terms of accuracy) than C5.0 and J48 in particular on small datasets.

7.4 CART

CART stands for Classification and Regression Trees. It was developed by Breiman *et al.* (1984) and is characterized by the fact that it constructs binary trees, namely each internal node has exactly two outgoing edges. The splits are selected using the Twoing Criteria and the obtained tree is pruned by Cost-Complexity Pruning. When provided, CART can consider misclassification costs in the tree induction. It also enables users to provide prior probability distribution.

An important feature of CART is its ability to generate regression trees. In regression trees, the leaves predict a real number and not a class. In case of regression, CART looks for splits that minimize the prediction squared error (the least-squared deviation). The prediction in each leaf is based on the weighted mean for node.

7.5 CHAID

Starting from the early Seventies, researchers in applied statistics developed procedures for generating decision trees [Kass (1980)]. Chi-squared-Automatic-Interaction-Detection (CHIAD) was originally designed to handle nominal attributes only. For each input attribute a_i, CHAID finds the pair of values in V_i that is least significantly different with respect to the target attribute. The significant difference is measured by the p value obtained from a statistical test. The statistical test used depends on the type of target attribute. An F test is used if the target attribute is continuous; a Pearson chi-squared test if it is nominal; and a likelihood ratio test if it is ordinal.

For each selected pair of values, CHAID checks if the p value obtained is greater than a certain merge threshold. If the answer is positive, it merges the values and searches for an additional potential pair to be merged. The process is repeated until no significant pairs are found.

The best input attribute to be used for splitting the current node is then selected, such that each child node is made of a group of homogeneous values of the selected attribute. Note that no split is performed if the adjusted p value of the best input attribute is not less than a certain split threshold. This procedure stops also when one of the following conditions is fulfilled:

(1) Maximum tree depth is reached.
(2) Minimum number of cases in a node for being a parent is reached, so it cannot be split any further.
(3) Minimum number of cases in a node for being a child node is reached.

CHAID handles missing values by treating them all as a single valid category. CHAID does not perform pruning.

7.6 QUEST

The Quick, Unbiased, Efficient Statistical Tree (QUEST) algorithm supports univariate and linear combination splits [Loh and Shih (1997)]. For each split, the association between each input attribute and the target attribute is computed using the ANOVA F-test or Levene's test (for ordinal and continuous attributes) or Pearson's chi-square (for nominal attributes). An ANOVA F-statistic is computed for each attribute. If the largest F-statistic exceeds a predefined threshold value, the attribute with the largest F-value is selected to split the node. Otherwise, Levene's test for unequal variances is computed for every attribute. If the largest Levene's statistic value is greater than a predefined threshold value, the attribute with the largest Levene value is used to split the node. If no attribute exceeded either threshold, the node is split using the attribute with the largest ANOVA F-value.

If the target attribute is multinomial, two-means clustering is used to create two super-classes. The attribute that obtains the highest association with the target attribute is selected for splitting. Quadratic Discriminant Analysis (QDA) is applied to find the optimal splitting point for the input attribute. QUEST has negligible bias and yields a binary decision tree. Ten-fold cross-validation is used to prune the trees.

7.7 Reference to Other Algorithms

Table 7.1 describes other decision tree algorithms available in the literature. Although there are many other algorithms which are not included in this table, nevertheless, most are a variation of the algorithmic framework presented in previous sections. A profound comparison of the above algorithms and many others has been conducted in [Lim *et al.* (2000)].

Table 7.1   Additional decision tree inducers.

Algorithm	Description	Reference
CAL5	Designed specifically for numerical-valued attributes.	[Muller and Wysotzki (1994)]
FACT	An earlier version of QUEST. Uses statistical tests to select an attribute for splitting each node and then uses discriminant analysis to find the split point.	[Loh and Vanichsetakul (1988)]
LMDT	Constructs a decision tree based on multivariate tests which are linear combinations of the attributes.	[Brodley and Utgoff (1995)]
T1	A one-level decision tree that classifies instances using only one attribute. Missing values are treated as a "special value". Support both continuous an nominal attributes.	[Holte (1993)]
PUBLIC	Integrates the growing and pruning by using MDL cost in order to reduce the computational complexity.	[Rastogi and Shim (2000)]
MARS	A multiple regression function is approximated using linear splines and their tensor products.	[Friedman (1991)]

7.8   Advantages and Disadvantages of Decision Trees

Several advantages of the decision tree as a classification tool appear in the literature:

(1) Decision trees are self-explanatory and when compacted they are also easy to follow. That is to say, if the decision tree has a reasonable number of leaves it can be grasped by non-professional users. Furthermore, since decision trees can be converted to a set of rules, this sort of representation is considered as comprehensible.
(2) Decision trees can handle both nominal and numeric input attributes.
(3) Decision tree representation is rich enough to represent any discrete-value classifier.
(4) Decision trees can handle datasets that may have errors.
(5) Decision trees can deal with handle datasets that may have missing values.
(6) Decision trees are considered to be a non-parametric method, i.e. decisions tress do not include any assumptions about the space distribution and on the classifier structure.

(7) When classification cost is high, decision trees may be attractive in that they ask only for the values of the features along a single path from the root to a leaf.

Among the disadvantages of decision trees are:

(1) Most of the algorithms (like ID3 and C4.5) require that the target attribute will have only discrete values.

(2) As decision trees use the "divide and conquer" method, they tend to perform well if a few highly relevant attributes exist, but less so if many complex interactions are present. One of the reasons for this happening is that other classifiers can compactly describe a classifier that would be very challenging to represent using a decision tree. A simple illustration of this phenomenon is the replication problem of decision trees [Pagallo and Huassler (1990)]. Since most decision trees divide the instance space into mutually exclusive regions to represent a concept, in some cases the tree should contain several duplications of the same subtree in order to represent the classifier. The replication problem forces duplication of subtrees into disjunctive concepts. For instance, if the concept follows the following binary function: $y = (A_1 \cap A_2) \cup (A_3 \cap A_4)$ then the minimal univariate decision tree that represents this function is illustrated in Figure 7.1. Note that the tree contains two copies of the same subtree.

(3) The greedy characteristic of decision trees leads to another disadvantage that should be pointed out. The over-sensitivity to the training set, to irrelevant attributes and to noise [Quinlan (1993)] make decision trees especially unstable: a minor change in one split close to the root will change the whole subtree below. Due to small variations in the

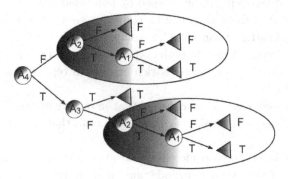

Fig. 7.1 Illustration of decision tree with replication.

training set, the algorithm may choose an attribute which is not truly the best one.

(4) The fragmentation problem causes partitioning of the data into smaller fragments. This usually happens if many features are tested along the path. If the data splits approximately equally on every split, then a univariate decision tree cannot test more than $O(logn)$ features. This puts decision trees at a disadvantage for tasks with many relevant features. Note that replication always implies fragmentation, but fragmentation may happen without any replication.

(5) Another problem refers to the effort needed to deal with missing values [Friedman *et al.* (1996)]. While the ability to handle missing values is considered to be advantage, the extreme effort which is required to achieve it is considered a drawback. The correct branch to take is unknown if a feature tested is missing, and the algorithm must employ special mechanisms to handle missing values. In order to reduce the occurrences of tests on missing values, C4.5 penalizes the information gain by the proportion of unknown instances and then splits these instances into subtrees. CART uses a much more complex scheme of surrogate features.

(6) The myopic nature of most of the decision tree induction algorithms is reflected by the fact that the inducers look only one level ahead. Specifically, the splitting criterion ranks possible attributes based on their immediate descendants. Such strategy prefers tests that score high in isolation and may overlook combinations of attributes. Using deeper lookahead strategies is considered to be computationally expensive and has not proven useful.

Chapter 8

Beyond Classification Tasks

8.1 Introduction

Up to this point, we have mainly focused on using decision trees for classification tasks (i.e. classification trees). However, decision trees can be used for other data mining tasks. In this chapter, we review the other common tasks that decision trees are used for, including: regression, clustering and survival analysis.

8.2 Regression Trees

Regression models map the input space into a real-value domain. For instance, a regressor can predict the demand for a certain product given its characteristics. Formally, the goal is to examine $y|X$ for a response y and a set of predictors X.

Regression trees are decision trees that deal with a continuous target. The basic idea is to combine decision trees and linear regression to forecast numerical target attribute based on a set of input attributes. These methods perform induction by means of an efficient recursive partitioning algorithm. The choice of the best split at each node of the tree is usually guided by a least squares error criterion.

Regression tree models are successfully used for day ahead forecasting of power consumption using input features such as temperature, day of the week and location.

CART and CHAID regression tree algorithms assign a constant value to the leaves. The constant value is usually the mean value of the corresponding leaf. RETIS and M5 algorithms are able to use linear regression models at the leaves. Linear regression is a well-known statistics method that was studied rigorously.

CART can be applied to both categorical and quantitative response variables. When CART is applied with a quantitative response variable, the procedure is known as "Regression Trees". At each step, heterogeneity is now measured by the within-node sum of squares of the response:

$$i(\tau) = \sum (y_i - \bar{y}(\tau))^2, \qquad (8.1)$$

where for node τ the summation is over all cases in that node, and $\bar{y}(\tau)$ is the mean of those cases. The heterogeneity for each potential split is the sum of the two sums of squares for the two nodes that would result. The split is chosen that reduces most this within-nodes sum of squares; the sum of squares of the parent node is compared to the combined sums of squares from each potential split into two offspring nodes. Generalization to Poisson regression (for count data) follows with the deviance used in place of the sum of squares.

Several software packages provide implementation of regression tree models. MATLAB provides the REPTree function that fits a regression tree model according to the threshold and tree pruning setting. The `party` package in R provides a set of tools for training regression trees. Section 10.3 presents a walk-through-guide for building Regression Trees in R.

8.3 Survival Trees

Survival analysis is a collection of statistical procedures for data analysis for which the outcome variable of interest is the time until an event occurs. An event might be a death, machine end of life, disease incidence, component failure, recovery or any designated experience of interest that may happen to an individual/object on which the study is focused.

The main goals of survival analysis are estimating the relative effects of risk factors and predicting survival probabilities/survival times. Cox's proportional hazards model is probably the most obvious way to fulfill the first goal by assuming there is a linear association between survival time and covariates.

Survival analysis has been used extensively in medical research. Most of the work in the medical field focuses on studying survival curves of patients suffering from different ailments. However, survival analysis can be used in the engineering domain. For example, Eyal *et al.* (2014) show that survival analysis can be used to predict failures of automobiles. Automobiles can be considered analogous to humans due to their complexity and the wide variety of factors which impact their life expectancy.

In order to learn the above characteristics of a population or group of components, speaking in terms of engineering systems, a sufficient amount of data is needed. The data should include enough instances of objects in the population, information about several properties of each individual (values of the explanatory variables), and the time of failure or at least the maximal time in which a subject is known to have survived. The basic terms of survival analysis are described below.

In survival analysis, tree structures are used for analyzing multi-dimensional data by partitioning it and identifying local structures in it. Tree methods are non-parametric, since they do not assume any distributional properties about the data. Tree-based methods for univariate and multivariate survival data have been proposed and evaluated by many authors. Some of these works suggest extensions to the CART algorithm. The leaves of the tree hold the hazard functions. The hazard function is the probability that an individual will experience an event (for example, death) within a small time interval, given that the individual has survived up to the beginning of the interval.

Some survival trees are based on conditional hypothesis testing. This framework provides a solution to models with continuous and categorical data and includes procedures applicable to censored, ordinal, or multivariate responses. In this framework, the conditional distribution of statistics to measure the association between responses and factors. This would serve as a basis for unbiased selection among factors. This algorithm, known as Conditional Inference Trees (C-Tree algorithm), uses classical statistical tests to select a split point. It is based on the minimum p-value among all tests of independence between the response variable and each factor, where p-value is the probability incorrectly rejecting the null hypothesis. This framework derives unbiased estimates of factors and correctly handles ordinal response variables. Statistically motivated stopping criteria implemented via hypothesis tests yield a predictive performance that is equivalent to the optimally pruned trees. Based on this observation, they offered an intuitive and computationally efficient solution to the overfitting problem.

In the recent years, survival tree methods became popular tools for survival analysis. As survival trees are non-parametric models, they do not require predefined distributional assumptions. When a single tree framework is used, the data is split only by a subset of factors and the rest are disregarded due to the trees stopping conditions, e.g. minimum number of observations in a terminal node. Therefore, a single tree-based method may not offer information on the influence of many of the factors on the behavior of the component. Ensemble tree-based algorithms are strong methods which overcome this limitation.

The survival trees method is highly popular among the tree-based methods. This method is useful for identifying factors that may influence a failure event and the mileage or time to an event of interest. Survival trees do not require any defined distribution assumptions and they tend to be resistant to the influence of outliers. When a single tree framework is used, the data are split by only a subset of factors and the rest are disregarded due to the trees stopping conditions, e.g. minimum number of observations in a terminal node. Therefore, a single tree-based method may not offer information on the influence of many of the factors on the behavior of the component. In order to overcome this limitation, a new ensemble approach is proposed.

The Random Survival Forests (RSF) is a method for the analysis of right-censored survival data. Both Random Forest (RF) and RSF are very efficient algorithms for analyzing large multidimensional datasets. However, due to their random nature they are not always intuitive and comprehensible to the user. Different trees in the forest might yield conflicting interpretations. In contrast to the RF, the C-Forest function in R creates random forests from unbiased classification trees based on a conditional inference framework.

Like in classification trees, also in survival trees the splitting criterion that is very crucial to the success of the algorithm. Bou-Hamad *et al.* (2011) provide a very detailed comparison of splitting criteria. Most of the existing algorithms are using statistical tests for choosing the best split. One possible approach is to use the logrank statistic to compare the two groups formed by the children nodes. The chosen split is the one with the largest significant test statistic value. The use of the logrank test leads to a split which assures the best separation of the median survival times in the two children nodes. Another option is to use the likelihood ratio statistic (LRS) under an assumed model to measure the dissimilarity between the two children nodes. Another option is to use the KolmogorovSmirnov statistic to compare the survival curves of the two nodes. Some researchers suggest to select the split based on residuals obtained from fitting a model. The degree of randomness of the residuals is quantified and the split that appears the least random is selected. The `party` package in R provides a set of tools for training survival trees. Section 10.3 presents a walk-through-guide for building Regression Trees in R.

8.4 Clustering Tree

Clustering groups data instances into subsets in such a manner that similar instances are grouped together, while different instances belong to different groups. The instances are thereby organized into an efficient representation that characterizes the population being sampled. Formally, the clustering structure is represented as a set of subsets $C = C_1, \ldots, C_k$ of S, such that: $S = \bigcup_{i=1}^{k} C_i$ and $C_i \cap C_j = \emptyset$ for $i \neq j$. Consequently, any instance in S belongs to exactly one and only one subset.

Clustering of objects is as ancient as the human need for describing the salient characteristics of men and objects and identifying them with a type. Therefore, it embraces various scientific disciplines: from mathematics and statistics to biology and genetics, each of which uses different terms to describe the topologies formed using this analysis. From biological "taxonomies", to medical "syndromes" and genetic "genotypes" to manufacturing "group technology" — the problem is identical: forming categories of entities and assigning individuals to the proper groups within it. A clustering tree is a decision tree where the leaves do not contain classes but each node of a tree corresponds to a concept or a cluster, and the tree as a whole thus represents a kind of taxonomy or a hierarchy. To induce clustering trees, Blockeel *et al.* (1998) introduce the top-down induction of clustering trees which adapt the basic top-down induction of decision trees method towards clustering. To this end, a distance measure is used to compute the distance between two examples. Specifically, in order to compute the distance between two sets of instances, they employ a function that induces a prototype of a set instances. Thus, the distance between two set of instances is calculated as the distance between their prototypes. Given a distance measure for clusters and the view that each node of a tree corresponds to a cluster, the decision tree algorithm selects in each node the test that will maximize the distance between the resulting clusters in its subnodes. Each node in the tree corresponds to a cluster of examples, and the hierarchical structure of the tree shows the way that clusters are split into subclusters. The test in a node can be seen as a discriminant description of the two clusters in which the current cluster of examples is divided. One cluster is described by saying that the test succeeds, the other by saying that it fails.

8.4.1 *Distance Measures*

Since clustering is the grouping of similar instances/objects, some sort of measure that can determine whether two objects are similar or dissimilar is required. There are two main type of measures used to estimate this relation: distance measures and similarity measures.

Many clustering methods use distance measures to determine the similarity or dissimilarity between any pair of objects. It is useful to denote the distance between two instances x_i and x_j as: $d(x_i, x_j)$. A valid distance measure should be symmetric and obtains its minimum value (usually zero) in case of identical vectors. The distance measure is called a metric distance measure if it also satisfies the following properties:

(1) Triangle inequality $d(x_i, x_k) \leq d(x_i, x_j) + d(x_j, x_k)$ $\forall x_i, x_j, x_k \in S$.
(2) $d(x_i, x_j) = 0 \Rightarrow x_i = x_j$ $\forall x_i, x_j \in S$.

8.4.2   *Minkowski: Distance Measures for Numeric Attributes*

Given two p-dimensional instances, $x_i = (x_{i1}, x_{i2}, \ldots, x_{ip})$ and $x_j = (x_{j1}, x_{j2}, \ldots, x_{jp})$, the distance between the two data instances can be calculated using the Minkowski metric:

$$d(x_i, x_j) = (|x_{i1} - x_{j1}|^g + |x_{i2} - x_{j2}|^g + \cdots + |x_{ip} - x_{jp}|^g)^{1/g} \,.$$

The commonly used Euclidean distance between two objects is achieved when $g = 2$. Given $g = 1$, the sum of absolute paraxial distances (Manhattan metric) is obtained, and with $g = \infty$ one gets the greatest of the paraxial distances (Chebychev metric).

The measurement unit used can affect the clustering analysis. To avoid the dependence on the choice of measurement units, the data should be standardized. Standardizing measurements attempts to give all variables an equal weight. However, if each variable is assigned with a weight according to its importance, then the weighted distance can be computed as:

$$d(x_i, x_j) = (w_1 |x_{i1} - x_{j1}|^g + w_2 |x_{i2} - x_{j2}|^g + \cdots + w_p |x_{ip} - x_{jp}|^g)^{1/g} \,,$$

where $w_i \in [0, \infty)$.

8.4.2.1   *Distance Measures for Binary Attributes*

The distance measure described in the last section may be easily computed for continuous-valued attributes. In the case of instances described by categorical, binary, ordinal or mixed type attributes, the distance measure should be revised.

In the case of binary attributes, the distance between objects may be calculated based on a contingency table. A binary attribute is symmetric if both of its states are equally valuable. In that case, using the simple matching coefficient can assess dissimilarity between two objects:

$$d(x_i, x_j) = \frac{r + s}{q + r + s + t},$$

where q is the number of attributes that equal 1 for both objects; t is the number of attributes that equal 0 for both objects; and s and r are the number of attributes that are unequal for both objects.

A binary attribute is asymmetric, if its states are not equally important (usually the positive outcome is considered more important). In this case, the denominator ignores the unimportant negative matches (t). This is called the Jaccard coefficient:

$$d(x_i, x_j) = \frac{r + s}{q + r + s}.$$

8.4.2.2 *Distance Measures for Nominal Attributes*

When the attributes are *nominal*, two main approaches may be used:

(1) Simple matching:

$$d(x_i, x_j) = \frac{p - m}{p},$$

where p is the total number of attributes and m is the number of matches.
(2) Creating a binary attribute for each state of each nominal attribute and computing their dissimilarity as described above.

8.4.2.3 *Distance Metrics for Ordinal Attributes*

When the attributes are *ordinal*, the sequence of the values is meaningful. In such cases, the attributes can be treated as numeric ones after mapping their range onto [0,1]. Such mapping may be carried out as follows:

$$z_{i,n} = \frac{r_{i,n} - 1}{M_n - 1},$$

where $z_{i,n}$ is the standardized value of attribute a_n of object i. $r_{i,n}$ is that value before standardization, and M_n is the upper limit of the domain of attribute a_n (assuming the lower limit is 1).

8.4.2.4   *Distance Metrics for Mixed-Type Attributes*

In the cases where the instances are characterized by attributes of *mixed-type*, one may calculate the distance by combining the methods mentioned above. For instance, when calculating the distance between instances i and j using a metric such as the Euclidean distance, one may calculate the difference between nominal and binary attributes as 0 or 1 ("match" or "mismatch", respectively), and the difference between numeric attributes as the difference between their normalized values. The square of each such difference will be added to the total distance. Such calculation is employed in many clustering algorithms presented below.

The dissimilarity $d(x_i, x_j)$ between two instances, containing p attributes of mixed types, is defined as:

$$d(x_i, x_j) = \frac{\sum_{n=1}^{p} \delta_{ij}^{(n)} d_{ij}^{(n)}}{\sum_{n=1}^{p} \delta_{ij}^{(n)}},$$

where the indicator $\delta_{ij}^{(n)} = 0$ if one of the values is missing. The contribution of attribute n to the distance between the two objects $d^{(n)}(x_i, x_j)$ is computed according to its type:

- If the attribute is binary or categorical, $d^{(n)}(x_i, x_j) = 0$ if $x_{in} = x_{jn}$, otherwise $d^{(n)}(x_i, x_j) = 1$.
- If the attribute is continuous-valued, $d_{ij}^{(n)} = \frac{|x_{in} - x_{jn}|}{\max_h x_{hn} - \min_h x_{hn}}$, where h runs over all non-missing objects for attribute n.
- If the attribute is ordinal, the standardized values of the attribute are computed first and then, $z_{i,n}$ is treated as continuous-valued.

8.4.3   *Similarity Functions*

An alternative concept to that of the distance is the similarity function $s(x_i, x_j)$ that compares the two vectors x_i and x_j. This function should be symmetrical (namely $s(x_i, x_j) = s(x_j, x_i)$) and have a large value when x_i and x_j are somehow "similar" and constitute the largest value for identical vectors.

A similarity function where the target range is [0,1] is called a dichotomous similarity function. In fact, the measures described in the previous sections for calculating the "distances" in the case of binary and nominal attributes may be easily converted to similarity functions, by subtracting the distance measure from 1.

8.4.3.1 *Cosine Measure*

When the angle between the two vectors is a meaningful measure of their similarity, the normalized inner product may be an appropriate similarity measure:

$$s(x_i, x_j) = \frac{x_i^T \cdot x_j}{\|x_i\| \cdot \|x_j\|}.$$

8.4.3.2 *Pearson Correlation Measure*

The normalized Pearson correlation is defined as:

$$s(x_i, x_j) = \frac{(x_i - \bar{x}_i)^T \cdot (x_j - \bar{x}_j)}{\|x_i - \bar{x}_i\| \cdot \|x_j - \bar{x}_j\|},$$

where $\bar{x}_i$ denotes the average feature value of x over all dimensions.

8.4.3.3 *Extended Jaccard Measure*

The extended Jaccard measure is defined as:

$$s(x_i, x_j) = \frac{x_i^T \cdot x_j}{\|x_i\|^2 + \|x_j\|^2 - x_i^T \cdot x_j}.$$

8.4.3.4 *Dice Coefficient Measure*

The dice coefficient measure is similar to the extended Jaccard measure and it is defined as:

$$s(x_i, x_j) = \frac{2x_i^T \cdot x_j}{\|x_i\|^2 + \|x_j\|^2}.$$

8.4.4 *The OCCT Algorithm*

Dror *et al.* (2014) recently introduced the One-Class Clustering Tree algorithm (OCCT) which is a clustering tree for implementing One-to-Many data linkage. Data linkage refers to the task of matching entities from two different data sources that do not share a common identifier (i.e. a foreign key). Data linkage is usually performed among entities of the same type. It is common to divide data linkage into two types, namely, one-to-one and one-to-many. In one-to-one data linkage, the goal is to associate one record in the first table with a single matching record in the second table. In the case of one-to-many data linkage, the goal is to associate one record in the first table with one or more matching records in the second table. The OCCT algorithm characterizes the entities that should be linked together. The tree is built such that it is easy to understand and transform into association rules, i.e. the inner nodes consist only of features describing the first set of entities, while the leaves of the tree represent features of their matching entities from the second dataset. OCCT can be applied with four different splitting criteria:

- Coarse-grained Jaccard (CGJ) coefficient — It is based on the Jaccard similarity coefficient described above. It aims to choose the splitting attribute which leads to the smallest possible similarity between the subsets (i.e. an attribute that generates subsets that are different from each other as much as possible). In order to do so, we need examine each of the possible splitting attributes and measure the similarity between the subsets.
- Fine-grained Jaccard (FGJ) coefficient — The fine-grained Jaccard coefficient is capable of identifying partial record matches, as opposed to the coarse-grained method, which identifies exact matches only. It not only considers records which are exactly identical, but also checks to what extent each possible pair of records is similar.
- Least probable intersections (LPI) — In this measure the optimal splitting attribute is the attribute that leads to the minimum amount of instances that are shared between two item-sets. The criterion relies on the cumulative distribution function (CDF) of the Poisson distribution and described in details in the next chapter.
- Maximum likelihood estimation (MLE) — Given a candidate split, a probabilistic model is trained (such as decision tree) for each of the split's subsets. The idea is to choose the split that achieves the maximal likelihood.

8.5   Hidden Markov Model Trees

Hidden Markov Model is a method for sequence learning which is capable to estimate the probability of sequences by training from data. HMM is a type of dynamic Bayesian network (DBN). It is a stochastic process with an underlying unobservable (hidden) stochastic process that can only be observed through another set of stochastic processes that produce the sequence of observed symbols. HMM can be viewed as a specific instance of a state-space model in which the latent variables are discrete. In HMM, the probability distribution of z_n depends on the state of the previous latent variable z_{n-1} through a conditional distribution $p(z_n|z_{n-1})$. The following characterize a HMM:

- N — the number of states in the model. The individual states are denoted as $Z = \{z_1, z_2 \ldots z_N\}$ and the state at time t as q_t.
- M — the number of distinct observation symbols per state. The observation symbols correspond to the physical output of the system being modeled. The symbols are represented as $X = \{x_1, x_2 \ldots x_M\}$.
- The state transition probability distribution $A = \{a_{i,j}\}$ where $a_{i,j} = P[q_{t+1} = z_j | q_t = z_i]$ $1 \leq i, j \leq N$.
- The observation symbol probability distribution in state j, $B = \{b_i(k)\}$ where $b_i(k) = P[x_k \, at \, t \, |q_t = z_j], \begin{array}{l} 1 \leq j \leq N \\ 1 \leq k \leq M \end{array}$.
- The initial state distribution $\pi = \{\pi_i\}$ where $\pi = P[q_1 = z_i]$, $1 \leq i \leq N$.

Antwarg *et al.* (2012) present the notion of HMM tree. Each node in the tree is a HMM which uses the same states from the higher level or only some of them but with different transition probabilities. Because the number of available training instances drops as we move down the tree, the number of hidden states should generally drop accordingly. In particular, if the number of observations is very large, then we can choose a large number of hidden states to capture more features. The hierarchical structure that forms a tree is used to differentiate between cases and better estimate HMM parameters.

Consider the task of intention prediction which aims to predict what the user wants to accomplish when performing a certain sequence of activities. Predicting user intentions when using a system can improve the services provided to users by adjusting the system services to their needs. This goal is achieved by training a specific learning algorithm in order to generate models that will maximize the accuracy of the prediction. The challenge in predicting the intention of the user given a sequence of interactions can be categorized as a problem with a sequential problem space which is commonly solved using sequence learning algorithms.

Using intention prediction methods will enable a company to improve the services provided to users by adjusting the system services to their needs (e.g. the interface). Predicting user intentions can be also used for assisting users to perform or complete tasks, to alert them regarding the availability of features, and to increase their general knowledge. Effective assistance will allow users to acquire the new skills and knowledge they need to easily operate an unfamiliar device or function.

Different users tend to select different sequences for accomplishing the same goal. Specifically, the user's attributes and context (such as age or the operating system) indicate which sequence the user will eventually perform. For example, if a young male uses a system, it is possible to use the model to predict the goal that he intends to accomplish and provide him with a user interface (UI) more appropriate to his usage and intentions.

The reason for using hidden Markov models is that the sequence of actions that users perform is not always observable but can only be observed through another set of stochastic processes that produce the sequence of observations. For example, in a mobile device the sequence of buttons that the user pressed is unknown (hidden) but the sequence of screens that was created from using these buttons is known (observable). Thus, we can learn the sequence of buttons from the sequence of screens using HMM.

Figure 8.1 illustrates a HMM tree. In this case, the tree is branched according to the user's attributes and each node in the tree consists of

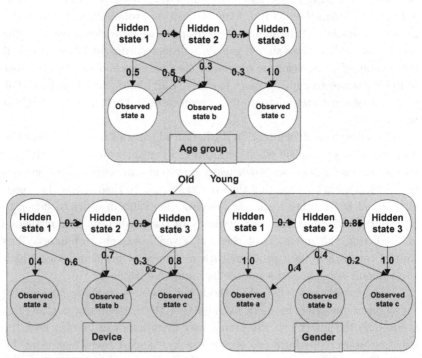

Fig. 8.1   Structure of attribute-driven HMM tree. Each node in the hierarchical structure contains a model and an attribute. All nodes contain the same model but with different transition probabilities.

a single HMM. When the user performs a new task, we first employ her attributes to find the suitable node in each of the goal trees. Then, based on the actions the user has already performed in implementing this task, we anticipate the goal she is trying to accomplish and the action she intends to perform next.

In a typical sequence learning problem, a training set of sequences $S = \{s_1, s_2, \ldots, s_m\}$ is given. Each sequence $s_j \in S$ is an ordered set of n_j elements (actions) $\{e_1, e_2, \ldots, e_{n_i}\}$. G denotes the set of all possible goals (for example, in an email application G = {'Add recipient', 'Send an email', 'Read email'}). Each training sequence is associated with one goal and several characterizing attributes. The notation U denotes the set of input attributes containing η attributes: $U = \{v_1, \ldots, v_\eta\}$. The domain (possible values for each attribute) of an attribute is denoted by $dom(v_i)$. User space (the set of all possible users) is defined as a Cartesian product of all the input attribute domains. The input in the problem consists of a set of m records and is denoted as $Train = (\langle s_1, g_1, u_1 \rangle, \ldots, \langle s_m, g_m, u_m \rangle)$ where $s_q \in S, g_q \in G, u_q \in U$.

The notation L represents a probabilistic sequence learning algorithm such as HMM. We mainly focus on HMM, but the same algorithm can be used with other base models, for example, conditional random field (CRF) as a base model. These algorithms generate models that can estimate the conditional probability of a goal g given a sequence and the input user attributes. Let λ represent a probabilistic model which was induced by activating L onto dataset $Train$. In this case, we would like to estimate the conditional probability $p_\lambda(G = g_j | s_q, u_q)$ of a sequence s_q that was generated by user u_q. Thus, the aim of intention prediction is to find the most accurate probability estimations.

As indicated in Figure 8.1, we are using a tree structure to improve the accuracy of training models. For each goal in the system, a different tree is generated. This structure is built using user attributes in an attempt to differentiate between various usage behaviors in the system. For example, in Figure 1 we are employing the age, gender and device for differentiating between usage behaviors. In this structure, each node contains a model and an attribute v_i that splits the node. Assuming this tree structure, the problem can be formally phrased as follows:

Given a sequence learning algorithm L and a training set $Train$ with input sessions set S, users U and goals G, the aim is to find an optimal set of trees (a tree for each goal). Optimality is defined in terms of minimizing prediction errors.

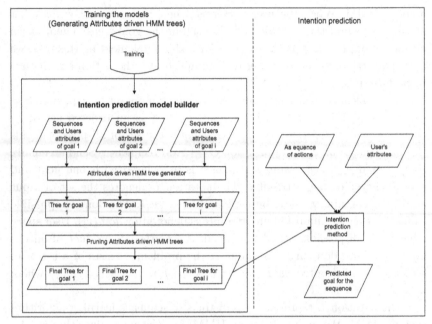

Fig. 8.2   Overall diagram of the attribute-driven HMM tree-based method for intention prediction.

We assume that L is an algorithm for training HMMs. Particularly, the model λ in each of the tree's nodes is trained using the Baum–Welch algorithm and the probability $p_\lambda(G = g_j|s_q, u_q)$ is estimated using the forward–backward algorithm as we show below.

Figure 8.2 presents the HMM training process schematically. The left side in Figure 8.2 specifies the generation of the models used for intention prediction based on an attribute-driven HMM tree for each possible goal. The input for this process is a set of user action sequences divided into goals and user attributes. The output of the process is a tree for each goal based on different usage behavior of users in attaining this goal, and user attributes. The right side of the figure presents the prediction process. The inputs for the process are: the goal trees generated during the model generation phase, a specific user session (i.e. a sequence of actions), and the attributes of a user. The output is the predicted goal that the specific user was trying to accomplish in this sequence (i.e. the goal with the highest probability estimation).

Chapter 9

Decision Forests

9.1 Introduction

The main idea of an ensemble methodology is to combine a set of models, each of which solves the same original task, in order to obtain a better composite global model, with more accurate and reliable estimates or decisions than can be obtained from using a single model. The idea of building a predictive model by integrating multiple models has been under investigation for a long time. In fact, ensemble methodology imitates our second nature to seek several opinions before making any crucial decision. We weigh individual opinions, and combine them to reach our final decision [Polikar (2006)].

It is well known that ensemble methods can be used for improving prediction performance. Researchers from various disciplines such as statistics, machine learning, pattern recognition, and data mining considered the use of ensemble methodology. This chapter presents an updated survey of ensemble methods in classification tasks. The chapter provides a profound descriptions of the various combining methods, ensemble diversity generator and ensemble size determination.

In the literature, the term "ensemble methods" is usually reserved for collections of models that are minor variants of the same basic model. Nevertheless, in this chapter we also cover hybridization of models that are not from the same family. The latter is also referred in the literature as "multiple classifier systems."

9.2 Back to the Roots

Marie Jean Antoine Nicolas de Caritat, marquis de Condorcet (1743–1794) was a French mathematician who among others wrote in 1785 the Essay on the Application of Analysis to the Probability of Majority Decisions. This work presented the well-known Condorcet's jury theorem. The theorem refers to a jury of voters who need to make a decision regarding a binary outcome (for example, to convict or not a defendant). If each voter has a probability p of being correct and the probability of a majority of voters being correct is M then:

- $p > 0.5$ implies $M > p$.
- Also M approaches 1, for all $p > 0.5$ as the number of voters approaches infinity.

This theorem has two major limitations: the assumption that the votes are independent; and that there are only two possible outcomes. Nevertheless, if these two preconditions are met, then a correct decision can be obtained by simply combining the votes of a large enough jury that is composed of voters whose judgments are slightly better than a random vote.

Originally, the Condorcet Jury Theorem was written to provide a theoretical basis for democracy. Nonetheless, the same principle can be applied in pattern recognition. A strong learner is an inducer that is given a training set consisting of labeled data and produces a classifier which can be arbitrarily accurate. A weak learner produces a classifier which is only slightly more accurate than random classification. The formal definitions of weak and strong learners are beyond the scope of this book. The reader is referred to [Schapire (1990)] for these definitions under the PAC theory. A decision stump inducer is one example of a weak learner. A Decision Stump is a one-level Decision Tree with either a categorical or a numerical class label.

For the sake of clarity, let us demonstrate the ensemble idea by applying it to the Labor dataset presented in Table 9.1. Each instance in the table stands for a collective agreement reached in the business and personal services sectors (such as teachers and nurses) in Canada during the years 1987–1988. The aim of the learning task is to distinguish between acceptable and unacceptable agreements (as classified by experts in the field). The selected input-features that characterize the agreement are:

- Dur — the duration of agreement
- Wage — wage increase in first year of contract
- Stat — number of statutory holidays
- Vac — number of paid vacation days

Table 9.1 The labor dataset.

Dur	Wage	Stat	Vac	Dis	Dental	Ber	Health	Class
1	5	11	average	?	?	yes	?	good
2	4.5	11	below	?	full	?	full	good
?	?	11	generous	yes	half	yes	half	good
3	3.7	?	?	?	?	yes	?	good
3	4.5	12	average	?	half	yes	half	good
2	2	12	average	?	?	?	?	good
3	4	12	generous	yes	none	yes	half	good
3	6.9	12	below	?	?	?	?	good
2	3	11	below	yes	half	yes	?	good
1	5.7	11	generous	yes	full	?	?	good
3	3.5	13	generous	?	?	yes	full	good
2	6.4	15	?	?	full	?	?	good
2	3.5	10	below	no	half	?	half	bad
3	3.5	13	generous	?	full	yes	full	good
1	3	11	generous	?	?	?	?	good
2	4.5	11	average	?	full	yes	?	good
1	2.8	12	below	?	?	?	?	good
1	2.1	9	below	yes	half	?	none	bad
1	2	11	average	no	none	no	none	bad
2	4	15	generous	?	?	?	?	good
2	4.3	12	generous	?	full	?	full	good
2	2.5	11	below	?	?	?	?	bad
3	3.5	?	?	?	?	?	?	good
2	4.5	10	generous	?	half	?	full	good
1	6	9	generous	?	?	?	?	good
3	2	10	below	?	half	yes	full	bad
2	4.5	10	below	yes	none	?	half	good
2	3	12	generous	?	?	yes	full	good
2	5	11	below	yes	full	yes	full	good
3	2	10	average	?	?	yes	full	bad
3	4.5	11	average	?	half	?	?	good
3	3	10	below	yes	half	yes	full	bad
2	2.5	10	average	?	?	?	?	bad
2	4	10	below	no	none	?	none	bad
3	2	10	below	no	half	yes	full	bad
2	2	11	average	yes	none	yes	full	bad
1	2	11	generous	no	none	no	none	bad
1	2.8	9	below	yes	half	?	none	bad
3	2	10	average	?	?	yes	none	bad
2	4.5	12	average	yes	full	yes	half	good
1	4	11	average	no	none	no	none	bad
2	2	12	generous	yes	none	yes	full	bad
2	2.5	12	average	?	?	yes	?	bad
2	2.5	11	below	?	?	yes	?	bad
2	4	10	below	no	none	?	none	bad
2	4.5	10	below	no	half	?	half	bad

(*Continued*)

Table 9.1   (*Continued*)

Dur	Wage	Stat	Vac	Dis	Dental	Ber	Health	Class
2	4.5	11	average	?	full	yes	full	good
2	4.6	?	?	yes	half	?	half	good
2	5	11	below	yes	?	?	full	good
2	5.7	11	average	yes	full	yes	full	good
2	7	11	?	yes	full	?	?	good
3	2	?	?	yes	half	yes	?	good
3	3.5	13	generous	?	?	yes	full	good
3	4	11	average	yes	full	?	full	good
3	5	11	generous	yes	?	?	full	good
3	5	12	average	?	half	yes	half	good
3	6	9	generous	yes	full	yes	full	good

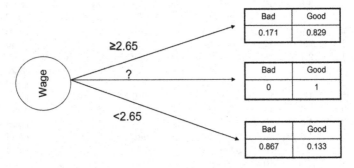

Fig. 9.1   Decision stump classifier for solving the labor classification task.

- Dis — employer's help during employee longterm disability
- Dental — contribution of the employer towards a dental plan
- Ber — employer's financial contribution in the costs of bereavement
- Health — employer's contribution towards the health plan.

Applying a Decision Stump inducer on the Labor dataset results in the model that is depicted in Figure 9.1. Using 10-folds cross-validation, the estimated generalized accuracy of this model is 59.64%.

Next, we execute an ensemble algorithm using Decision Stump as the base inducer and train four decision trees. Specifically we use the Bagging (bootstrap aggregating) ensemble method. Bagging is simple yet effective method for generating an ensemble of classifiers or in this case forest of decision trees. Each decision tree in the ensemble is trained on a sample of instances taken with replacement (allowing repetitions) from the original training set. Consequently, in each iteration some of the original instances from S may appear more than once and some may not be included at all. Table 9.2 indicates for each instance the number of times it was sampled in every iteration.

Figure 9.2 presents the four trees that were built. The estimated generalized accuracy of this forest rises from 59.64% to 77.19%

Table 9.2   The bagging sample sizes for the labor dataset.

Instance	Iteration 1	Iteration 2	Iteration 3	Iteration 4
1			1	1
2	1	1	1	1
3	2	1	1	1
4	1	1		
5		1	2	1
6	2	1		1
7		1	1	1
8	1		1	1
9		2		
10	1	1	2	
11		1		1
12	1	1	1	
13		1	1	2
14	1	1		2
15	1		1	1
16	2	3	2	1
17	1			
18	1	2	2	1
19	1			2
20		1	3	
21	2		1	1
22	2	1	1	
23		1	2	1
24	1	1		1
25	2	2	1	2
26	1	1	1	1
27		1		
28	2	1	1	1
29	1		1	1
30	1	1		
31		1	1	3
32	2	1	2	
33	1			1
34	2	2	1	
35				2
36	1	1	1	1
37		2	1	
38	2	1		1

(*Continued*)

Table 9.2   (*Continued*)

Instance	Iteration 1	Iteration 2	Iteration 3	Iteration 4
39	2	1	1	
40	1	1	1	2
41	1	2	2	2
42		3	2	1
43	2			1
44	1	2	1	3
45	3	1	2	1
46	1		1	2
47	1	1	2	1
48		1	1	1
49	1	2	1	2
50	2		1	1
51	1	1	1	1
52	1	1	1	
53	1	2	2	2
54	1	1		
55			2	2
56	1	1	1	1
57	1	1	2	1
Total	57	57	57	57

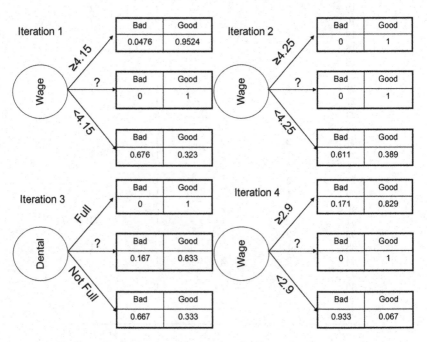

Fig. 9.2   Decision stumps for solving the labor classification task.

One of the basic questions that has been investigated in ensemble learning is: "Can a collection of weak classifiers create a single strong one?". Applying the Condorcet Jury Theorem insinuates that this goal might be achieved. Namely, construct an ensemble that (a) consists of independent classifiers, each of which correctly classifies a pattern with a probability of $p > 0.5$; and (b) has a probability of $M > p$ to jointly classify a pattern to its correct class.

Sir Francis Galton (1822–1911) was an English philosopher and statistician that conceived the basic concept of standard deviation and correlation. While visiting a livestock fair, Galton was intrigued by a simple weight-guessing contest. The visitors were invited to guess the weight of an ox. Hundreds of people participated in this contest, but no one succeeded to guess the exact weight: 1,198 pounds. Nevertheless, surprisingly enough, Galton found out that the average of all guesses came quite close to the exact weight: 1,197 pounds. Similarly to the Condorcet jury theorem, Galton revealed the power of combining many simplistic predictions in order to obtain an accurate prediction.

James Michael Surowiecki, an American financial journalist, published in 2004 the book "The Wisdom of Crowds: Why the Many Are Smarter Than the Few and How Collective Wisdom Shapes Business, Economies, Societies and Nations". Surowiecki argues, that under certain controlled conditions, the aggregation of information from several sources, results in decisions that are often superior to those that could have been made by any single individual — even experts.

Naturally, not all crowds are wise (for example, greedy investors of a stock market bubble). Surowiecki indicates that in order to become wise, the crowd should comply with the following criteria:

- **Diversity of opinion** — Each member should have private information even if it is just an eccentric interpretation of the known facts.
- **Independence** — Members' opinions are not determined by the opinions of those around them.
- **Decentralization** — Members are able to specialize and draw conclusions based on local knowledge.
- **Aggregation** — Some mechanism exists for turning private judgments into a collective decision.

In statistics, the idea of building a predictive model that integrates multiple models has been investigated for a long time. The history of ensemble methods dates back to as early as 1977 with Tukeys Twicing

[1]: an ensemble of two linear regression models. Tukey suggested to fit the first linear regression model to the original data and the second linear model to the residuals. Two years later, Dasarathy and Sheela (1979) suggested to partition the input space using two or more classifiers. The main progress in the field was achieved during the Nineties. Hansen and Salamon (1990) suggested an ensemble of similarly configured neural networks to improve the predictive performance of a single one. At the same time Schapire (1990) laid the foundations for the award winning AdaBoost [Freund and Schapire (1996)] algorithm by showing that a strong classifier in the *probably approximately correct* (PAC) sense can be generated by combining "weak" classifiers (that is, simple classifiers whose classification performance is only slightly better than random classification). Ensemble methods can also be used for improving the quality and robustness of unsupervised tasks. Nevertheless, in this book we focus on classifier ensembles.

In the past few years, experimental studies conducted by the machine-learning community show that combining the outputs of multiple classifiers reduces the generalization error [Domingos (1996); Quinlan (1996); Bauer and Kohavi (1999); Opitz and Maclin (1999)] of the individual classifiers. Ensemble methods are very effective, mainly due to the phenomenon that various types of classifiers have different "inductive biases" [Mitchell (1997)]. Indeed, ensemble methods can effectively make use of such diversity to reduce the variance-error [Tumer and Ghosh (1996)] [Ali and Pazzani (1996)] without increasing the bias-error. In certain situations, an ensemble method can also reduce bias-error, as shown by the theory of large margin classifiers [Bartlett and Shawe-Taylor (1998)].

The ensemble methodology is applicable in many fields such as: finance [Leigh *et al.* (2002)]; bioinformatics [Tan *et al.* (2003)]; medicine [Mangiameli *et al.* (2004)], cheminformatics [Merkwirth *et al.* (2004)]; manufacturing [Maimon and Rokach (2004)]; geography [Bruzzone *et al.* (2004)] and pattern recognition [Pang *et al.* (2003)].

Given the potential usefulness of ensemble methods, it is not surprising that a vast number of methods is now available to researchers and practitioners. Several surveys on ensemble are available in the literature, such as [Clemen (1989)] for forecasting methods or [Dietterich (2000b)] for machine learning. Nevertheless, this survey proposes an updated and profound description of issues related to ensemble of classifiers. This chapter aims to organize all significant methods developed in this field into a coherent and unified catalog.

A typical ensemble framework for classification tasks contains the following building blocks:

(1) Training set — A labeled dataset used for ensemble training. In semi-supervised methods of ensemble generation, such as ASSEMBLE [Bennett *et al.* (2002)], unlabeled instances can be also used for the creation of the ensemble.
(2) Inducer — The inducer is an induction algorithm that obtains a training set and forms a classifier that represents the generalized relationship between the input attributes and the target attribute.
(3) Ensemble generator — This component is responsible for generating the diverse classifiers.
(4) Combiner — The combiner is responsible for combining the classifications of the various classifiers.

We use the notation $M_i = I(S_i)$ for representing a classifier M_i which was induced by inducer I on a training set S_i. The notation of $M_t, \alpha_t; t = 1, \ldots, T$ represents an ensemble of T classifiers.

The nature of each building block and the relation between them characterizes the ensemble framework design. The following list describes the main properties.

(1) Classifier dependency — During the classifier training how does each classifier affect the other classifiers? Classifiers may be dependent or independent.
(2) Diversity generator — In order to make the ensemble more effective, there should be some sort of diversity between the classifiers [Kuncheva (2005)]. Diversity may be obtained through different presentations of the input data, as in bagging, variations in learner design, or by adding a penalty to the outputs to encourage diversity.
(3) Ensemble size — The number of classifiers in the ensemble and how the undesirable classifiers are removed from the ensemble.
(4) Inducer usage — This property indicates the relation between the ensemble generator and the inducer used. Some ensemble have been specifically designed for a certain inducer and cannot have been used for other inducers.
(5) Combiner usage — This property specifies the relation between the ensemble generator and the combiner.
(6) Training data overlap — This property indicates which portion of the input data, used to induce a certain classifier, was also used to train other classifiers.

The issues of classifier dependency and diversity are very closely linked. More specifically, it can be argued that any effective method for generating diversity results in dependent classifiers (otherwise obtaining diversity is just luck). Nevertheless, as we will explain later one can independently create the classifiers and then, as a post-processing step, select the most diverse classifiers. Naturally there might be other properties which can be used to differentiate an ensemble scheme. We begin by surveying various combination methods. Following that we discuss and describe each one of the above-mentioned properties in details.

9.3   Combination Methods

There are two main methods for combining classifiers: weighting methods and meta-learning. The weighting methods are best suited for problems where the individual classifiers perform the same task and have comparable success or when we would like to avoid problems associated with added learning (such as overfitting or long training time).

9.3.1   *Weighting Methods*

When combining classifiers with weights, a classifier's classification has a strength proportional to its assigned weight. The assigned weight can be fixed or dynamically determined for the specific instance to be classified.

9.3.1.1   *Majority Voting*

In this combining scheme, a classification of an unlabeled instance is performed according to the class that obtains the highest number of votes (the most frequent vote). This method is also known as the plurality vote (PV) or the basic ensemble method (BEM). This approach has frequently been used as a combining method for comparing newly proposed methods.

Mathematically, it can be written as:

$$class(x) = \underset{c_i \in dom(y)}{\arg\max} \left(\sum_k g\left(y_k(x), c_i\right) \right), \qquad (9.1)$$

where $y_k(x)$ is the classification of the k'th classifier and $g(y, c)$ is an indicator function defined as:

$$g(y, c) = \begin{cases} 1 & y = c \\ 0 & y \neq c \end{cases}. \qquad (9.2)$$

Note that in case of a probabilistic classifier, the crisp classification $y_k(x)$ is usually obtained as follows:

$$y_k(x) = \arg\max_{c_i \in dom(y)} \hat{P}_{M_k}(y = c_i \,|\, x), \tag{9.3}$$

where M_k denotes classifier k and $\hat{P}_{M_k}(y = c \,|\, x)$ denotes the probability of y obtaining the value c given an instance x.

9.3.1.2 *Performance Weighting*

The weight of each classifier can be set proportional to its accuracy performance on a validation set [Opitz and Shavlik (1996)]:

$$\alpha_i = \frac{(1 - E_i)}{\sum\limits_{j=1}^{T}(1 - E_j)}, \tag{9.4}$$

where E_i is a normalization factor which is based on the performance evaluation of classifier i on a validation set.

9.3.1.3 *Distribution Summation*

The idea of the distribution summation combining method is to sum up the conditional probability vector obtained from each classifier [Clark and Boswell (1991)]. The selected class is chosen according to the highest value in the total vector. Mathematically, it can be written as:

$$Class(x) = \underset{c_i \in dom(y)}{\operatorname{argmax}} \sum_k \hat{P}_{M_k}(y = c_i \,|\, x). \tag{9.5}$$

9.3.1.4 *Bayesian Combination*

In the Bayesian combination method the weight associated with each classifier is the posterior probability of the classifier given the training set [Buntine (1990)].

$$Class(x) = \underset{c_i \in dom(y)}{\operatorname{argmax}} \sum_k P(M_k \,|\, S) \cdot \hat{P}_{M_k}(y = c_i \,|\, x), \tag{9.6}$$

where $P(M_k|S)$ denotes the probability that the classifier M_k is correct given the training set S. The estimation of $P(M_k|S)$ depends on the classifier's representation. To estimate this value for decision trees the reader is referred to [Buntine (1990)].

9.3.1.5 *Dempster–Shafer*

The idea of using the Dempster–Shafer theory of evidence [Buchanan and Shortliffe (1984)] for combining classifiers has been suggested in [Shilen (1990)]. This method uses the notion of basic probability assignment defined for a certain class c_i given the instance x:

$$bpa(c_i, x) = 1 - \prod_k \left(1 - \hat{P}_{M_k}(y = c_i \,|x)\right). \tag{9.7}$$

Consequently, the selected class is the one that maximizes the value of the belief function:

$$Bel(c_i, x) = \frac{1}{A} \cdot \frac{bpa(c_i, x)}{1 - bpa(c_i, x)}, \tag{9.8}$$

where A is a normalization factor defined as:

$$A = \sum_{\forall c_i \in dom(y)} \frac{bpa(c_i, x)}{1 - bpa(c_i, x)} + 1. \tag{9.9}$$

9.3.1.6 *Vogging*

The idea behind the vogging approach (Variance Optimized Bagging) is to optimize a linear combination of base-classifiers so as to aggressively reduce variance while attempting to preserve a prescribed accuracy [Derbeko *et al.* (2002)]. For this purpose, Derbeko *et al.* implemented the Markowitz Mean-Variance Portfolio Theory that is used for generating low variance portfolios of financial assets.

9.3.1.7 *Naïve Bayes*

Using Bayes' rule, one can extend the naïve Bayes idea for combining various classifiers:

$$Class(x) = \operatorname*{argmax}_{\substack{c_j \in dom(y) \\ \hat{P}(y=c_j)>0}} \hat{P}(y = c_j) \cdot \prod_{k=1} \frac{\hat{P}_{M_k}(y = c_j \,|x)}{\hat{P}(y = c_j)}. \tag{9.10}$$

9.3.1.8 *Entropy Weighting*

The idea in this combining method is to give each classifier a weight that is inversely proportional to the entropy of its classification vector.

$$Class(x) = \operatorname*{argmax}_{\substack{c_i \in dom(y) \\ k:c_i = \operatorname*{argmax}_{c_j \in dom(y)} \hat{P}_{M_k}(y=c_j|x)}} \sum E(M_k, x), \tag{9.11}$$

where:

$$E(M_k, x) = -\sum_{c_j} \hat{P}_{M_k}(y = c_j \,|\, x) \log(\hat{P}_{M_k}(y = c_j \,|\, x).) \qquad (9.12)$$

9.3.1.9 *Density-based Weighting*

If the various classifiers were trained using datasets obtained from different regions of the instance space, it might be useful to weight the classifiers according to the probability of sampling x by classifier M_k, namely:

$$Class(x) = \operatorname*{argmax}_{c_i \in dom(y)} \sum_{k : c_i = \operatorname*{argmax}_{c_j \in dom(y)} \hat{P}_{M_k}(y = c_j | x)} \hat{P}_{M_k}(x). \qquad (9.13)$$

The estimation of $\hat{P}_{M_k}(x)$ depends on the classifier representation and can not always be estimated.

9.3.1.10 *DEA Weighting Method*

Recently there has been attempt to use the data envelop analysis (DEA) methodology [Charnes *et al.* (1978)] in order to assign weights to different classifiers [Sohn and Choi (2001)]. These researchers argue that the weights should not be specified according to a single performance measure, but should be based on several performance measures. Because there is a trade-off among the various performance measures, the DEA is employed in order to figure out the set of efficient classifiers. In addition, DEA provides inefficient classifiers with the benchmarking point.

9.3.1.11 *Logarithmic Opinion Pool*

According to the logarithmic opinion pool [Hansen (2000)], the selection of the preferred class is performed according to:

$$Class(x) = \operatorname*{argmax}_{c_j \in dom(y)} e^{\sum_k \alpha_k \cdot \log(\hat{P}_{M_k}(y = c_j | x))}, \qquad (9.14)$$

where α_k denotes the weight of the k-th classifier, such that:

$$\alpha_k \geq 0; \quad \sum \alpha_k = 1. \qquad (9.15)$$

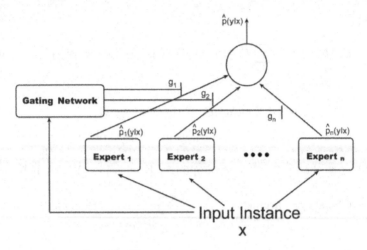

Fig. 9.3   Illustration of n-expert structure.

9.3.1.12   *Gating Network*

Figure 9.3 illustrates an n-expert structure. Each expert outputs the conditional probability of the target attribute given the input instance. A gating network is responsible for combining the various experts by assigning a weight to each network. These weights are not constant but are functions of the input instance x. The gating network selects one or a few experts (classifiers) which appear to have the most appropriate class distribution for the example. In fact, each expert specializes on a small portion of the input space.

An extension to the basic mixture of experts, known as hierarchical mixtures of experts (HME), has been proposed in [Jordan and Jacobs (1994)]. This extension decomposes the space into sub-spaces, and then recursively decomposes each sub-space into sub-spaces.

Variations of the basic mixture of experts methods have been developed to accommodate specific domain problems. A specialized modular networks called the Meta-p_i network has been used to solve the vowel-speaker problem [Hampshire and Waibel (1992); Peng *et al.* (1996)]. There have been other extensions, such as nonlinear gated experts for time-series [Weigend *et al.* (1995)]; revised modular network for predicting the survival of AIDS patients [Ohno-Machado and Musen (1997)]; and a new approach for combining multiple experts for improving handwritten numeral recognition [Rahman and Fairhurst (1997)].

9.3.1.13 *Order Statistics*

Order statistics can be used to combine classifiers [Tumer and Ghosh (2000)]. These combiners offer the simplicity of a simple weighted combination method together with the generality of meta-combination methods (see the following section). The robustness of this method is helpful when there are significant variations among classifiers in some part of the instance space.

9.3.2 *Meta-combination Methods*

Meta-learning means learning from the classifiers produced by the inducers and from the classifications of these classifiers on training data. The following sections describe the most well-known meta-combination methods.

9.3.2.1 *Stacking*

Stacking is a technique for achieving the highest generalization accuracy [Wolpert (1992)]. By using a meta-learner, this method tries to induce which classifiers are reliable and which are not. Stacking is usually employed to combine models built by different inducers. The idea is to create a meta-dataset containing a tuple for each tuple in the original dataset. However, instead of using the original input attributes, it uses the predicted classifications by the classifiers as the input attributes. The target attribute remains as in the original training set. A test instance is first classified by each of the base classifiers. These classifications are fed into a meta-level training set from which a meta-classifier is produced. This classifier combines the different predictions into a final one.

It is recommended that the original dataset should be partitioned into two subsets. The first subset is reserved to form the meta-dataset and the second subset is used to build the base-level classifiers. Consequently, the meta-classifier predications reflect the true performance of base-level learning algorithms.

Stacking performance can be improved by using output probabilities for every class label from the base-level classifiers. In such cases, the number of input attributes in the meta-dataset is multiplied by the number of classes.

It has been shown that with stacking the ensemble performs (at best) comparably to selecting the best classifier from the ensemble by cross-validation [Džeroski and Ženko (2004)]. In order to improve the existing stacking approach, they employed a new multi-response model tree to learn at the meta-level and empirically showed that it performs better than existing stacking approaches and better than selecting the best classifier by cross-validation.

The SCANN (for Stacking, Correspondence Analysis and Nearest Neighbor) combining method [Merz (1999)] uses the strategies of stacking and correspondence analysis. Correspondence analysis is a method for geometrically modeling the relationship between the rows and columns of a matrix whose entries are categorical. In this context Correspondence Analysis is used to explore the relationship between the training examples and their classification by a collection of classifiers.

A nearest neighbor method is then applied to classify unseen examples. Here, each possible class is assigned coordinates in the space derived by correspondence analysis. Unclassified examples are mapped into the new space, and the class label corresponding to the closest class point is assigned to the example.

9.3.2.2 *Arbiter Trees*

According to Chan and Stolfo's approach [Chan and Stolfo (1993)], an arbiter tree is built in a bottom-up fashion. Initially, the training set is randomly partitioned into k disjoint subsets. The arbiter is induced from a pair of classifiers and recursively a new arbiter is induced from the output of two arbiters. Consequently for k classifiers, there are $\log_2(k)$ levels in the generated arbiter tree.

The creation of the arbiter is performed as follows. For each pair of classifiers, the union of their training dataset is classified by the two classifiers. A selection rule compares the classifications of the two classifiers and selects instances from the union set to form the training set for the arbiter. The arbiter is induced from this set with the same learning algorithm used in the base level. The purpose of the arbiter is to provide an alternate classification when the base classifiers present diverse classifications. This arbiter, together with an arbitration rule, decides on a final classification outcome, based upon the base predictions. Figure 9.4 shows how the final classification is selected based on the classification of two base classifiers and a single arbiter.

The process of forming the union of data subsets; classifying it using a pair of arbiter trees; comparing the classifications; forming a training set; training the arbiter; and picking one of the predictions, is recursively performed until the root arbiter is formed. Figure 9.5 illustrates an arbiter tree created for $k = 4$. $T_1 - T_4$ are the initial four training datasets from

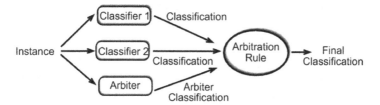

Fig. 9.4 A prediction from two base classifiers and a single arbiter.

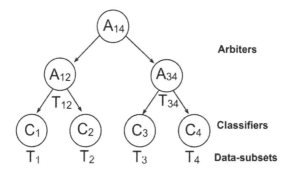

Fig. 9.5 Sample arbiter tree.

which four classifiers $M_1 - M_4$ are generated concurrently. T_{12} and T_{34} are the training sets generated by the rule selection from which arbiters are produced. A_{12} and A_{34} are the two arbiters. Similarly, T_{14} and A_{14} (root arbiter) are generated and the arbiter tree is completed.

There are several schemes for arbiter trees; each is characterized by a different selection rule. Here are three versions of selection rules:

- Only instances with classifications that disagree are chosen (group 1).
- Like group 1 defined above, plus instances where their classifications agree but are incorrect (group 2).
- Like groups 1 and 2 defined above, plus instances that have the same correct classifications (group 3).

Of the two versions of arbitration rules that have been implemented, each corresponds to the selection rule used for generating the training data at that level:

- For selection rules 1 and 2, a final classification is made by a majority vote of the classifications of the two lower levels and the arbiter's own classification, with preference given to the latter.

- For selection rule 3, if the classifications of the two lower levels are not equal, the classification made by the sub-arbiter based on the first group is chosen. In case this is not true and the classification of the sub-arbiter constructed on the third group equals those of the lower levels, then this is the chosen classification. In any other case, the classification of the sub-arbiter constructed on the second group is chosen. In fact it is possible to achieve the same accuracy level as in the single mode applied to the entire dataset but with less time and memory requirements [Chan and Stolfo (1993)]. More specifically, it has been shown that this meta-learning strategy required only around 30% of the memory used by the single model case. This last fact, combined with the independent nature of the various learning processes, make this method robust and effective for massive amounts of data. Nevertheless, the accuracy level depends on several factors such as the distribution of the data among the subsets and the pairing scheme of learned classifiers and arbiters in each level. The decision regarding any of these issues may influence performance, but the optimal decisions are not necessarily known in advance, nor initially set by the algorithm.

9.3.2.3 *Combiner Trees*

The way combiner trees are generated is very similar to arbiter trees. Both are trained bottom-up. However, a combiner, instead of an arbiter, is placed in each non-leaf node of a combiner tree [Chan and Stolfo (1997)]. In the combiner strategy, the classifications of the learned base classifiers form the basis of the meta-learner's training set. A composition rule determines the content of training examples from which a combiner (meta-classifier) will be generated. In classifying an instance, the base classifiers first generate their classifications and based on the composition rule, a new instance is generated. The aim of this strategy is to combine the classifications from the base classifiers by learning the relationship between these classifications and the correct classification. Figure 9.6 illustrates the result obtained from two base classifiers and a single combiner.

Two schemes for composition rules were proposed. The first one is the stacking scheme. The second is like stacking with the addition of the instance input attributes. It has been shown that the stacking scheme *per se* does not perform as well as the second scheme [Chan and Stolfo (1995)]. Although there is information loss due to data partitioning, combiner trees can sustain the accuracy level achieved by a single classifier. In a few cases, the single classifier's accuracy was consistently exceeded.

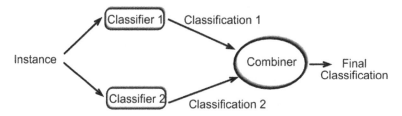

Fig. 9.6   A prediction from two base classifiers and a single combiner.

9.3.2.4   *Grading*

This technique uses "graded" classifications as meta-level classes [Seewald and Furnkranz (2001)]. The term "graded" is used in the sense of classifications that have been marked as correct or incorrect. The method transforms the classification made by the k different classifiers into k training sets by using the instances k times and attaching them to a new binary class in each occurrence. This class indicates whether the kth classifier yielded a correct or incorrect classification, compared to the real class of the instance.

For each base classifier, one meta-classifier is learned whose task is to classify when the base classifier will misclassify. At classification time, each base classifier classifies the unlabeled instance. The final classification is derived from the classifications of those base classifiers that are classified to be correct by the meta-classification schemes. In case several base classifiers with different classification results are classified as correct, voting, or a combination considering the confidence estimates of the base classifiers, is performed. Grading may be considered as a generalization of cross-validation selection [Schaffer (1993)], which divides the training data into k subsets, builds $k - 1$ classifiers by dropping one subset at a time and then uses it to find a misclassification rate. Finally, the procedure simply chooses the classifier corresponding to the subset with the smallest misclassification. Grading tries to make this decision separately for each and every instance by using only those classifiers that are predicted to classify that instance correctly. The main difference between grading and combiners (or stacking) is that the former does not change the instance attributes by replacing them with class predictions or class probabilities (or adding them to it). Instead it modifies the class values. Furthermore, in grading several sets of meta-data are created, one for each base classifier. Several meta-level classifiers are learned from those sets.

The main difference between grading and arbiters is that arbiters use information about the disagreements of classifiers for selecting a training set; grading uses disagreement with the target function to produce a new training set.

9.4 Classifier Dependency

This property indicates whether the various classifiers are dependent or independent. In a dependent framework the outcome of a certain classifier affects the creation of the next classifier. Alternatively each classifier is built independently and their results are combined in some fashion. Some researchers refer to this property as "the relationship between modules" and distinguish between three different types: successive, cooperative and supervisory [Sharkey (1996)]. Roughly speaking, "successive" refers to "dependent" while "cooperative" refers to "independent". The last type applies to those cases in which one model controls the other model.

9.4.1 *Dependent Methods*

In dependent approaches for learning ensembles, there is an interaction between the learning runs. Thus it is possible to take advantage of knowledge generated in previous iterations to guide the learning in the next iterations. We distinguish between two main approaches for dependent learning, as described in the following sections [Provost and Kolluri (1997)].

9.4.1.1 *Model-guided Instance Selection*

In this dependent approach, the classifiers that were constructed in previous iterations are used for manipulating the training set for the following iteration (see Figure 9.7). One can embed this process within the basic learning algorithm. These methods usually ignore all data instances on which their initial classifier is correct and only learn from misclassified instances.

The most well-known model-guided instance selection is boosting. Boosting (also known as arcing adaptive resampling and combining) is a general method for improving the performance of a weak learner (such as classification rules or decision trees). The method works by repeatedly running a weak learner (such as classification rules or decision trees), on various distributed training data. The classifiers produced by the weak learners are then combined into a single composite strong classifier in

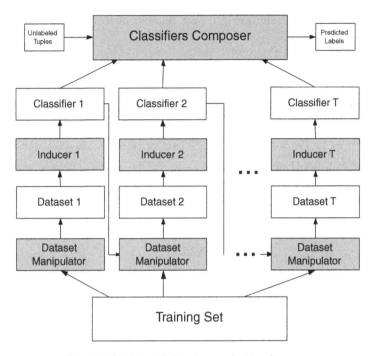

Fig. 9.7 Model-guided instance selection diagram.

order to achieve a higher accuracy than the weak learners classifiers would have had.

Freund and Schapire (1996) introduced the AdaBoost algorithm. The main idea of this algorithm is to assign a weight in each example in the training set. In the beginning, all weights are equal, but in every round, the weights of all misclassified instances are increased while the weights of correctly classified instances are decreased. As a consequence, the weak learner is forced to focus on the difficult instances of the training set. This procedure provides a series of classifiers that complement one another.

The pseudo-code of the AdaBoost algorithm is described in Figure 9.8. The algorithm assumes that the training set consists of m instances, labeled as -1 or $+1$. The classification of a new instance is made by voting on all classifiers $\{M_t\}$, each having a weight of α_t. Mathematically, it can be written as:

$$H(x) = sign\left(\sum_{t=1}^{T} \alpha_t \cdot M_t(x)\right). \tag{9.16}$$

Require: I (a weak inducer), T (the number of iterations), S (training set)

Ensure: $M_t, \alpha_t; t = 1, \ldots, T$

1: $t \leftarrow 1$
2: $D_1(i) \leftarrow 1/m; i = 1, \ldots, m$
3: **repeat**
4:   Build Classifier M_t using I and distribution D_t
5:   $\varepsilon_t \leftarrow \sum\limits_{i:M_t(x_i) \neq y_i} D_t(i)$
6:   **if** $\varepsilon_t > 0.5$ **then**
7:     $T \leftarrow t - 1$
8:     exit Loop.
9:   **end if**
10: $\alpha_t \leftarrow \quad \frac{1}{2}\ln(\frac{1-\varepsilon_t}{\varepsilon_t})$
11: $D_{t+1}(i) = D_t(i) \cdot e^{-\alpha_t y_t M_t(x_i)}$
12: Normalize D_{t+1} to be a proper distribution.
13: $t++$
14: **until** $t > T$

Fig. 9.8   The AdaBoost algorithm.

For using the boosting algorithm with decision trees, the decision tree inducer should be able to handle weighted instances. Some decision trees inducers (such as C4.5) can provide different treatments to different instances. This is performed by weighting the contribution of each instance in the analysis according to a provided weight (between 0 and 1). If weighted instances are used, then one may obtain probability vectors in the leaf nodes that consist of irrational numbers. This can be explained by the fact that counting weighted instances is not necessarily summed up with an integer number.

The basic AdaBoost algorithm, described in Figure 9.8, deals with binary classification. Freund and Schapire (1996) describe two versions of the AdaBoost algorithm (AdaBoost.M1, AdaBoost.M2), which are equivalent for binary classification and differ in their handling of multiclass classification problems. Figure 9.9 describes the pseudo-code of AdaBoost.M1. The classification of a new instance is performed according to the following equation:

$$H(x) = \underset{y \in dom(y)}{\text{argmax}} \left(\sum_{t:M_t(x)=y} \log \frac{1}{\beta_t} \right), \qquad (9.17)$$

where β_t is defined in Figure 9.9.

Require: I (a weak inducer), T (the number of iterations), S (the training set)

Ensure: $M_t, \beta_t; t = 1, \ldots, T$

1: $t \leftarrow 1$

2: $D_1(i) \leftarrow 1/m; i = 1, \ldots, m$

3: **repeat**

4:     Build Classifier M_t using I and distribution D_t

5:     $\varepsilon_t \leftarrow \sum\limits_{i:M_t(x_i) \neq y_i} D_t(i)$

6:     **if** $\varepsilon_t > 0.5$ **then**

7:         $T \leftarrow t - 1$

8:         exit Loop.

9:     **end if**

10:    $\beta_t \leftarrow \frac{\varepsilon_t}{1 - \varepsilon_t}$

11:    $D_{t+1}(i) = D_t(i) \cdot \begin{cases} \beta_t & M_t(x_i) = y_i \\ 1 & Otherwise \end{cases}$

12:    Normalize D_{t+1} to be a proper distribution.

13:    $t{+}{+}$

14: **until** $t > T$

Fig. 9.9   The AdaBoost.M.1 algorithm.

All boosting algorithms presented here assume that the weak inducers which are provided can cope with weighted instances. If this is not the case, an unweighted dataset is generated from the weighted data by a resampling technique. Namely, instances are chosen with a probability according to their weights (until the dataset becomes as large as the original training set).

Boosting seems to improve performance for two main reasons:

(1) It generates a final classifier whose error on the training set is small by combining many hypotheses whose error may be large.
(2) It produces a combined classifier whose variance is significantly lower than those produced by the weak learner.

On the other hand, boosting sometimes leads to a deterioration in generalization performance. According to Quinlan (1996), the main reason for boosting's failure is overfitting. The objective of boosting is to construct a composite classifier that performs well on the data, but a large number of iterations may create a very complex composite classifier, that is significantly less accurate than a single classifier. A possible way to avoid overfitting is by keeping the number of iterations as small as possible. It has been shown that boosting approximates a large margin classifier such as the SVM [Rudin *et al.* (2004)].

Another important drawback of boosting is that it is difficult to understand. The resulting ensemble is considered to be less comprehensible since the user is required to capture several classifiers instead of a single classifier. Despite the above drawbacks, Breiman (1996) refers to the boosting idea as the most significant development in classifier design of the Nineties.

9.4.1.2 *Incremental Batch Learning*

In this method, the classification produced in one iteration is given as "prior knowledge" to the learning algorithm in the following iteration. The learning algorithm uses the current training set together with the classification of the former classifier for building the next classifier. The classifier constructed at the last iteration is chosen as the final classifier.

9.4.2 *Independent Methods*

In independent ensemble methodology, the original dataset is partitioned into several subsets from which multiple classifiers are induced (please see Figure 9.10). The subsets created from the original training set may be disjointed (mutually exclusive) or overlapping. A combination procedure is then applied in order to produce a single classification for a given instance. Since the method for combining the results of induced classifiers is usually independent of the induction algorithms, it can be used with different inducers at each subset. Moreover, this methodology can be easily parallelized. These independent methods aim either at improving the predictive power of classifiers or decreasing the total execution time. The following sections describe several algorithms that implement this methodology.

9.4.2.1 *Bagging*

The most well-known independent method is bagging (bootstrap aggregating). The method aims to increase accuracy by creating an improved composite classifier, I^*, by amalgamating the various outputs of learned classifiers into a single prediction.

Figure 9.11 presents the pseudo-code of the bagging algorithm [Breiman (1996)]. Each classifier is trained on a sample of instances taken with a

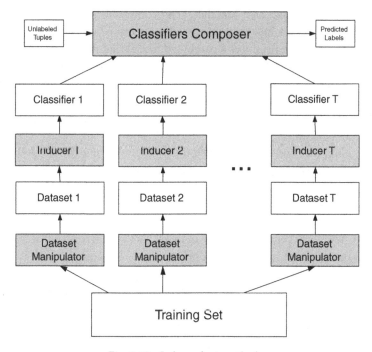

Fig. 9.10 Independent methods.

Require: I (an inducer), T (the number of iterations), S (the training set), μ (the sub-sample size).
Ensure: $M_t; t = 1, \ldots, T$
1: $t \leftarrow 1$
2: **repeat**
3:     $S_t \leftarrow$ Sample μ instances from S with replacement.
4:     Build classifier M_t using I on S_t
5:     $t++$
6: **until** $t > T$

Fig. 9.11 The bagging algorithm.

replacement from the training set. Usually each sample size is equal to the size of the original training set.

Note that since sampling with replacement is used, some of the original instances of S may appear more than once in S_t and some may not be included at all. To classify a new instance, each classifier returns the class prediction for the unknown instance. The composite bagged classifier, I^*, returns the class that has been predicted most often (voting method). The result is that bagging produces a combined model that often performs better than the single model built from the original single data. Breiman (1996) notes that this is true especially for unstable inducers because bagging can eliminate their instability. In this context, an inducer is considered unstable if perturbing the learning set can cause significant changes in the constructed classifier.

Bagging, like boosting, is a technique for improving the accuracy of a classifier by producing different classifiers and combining multiple models. They both use a kind of voting for classification in order to combine the outputs of the different classifiers of the same type. In boosting, unlike bagging, each classifier is influenced by the performance of those built before with the new classifier trying to pay more attention to errors that were made in the previous ones and to their performances. In bagging, each instance is chosen with equal probability, while in boosting, instances are chosen with a probability proportional to their weight. Furthermore, according to Quinlan (1996), as mentioned above, bagging requires that the learning system should not be stable, where boosting does not preclude the use of unstable learning systems, provided that their error rate can be kept below 0.5.

9.4.2.2 *Wagging*

Wagging is a variant of bagging [Bauer and Kohavi (1999)] in which each classifier is trained on the entire training set, but each instance is stochastically assigned a weight. Figure 9.12 presents the pseudo-code of the wagging algorithm.

Require: I (an inducer), T (the number of iterations), S (the training set), d (weighting distribution).

Ensure: $M_t; t = 1, \ldots, T$

1: $t \leftarrow 1$

2: **repeat**

3:     $S_t \leftarrow S$ with random weights drawn from d.

4:     Build classifier M_t using I on S_t

5:     $t + +$

6: **until** $t > T$

Fig. 9.12   The wagging algorithm.

In fact bagging can be considered to be wagging with allocation of weights from the Poisson distribution (each instance is represented in the sample a discrete number of times). Alternatively, it is possible to allocate the weights from the exponential distribution, because the exponential distribution is the continuous valued counterpart to the Poisson distribution [Webb (2000)].

9.4.2.3   *Random Forest*

A Random Forest ensemble uses a large number of individual, unpruned decision trees which are created by randomizing the split at each node of the decision tree [Breiman (2001)]. Each tree is likely to be less accurate than a tree created with the exact splits. But, by combining several of these "approximate" trees in an ensemble, we can improve the accuracy, often doing better than a single tree with exact splits.

The individual trees are constructed using the algorithm presented in Figure 9.13. The input parameter N represents the number of input variables that will be used to determine the decision at a node of the tree. This number should be much less than the number of attributes in the training set. Note that bagging can be thought of as a special case of random forests obtained when N is set to the number of attributes in the original training set. The IDT in Figure 9.13 represents any top-down decision tree induction algorithm with the following modification: the decision tree is not pruned and at each node, rather than choosing the best split among all attributes, the IDT randomly samples N of the attributes and chooses the best split from among those variables. The classification of an unlabeled instance is performed using majority vote.

Require: IDT (a decision tree inducer), T (the number of iterations), S (the training set), μ (the sub sample size). N (number of attributes used in each node)

Ensure: $M_t; t = 1, \ldots, T$

1: $t \leftarrow 1$
2: **repeat**
3:     $S_t \leftarrow$ Sample μ instances from S with replacement.
4:     Build classifier M_t using $IDT(N)$ on S_t
5:     $t++$
6: **until** $t > T$

Fig. 9.13   The random forest algorithm.

There are other ways to obtain random forests. For example, instead of using all the instances to determine the best split point for each feature, a sub-sample of the instances is used [Kamath and Cantu-Paz (2001)]. This sub-sample varies with the feature. The feature and split value that optimize the splitting criterion are chosen as the decision at that node. Since the split made at a node is likely to vary with the sample selected, this technique results in different trees which can be combined in ensembles.

Another method for randomization of the decision tree through histograms was proposed by Kamath *et al.* (2002). The use of histograms has long been suggested as a way of making the features discrete, while reducing the time to handle very large datasets. Typically, a histogram is created for each feature, and the bin boundaries used as potential split points. The randomization in this process is expressed by selecting the split point randomly in an interval around the best bin boundary.

Although the random forest was defined for decision trees, this approach is applicable to all types of classifiers. One important advantage of the random forest method is its ability to handle a very large number of input attributes [Skurichina and Duin (2002)]. Another important feature of the random forest is that it is fast.

9.4.2.4 *Rotation Forest*

Similarly to Random Forest, the aim of Rotation Forest is to independently build accurate and diverse set of classification trees. Recall that in Random Forest the diversity among the base trees is obtained by training each tree on a different bootstrap sample of the dataset and by randomizing the feature choice at each node. On the other hand, in Rotation forest the diversity among the base trees is acheived by training each tree on the whole dataset in a rotated feature space. Because tree induction algorithms split the input space using hyperplanes parallel to the feature axes, rotating the axes just before running the tree induction algorithm, may result with a very different classification tree.

More specifically the main idea is to use feature extraction methods to build a full feature set for each tree in the forest. To this end, we first randomly split the feature set into K mutually exclusive partitions. Then we use a principal component analysis (PCA) separately on each feature partition. PCA is a well-established statistical procedure that was invented in 1901 by Karl Pearson. The idea of PCA is to orthogonaly transforms possibly correlated features into a set of linearly uncorrelated features (called principal components). Each component is a linear combination of the original. The transformation guarantee that the first principal component has the largest possible variance. Every subsequent component has the highest variance possible under the constraint that is orthogonal to the previous components.

The principal components is used to construct the new set of features. The original dataset is transformed linearly into the new feature space to construct the new training set. This new training set is fed into the tree induction algorithm which train a classification tree. Note that different feature partitions will lead to different set of transformed features, thus different classification trees are generated.

Figure 9.14 presents the Rotation Forest pseudocode. For each one of the T base classifiers to be built, we divide the feature set into K

Rotation Forest

Require: I (a base inducer), S (the original training set), T (number of iterations), K (number of subsets),

1: **for** $i = 1$ to T **do**
2:     Split the feature set into K subsets: $F_{i,j}$ (for j=1..K)
3:     **for** $j = 1$ to K **do**
4:         Let $S_{i,j}$ be the dataset S for the features in $F_{i,j}$
5:         Eliminate from $S_{i,j}$ a random subset of classes
6:         Select a bootstrap sample from $S_{i,j}$ of size 75% of the number of objects in $S_{i,j}$. Denote the new set by $S'_{i,j}$
7:         Apply PCA on $S'_{i,j}$ to obtain the coefficients in a matrix $C_{i,j}$
8:     **end for**
9:     Arrange the $C_{i,j}$, for $j = 1$ to K in a rotation matrix R_i as in the equation:

$$R_i = \begin{bmatrix} a_{i,1}^{(1)}, a_{i,1}^{(2)}, \ldots, a_{i,1}^{(M_1)} & [0] & \cdots & [0] \\ [0] & a_{i,2}^{(1)}, a_{i,2}^{(2)}, \ldots, a_{i,2}^{(M_2)} \cdots & & [0] \\ \cdots & \cdots & \cdots & \cdots \\ [0] & [0] & \cdots a_{i,k}^{(1)}, a_{i,k}^{(2)}, \ldots, a_{i,k}^{(Mk)} \end{bmatrix}$$

10:     Construct R_i^a by rearranging the columns of R_i so as to match the order of features in F
11: **end for**
12: Build classifier M_i using (SR_i^a, X) as the training set

Fig. 9.14 The rotation forest.

disjoint subsets $F_{i,j}$ of equal size M. For every subset, we randomly select a non-empty subset of classes and then draw a bootstrap sample which includes 3/4 of the original sample. Then we apply PCA using only the features in $F_{i,j}$ and the selected subset of classes. The obtained coefficients of the principal components, $a_{i,1}^1, a_{i,1}^2, \ldots$, are employed to create the sparse "rotation" matrix R_i. Finally, we use SR_i from training the base classifier M_i. In order to classify an instance, we calculate the average confidence for each class across all classifiers, and then assign the instance to the class with the largest confidence.

The rotation forest algorithm is implemented as part of the Weka suite. The matlab code of rotation forest can be obtained from: http://www.mathworks.com/matlabcentral/fileexchange/38792-rotation-forest-algorithm.

The experimantal study conducted by the inventors of Rotation Forest, show that Rotation Forest outperforms random forest in terms of accuracy. However, Rotation Forest has two drawbacks. First, Rotation Forest is usually more computationally intensive than Random Forest. Mainly because the computational complexity of PCA is more than linear (more specially mn^2, where m is the number of instances and n is the number of features). Another drawback is that the nodes in the obtained trees are the transformed features and not the original features. This can make it harder for the user to understand the tree because instead of examining a single feature in each node of the tree, the user needs to examine a linear combination of the features in each node of the tree.

Zhang and Zhang (2008) present the RotBoost algorithm which combines the ideas of Rotation Forest and AdaBoost. RotBoost achieves an even lower prediction error than either one of the two algorithms. RotBoost is presented in Figure 9.15. In each iteration a new rotation matrix is generated and used to create a dataset. The AdaBoost ensemble is induced from this dataset.

In conclusion, Rotation Forest is an ensemble generation method which aims at building accurate and diverse classifiers [Rodriguez *et al.* (2006)]. The main idea is to apply feature extraction to subsets of features in order to reconstruct a full feature set for each classifier in the ensemble. Rotation Forest ensembles tend to generate base classifiers which are more accurate than those created by AdaBoost and by Random Forest, and more diverse than those created by bagging. Decision trees were chosen as the base classifiers because of their sensitivity to rotation of the feature axes, while remaining very accurate. Feature extraction is based on PCA which is a valuable

RotBoost

Require: I (a base inducer), S (the original training set), K (number of attribute subsets), T_1 (number of iterations for Rotation Forest), T_2 (number of iterations for AdaBoost).

1: **for** $s = 1, \cdots T_2$ **do**

2:   Use the steps similar in Rotation Forest to compute the rotation matrix, R_s^a and let $S^a = [X R_s^a Y]$ be the training set for classifier C_s.

3:   Initialize the weight distribution over S^a as $D_1(i) = 1/N (i = 1, 2, \cdots N)$.

4:   **for** $t = 1, \cdots T_2$ **do**

5:     According to the distribution D_t, perform N extractions randomly f or S^a with replacement to compose a new set S_t^a.

6:     Apply I to S_t^a to train a classifier C_t^a and then compute the error of C_t^a as $\epsilon_t = \Pr_{i \sim D_t}(C_t^a(\mathbf{x}_i) \neq y_i) = \sum_{i=1}^N Ind(C_t^a(\mathbf{x}_i) \neq y_i) D_t(i)$.

7:     **if** $\xi i_t > 0.5$ **then**

8:       set $D_t(i) = 1/N (i = 1, 2, \cdots N)$ and continue with the next loop iteration

9:     **end if**

10:    **if** $\epsilon_t = 0\rangle$ **then**

11:      set $\epsilon_t = 10^{-10}$

12:    **end if**

13:    Choose $\alpha_t = \dfrac{1}{2} \ln(\dfrac{1 - \epsilon_t}{\epsilon_t})$

14:    Update the distribution D_t over S^a as $D_{t+1}(i) = \dfrac{D_t(i)}{Z_t} \times \begin{cases} e^{-\alpha_t}, \text{if} C_t^a(\mathbf{x}_i) = y_i \\ e^{\alpha_t})\text{if} C_t^a(\mathbf{x}_i) \neq y_i \end{cases}$ where Z_t is a normalization factor being chosen so that D_{t+1} is a probability distribution over S^a.

15: **end for**

16: **end for**

Fig. 9.15   The RotBoost algorithm.

diversifying heuristic. Rotation Forest is a powerful method for generating an ensemble of classification trees. While it has gained less popularity than Random Forest, we highly recommend to prefer it over Random Forest especially if the predictive performance is the main criterion for success.

9.4.2.5   *Cross-validated Committees*

This procedure creates k classifiers by partitioning the training set into k-equal-sized sets and training, in turn, on all but the ith set. This method, first used by Gams (1989), employed 10-fold partitioning. Parmanto *et al.* (1996) have also used this idea for creating an ensemble of neural networks. Domingos (1996) used cross-validated committees to speed up his own rule induction algorithm RISE, whose complexity is $O(n^2)$, making it unsuitable for processing large databases. In this case, partitioning is applied by predetermining a maximum number of examples to which the algorithm can be applied at once. The full training set is randomly divided into approximately equal-sized partitions. RISE is then run on each partition separately. Each set of rules grown from the examples in partition p is tested on the examples in partition $p + 1$, in order to reduce overfitting and to improve accuracy.

9.5 Ensemble Diversity

In an ensemble, the combination of the output of several classifiers is only useful if they disagree about some inputs [Tumer and Ghosh (1996)].

Creating an ensemble in which each classifier is as different as possible while still being consistent with the training set is theoretically known to be an important feature for obtaining improved ensemble performance [Krogh and Vedelsby (1995)]. According to Hu (2001), diversified classifiers lead to uncorrelated errors, which in turn improve classification accuracy.

In the regression context, the bias-variance-covariance decomposition has been suggested to explain why and how diversity between individual models contribute toward overall ensemble accuracy. Nevertheless, in the classification context, there is no complete and agreed upon theory [Brown *et al.* (2005)]. More specifically, there is no simple analogue of variance–covariance decomposition for the zero–one loss function. Instead, there are several ways to define this decomposition. Each way has its own assumptions.

Sharkey (1999) suggested a taxonomy of methods for creating diversity in ensembles of neural networks. More specifically, Sharkey's taxonomy refers to four different aspects: the initial weights; the training data used; the architecture of the networks; and the training algorithm used.

Brown *et al.* (2005) suggest a different taxonomy which consists of the following branches: varying the starting points within the hypothesis space; varying the set of hypotheses that are accessible by the ensemble members (for instance by manipulating the training set); and varying the way each member traverses the space.

In this paper, we suggest the following taxonomy. Note however that the components of this taxonomy are not mutually exclusive, namely, there are a few algorithms which combine two of them.

(1) Manipulating the Inducer — We manipulate the way in which the base inducer is used. More specifically, each ensemble member is trained with an inducer that is differently manipulated.
(2) Manipulating the Training Sample — We vary the input that is used by the inducer for training. Each member is trained from a different training set.
(3) Changing the target attribute representation — Each classifier in the ensemble solve a different target concept.
(4) Partitioning the search space — Each member is trained on a different search sub-space.
(5) Hybridization — Diversity is obtained by using various base inducers or ensemble strategies.

9.5.1 *Manipulating the Inducer*

A simple method for gaining diversity is to manipulate the inducer used for creating the classifiers. Below we survey several strategies to gain this diversity.

9.5.1.1 *Manipulation of the Inducer's Parameters*

The base inducer usually can be controlled by a set of parameters. For example, the well-known decision tree inducer C4.5 has the confidence level parameter that greatly affect learning.

In the neural network community, there were several attempts to gain diversity by using different number of nodes. Nevertheless, these researches concludes that variation in numbers of hidden nodes is not effective method of creating diversity in neural network ensembles. Nevertheless the CNNE algorithm which simultaneously determines the ensemble size along with the number of hidden nodes in individual NNs, has shown encouraging results.

Another effective approach for ANNs is to use several network topologies. For instance, the Addemup algorithm [Opitz and Shavlik (1996)] uses genetic algorithm to select the network topologies composing the ensemble. Addemup trains with standard backpropagation, then selects groups of networks with a good error diversity according to the measurement of diversity.

9.5.1.2   *Starting Point in Hypothesis Space*

Some inducers can gain diversity by starting the search in the Hypothesis Space from different points. For example, the simplest way to manipulate the back-propagation inducer is to assign different initial weights to the network [Kolen and Pollack (1991)]. Experimental study indicates that the resulting networks differed in the number of cycles in which they took to converge upon a solution, and in whether they converged at all. While it is very simple way to gain diversity, it is now generally accepted that it is not sufficient for achieving good diversity [Brown *et al.* (2005)].

9.5.1.3   *Hypothesis Space Traversal*

These techniques alter the way the inducer traverses the space, thereby leading different classifiers to converge to different hypotheses [Brown *et al.* (2005)]. We differentiate between two techniques for manipulating the space traversal for gaining diversity: Random and Collective-Performance.

9.5.1.3.1   Random-based Strategy

The idea in this case is to "inject randomness" into the inducers in order to increase the independence among the ensemble's members. Ali and Pazzani (1996) propose to change the rule learning HYDRA algorithm in the following way: Instead of selecting the best literal at each stage (using, for instance, an information gain measure), the literal is selected randomly such that its probability of being selected is proportional to its measured value. A similar idea has been implemented for C4.5 decision trees [Dietterich (2000a)]. Instead of selecting the best attribute in each stage, it selects randomly (with equal probability) an attribute from the set of the best 20 attributes. Markov Chain Monte Carlo (MCMC) methods can also be used for introducing randomness in the induction process [Neal (1993)].

9.5.1.3.2   Collective-Performance-based Strategy

In this case the evaluation function used in the induction of each member is extended to include a penalty term that encourages diversity. The most studied penalty method is the Negative Correlation Learning [Liu (2005); Brown and Wyatt (2003); Rosen (1996)]. The idea of negative correlation learning is to encourage different individual classifiers in the ensemble to represent different sub-spaces of the problem. While simultaneously creating the classifiers, the classifiers may interact with each other in order to specialize (for instance by using a correlation penalty term in the error function to encourage such specialization).

9.5.2 *Manipulating the Training Samples*

In this method, each classifier is trained on a different variation or subset of the original dataset. This method is useful for inducers whose variance-error factor is relatively large (such as decision trees and neural networks). That is to say, small changes in the training set may cause a major change in the obtained classifier. This category contains procedures such as bagging, boosting and cross-validated committees.

9.5.2.1 *Resampling*

The distribution of tuples among the different classifier could be random as in the bagging algorithm or in the arbiter trees. Other methods distribute the tuples based on the class distribution such that the class distribution in each subset is approximately the same as that in the entire dataset. It has been shown that proportional distribution as used in combiner trees [Chan and Stolfo (1993)] can achieve higher accuracy than random distribution.

Instead of performing sampling with replacement, some methods (like AdaBoost or Wagging) manipulate the weights that are attached to each instance in the training set. The base inducer should be capable to take these weights into account. Recently, a novel framework was proposed in which each instance contributes to the committee formation with a fixed weight, while contributing with different individual weights to the derivation of the different constituent classifiers [Christensen *et al.* (2004)]. This approach encourages model diversity without biasing the ensemble inadvertently towards any particular instance.

9.5.2.2 *Creation*

The DECORATE algorithm [Melville and Mooney (2003)] is a dependent approach in which the ensemble is generated iteratively, learning a classifier at each iteration and adding it to the current ensemble. The first member is created by using the base induction algorithm on the original training set. The successive classifiers are trained on an artificial set that combines tuples from the original training set and also on some fabricated tuples. In each iteration, the input attribute values of the fabricated tuples are generated according to the original data distribution. On the other hand, the target values of these tuples are selected so as to differ maximally from the current ensemble predictions. Comprehensive experiments have demonstrated that this technique is consistently more accurate than the base classifier, Bagging and Random Forests. Decorate also obtains higher accuracy than boosting on small training sets, and achieves comparable performance on larger training sets.

9.5.2.3 *Partitioning*

Some argue that classic ensemble techniques (such as boosting and bagging) have limitations on massive datasets, because the size of the dataset can become a bottleneck [Chawla *et al.* (2004)]. Moreover, it is suggested that partitioning the datasets into random, disjoint partitions will not only overcome the issue of exceeding memory size, but will also lead to creating an ensemble of diverse and accurate classifiers, each built from a disjoint partition but with the aggregate processing all of the data. This can improve performance in a way that might not be possible by subsampling. In fact, empirical studies have shown that the performance of the multiple disjoint partition approach is equivalent to the performance obtained by popular ensemble techniques such as bagging. More recently, a framework for building thousands of classifiers that are trained from small subsets of data in a distributed environment was proposed [Chawla *et al.* (2004)]. It has been empirically shown that this framework is fast, accurate, and scalable.

Clustering techniques can be used to partitioning the sample. The cluster-based concurrent decomposition (CBCD) algorithm first clusters the instance space by using the K-means clustering algorithm. Then, it creates disjoint sub-samples using the clusters in such a way that each sub-sample is comprised of tuples from all clusters and hence represents the entire dataset. An inducer is applied in turn to each sub-sample. A voting mechanism is used to combine the classifiers classifications. Experimental study indicates that the CBCD algorithm outperforms the bagging algorithm.

9.5.3 *Manipulating the Target Attribute Representation*

In methods that manipulate the target attribute, instead of inducing a single complicated classifier, several classifiers with different and usually simpler representations of the target attribute are induced. This manipulation can be based on an aggregation of the original target's values (known as *Concept Aggregation*) or more complicated functions (known as *Function Decomposition*).

Classical concept aggregation replaces the original target attribute with a function, such that the domain of the new target attribute is smaller than the original one.

Concept aggregation has been used to classify free text documents into predefined topics [Buntine (1996)]. This application suggests breaking the topics up into groups (co-topics) and then, instead of predicting the document's topic directly, classifying the document into one of the co-topics. Another model is then used to predict the actual topic in that co-topic.

A general concept aggregation algorithm called *Error-Correcting Output Coding* (ECOC) which converts multi-class problems into multiple, two-class problems has been suggested by Dietterich and Bakiri (1995). A classifier is built for each possible binary partition of the classes. Experiments show that ECOC improves the accuracy of neural networks and decision trees on several multi-class problems from the UCI repository.

The idea to convert K class classification problems into K-two class classification problems has been proposed by [Anand *et al.* (1995)]. Each problem considers the discrimination of one class to the other classes. Lu and Ito [Lu and Ito (1999)] extend Anand's method and propose a new method for manipulating the data based on the class relations among the training data. By using this method, they divide a K class classification problem into a series of $K(K-1)/2$ two-class problems where each problem considers the discrimination of one class to each one of the other classes. The researchers used neural networks to examine this idea.

Function decomposition was originally developed in the Fifties and Sixties for designing switching circuits. It was even used as an evaluation mechanism for checker playing programs [Samuel (1967)]. This approach was later improved by Biermann *et al.* (1982). Recently, the machine learning community has adopted this approach. A manual decomposition of the problem and an expert-assisted selection of examples to construct rules for the concepts in the hierarchy was studied in [Michie (1995)]. Compared to standard decision tree induction techniques, structured induction exhibits about the same degree of classification accuracy with the increased transparency and lower complexity of the developed models. A general-purpose function decomposition approach for machine learning was proposed in [Zupan *et al.* (1998)]. According to this approach, attributes are transformed into new concepts in an iterative manner to create a hierarchy of concepts. A different function decomposition which can be applied in data mining is the Bi-Decomposition [Long (2003)]. In this approach, the original function is decomposed into two decomposition functions that are connected by a two-input operator called a "gate". Each of the decomposition functions depends on fewer variables than the original function. Recursive bi-decomposition represents a function as a structure of interconnected gates.

9.5.4 *Partitioning the Search Space*

The idea is that each member in the ensemble explores a different part of the search space. Thus, the original instance space is divided into several sub-spaces. Each sub-space is considered independently and the total model is a (possibly soft) union of such simpler models.

When using this approach, one should decide if the sub-spaces will overlap. At one extreme, the original problem is decomposed into several mutually exclusive sub-problems, such that each sub-problem is solved using a dedicated classifier. In such cases, the classifiers may have significant variations in their overall performance over different parts of the input space [Tumer and Ghosh (2000)]. At the other extreme, each classifier solves the same original task. In such cases, "If the individual classifiers are then appropriately chosen and trained properly, their performances will be (relatively) comparable in any region of the problem space. [Tumer and Ghosh (2000)]". However, usually the sub-spaces may have soft boundaries, namely sub-spaces are allowed to overlap.

There are two popular approaches for search space manipulations: divide and conquer approaches and feature subset-based ensemble methods.

9.5.4.1 *Divide and Conquer*

In the neural-networks community, Nowlan and Hinton (1991) examined the mixture of experts (ME) approach, which partitions the instance space into several sub-spaces and assigns different experts (classifiers) to the different sub-spaces. The sub-spaces, in ME, have soft boundaries (i.e. they are allowed to overlap). A gating network then combines the experts' outputs and produces a composite decision.

Some researchers have used clustering techniques to partition the space. The basic idea is to partition the instance space into mutually exclusive subsets using K-means clustering algorithm. An analysis of the results shows that the proposed method is well suited for datasets of numeric input attributes and that its performance is influenced by the dataset size and its homogeneity.

NBTree [Kohavi (1996)] is an instance space decomposition method that induces a decision tree and a Naïve Bayes hybrid classifier. Naïve Bayes, which is a classification algorithm based on Bayes' theorem and a Naïve independence assumption, is very efficient in terms of its processing time. To induce an NBTree, the instance space is recursively partitioned according to attributes values. The result of the recursive partitioning is a decision tree whose terminal nodes are Naïve Bayes classifiers. Since subjecting a terminal node to a Naïve Bayes classifier means that the hybrid classifier may classify two instances from a single hyper-rectangle region into distinct classes, the NBTree is more flexible than a pure decision tree. In order to decide when to stop the growth of the tree, NBTree compares two alternatives in terms of error estimation — partitioning into a hyper-rectangle region and inducing a single Naïve Bayes classifier. The error estimation is calculated by cross-validation, which significantly increases the overall processing time. Although NBTree applies a Naïve Bayes classifier to decision tree terminal nodes, classification algorithms other than Naïve Bayes are also applicable. However, the cross-validation estimations make the NBTree hybrid computationally expensive for more time-consuming algorithms such as neural networks.

More recently, Cohen *et al.* (2007) generalizes the NBTree idea and examines a decision-tree framework for space decomposition. According to this framework, the original instance-space is hierarchically partitioned into multiple sub-spaces and a distinct classifier (such as neural network) is assigned to each sub-space. Subsequently, an unlabeled, previously-unseen instance is classified by employing the classifier that was assigned to the sub-space to which the instance belongs.

The divide and conquer approach includes many other specific methods such as local linear regression, CART/MARS, adaptive sub-space models, etc [Johansen and Foss (1992); Ramamurti and Ghosh (1999); Holmstrom *et al.* (1997)].

9.5.4.2 *Feature Subset-based Ensemble Methods*

Another less common strategy for manipulating the search space is to manipulate the input attribute set. Feature subset-based ensemble methods are those that manipulate the input feature set for creating the ensemble members. The idea is to simply give each classifier a different projection of the training set. [Tumer and Oza]. Feature subset-based ensembles potentially facilitate the creation of a classifier for high dimensionality data sets without the feature selection drawbacks mentioned above. Moreover, these methods can be used to improve the classification performance due to the reduced correlation among the classifiers. Rokach and Maimon (2001) also indicate that the reduced size of the dataset implies faster induction of classifiers. Feature subset avoids the class under-representation which may happen in instance subsets methods such as bagging. There are three popular strategies for creating feature subset-based ensembles: random-based, reduct-based and collective-performance-based strategy.

9.5.4.2.1   Random-based Strategy

The most straightforward techniques for creating feature subset-based ensemble are based on random selection. Ho (1998) creates a forest of decision trees. The ensemble is constructed systematically by pseudo-randomly selecting subsets of features. The training instances are projected to each subset and a decision tree is constructed using the projected training samples. The process is repeated several times to create the forest. The classifications of the individual trees are combined by averaging the conditional probability of each class at the leaves (distribution summation). Ho shows that simple random selection of feature subsets may be an effective technique because the diversity of the ensemble members compensates for their lack of accuracy.

Bay (1999) proposed using simple voting in order to combine outputs from multiple KNN (K-Nearest Neighbor) classifiers, each having access only to a random subset of the original features. Each classifier employs the same number of features. A technique for building ensembles of simple Bayesian classifiers in random feature subsets was also examined [Tsymbal and Puuronen (2002)] for improving medical applications.

9.5.4.2.2   Reduct-based Strategy

A reduct is defined as the smallest feature subset which has the same predictive power as the whole feature set. By definition, the size of the ensembles that were created using reducts are limited to the number of features. There have been several attempts to create classifier ensembles by combining several reducts.

9.5.4.2.3 Collective-Performance-based Strategy

Cunningham and Carney (2000) introduced an ensemble feature selection strategy that randomly constructs the initial ensemble. Then, an iterative refinement is performed based on a hill-climbing search in order to improve the accuracy and diversity of the base classifiers. For all the feature subsets, an attempt is made to switch (include or delete) each feature. If the resulting feature subset produces a better performance on the validation set, that change is kept. This process is continued until no further improvements are obtained. Similarly, Zenobi and Cunningham (2001) suggest that the search for the different feature subsets will not be solely guided by the associated error but also by the disagreement or ambiguity among the ensemble members.

Tsymbal *et al.* (2004) compare several feature selection methods that incorporate diversity as a component of the fitness function in the search for the best collection of feature subsets. This study shows that there are some datasets in which the ensemble feature selection method can be sensitive to the choice of the diversity measure. Moreover, no particular measure is superior in all cases.

Gunter and Bunke (2004) suggest employing a feature subset search algorithm in order to find different subsets of the given features. The feature subset search algorithm not only takes the performance of the ensemble into account, but also directly supports diversity of subsets of features.

Combining genetic search with ensemble feature selection was also examined in the literature. Opitz and Shavlik (1996) applied GAs to ensembles using genetic operators that were designed explicitly for hidden nodes in knowledge-based neural networks. In a later research, Opitz (1999) used genetic search for ensemble feature selection. This genetic ensemble feature selection (GEFS) strategy begins by creating an initial population of classifiers where each classifier is generated by randomly selecting a different subset of features. Then, new candidate classifiers are continually produced by using the genetic operators of crossover and mutation on the feature subsets. The final ensemble is composed of the most fitted classifiers.

9.5.4.2.4 Feature Set Partitioning

Feature set partitioning is a particular case of feature subset-based ensembles in which the subsets are pairwise disjoint subsets. At the same time, feature set partitioning generalizes the task of feature selection which aims to provide a single representative set of features from which a classifier is constructed. Feature set partitioning, on the other hand, decomposes the original set of features into several subsets and builds a classifier for each subset. Thus, a set of classifiers is trained such that each classifier employs a different subset of the original feature set. Subsequently, an unlabeled instance is classified by combining the classifications of all classifiers.

Several researchers have shown that the partitioning methodology can be appropriate for classification tasks with a large number of features [Kusiak (2000)]. The search space of a feature subset-based ensemble contains the search space of feature set partitioning, and the latter contains the search space of feature selection. Mutually exclusive partitioning has some important and helpful properties:

(1) There is a greater possibility of achieving reduced execution time compared to non-exclusive approaches. Since most learning algorithms have computational complexity that is greater than linear in the number of features or tuples, partitioning the problem dimensionality in a mutually exclusive manner means a decrease in computational complexity [Provost and Kolluri (1997)].

(2) Since mutual exclusiveness entails using smaller datasets, the classifiers obtained for each sub-problem are smaller in size. Without the mutually exclusive restriction, each classifier can be as complicated as the classifier obtained for the original problem. Smaller classifiers contribute to comprehensibility and ease in maintaining the solution.

(3) According to Bay (1999), mutually exclusive partitioning may help avoid some error correlation problems that characterize feature subset based ensembles. However, Sharkey (1996) argues that mutually exclusive training sets do not necessarily result in low error correlation. This point is true when each sub-problem is representative.

(4) In feature subset-based ensembles, different classifiers might generate contradictive classifications using the same features. This inconsistency in the way a certain feature can affect the final classification may increase mistrust among end-users. We claim that end-users can grasp mutually exclusive partitioning much easier.

(5) The mutually exclusive approach encourages smaller datasets which are generally more practicable. Some data mining tools can process only limited dataset sizes (for instance, when the program requires that the entire dataset will be stored in the main memory). The mutually exclusive approach can ensure that data mining tools can be scaled fairly easily to large datasets [Chan and Stolfo (1997)].

In the literature, there are several works that deal with feature set partitioning. In one research, the features are grouped according to the feature type: nominal value features, numeric value features and text value features [Kusiak (2000)]. A similar approach was also used for developing the linear Bayes classifier [Gama (2000)]. The basic idea consists of aggregating the features into two subsets: the first subset containing only the nominal features and the second only the continuous features.

In another research, the feature set was decomposed according to the target class [Tumer and Ghosh (1996)]. For each class, the features with low correlation relating to that class were removed. This method was applied on a feature set of 25 sonar signals where the target was to identify the meaning of the sound (whale, cracking ice, etc.). Feature set partitioning has also been used for radar-based volcano recognition [Cherkauer (1996)]. The researcher manually decomposed a feature set of 119 into 8 subsets. Features that were based on different image processing operations were grouped together. As a consequence, for each subset, four neural networks with different sizes were built. A new combining framework for feature set partitioning has been used for text-independent speaker identification [Chen *et al.* (1997)]. Other researchers manually decomposed the features set of a certain truck backer-upper problem and reported that this strategy has important advantages [Jenkins and Yuhas (1993)].

The feature set decomposition can be obtained by grouping features based on pairwise mutual information, with statistically similar features assigned to the same group [Liao and Moody (2000)]. For this purpose, one can use an existing hierarchical clustering algorithm. As a consequence, several feature subsets are constructed by selecting one feature from each group. A neural network is subsequently constructed for each subset. All networks are then combined.

In statistics literature, the well-known feature-oriented ensemble algorithm is the MARS algorithm [Friedman (1991)]. In this algorithm, a multiple regression function is approximated using linear splines and their tensor products. It has been shown that the algorithm performs an ANOVA decomposition, namely, the regression function is represented as a grand total of several sums. The first sum is of all basic functions that involve only a single attribute. The second sum is of all basic functions that involve exactly two attributes, representing (if present) two-variable interactions. Similarly, the third sum represents (if present) the contributions from three-variable interactions, and so on.

A general framework that searches for helpful feature set partitioning structures has also been proposed [Rokach and Maimon (2005b)]. This framework nests many algorithms, two of which are tested empirically over a set of benchmark datasets. The first algorithm performs a serial search while using a new Vapnik–Chervonenkis dimension bound for multiple oblivious trees as an evaluating scheme. The second algorithm performs a multi-search while using a wrapper evaluating scheme. This work indicates that feature set decomposition can increase the accuracy of decision trees.

9.5.5 *Multi-Inducers*

In Multi-Inducer strategy, diversity is obtained by using different types of inducers [Michalski and Tecuci (1994)]. Each inducer contains an explicit or implicit bias [Mitchell (1980)] that leads it to prefer certain generalizations over others. Ideally, this multi-inducer strategy would always perform as well as the best of its ingredients. Even more ambitiously, there is hope that this combination of paradigms might produce synergistic effects, leading to levels of accuracy that neither atomic approach by itself would be able to achieve.

Most research in this area has been concerned with combining empirical approaches with analytical methods (see for instance [Towell and Shavlik (1994)]). Woods *et al.* (1997) combine four types of base inducers (decision trees, neural networks, *k*-nearest neighbor, and quadratic Bayes). They then estimate local accuracy in the feature space to choose the appropriate classifier for a given new unlabled instance. Wang *et al.* (2004) examined the usefulness of adding decision trees to an ensemble of neural networks. The researchers concluded that adding a few decision trees (but not too many) usually improved the performance. Langdon *et al.* (2002) proposed using Genetic Programming to find an appropriate rule for combining decision trees with neural networks.

The model class selection (MCS) system fits different classifiers to different sub-spaces of the instance space, by employing one of three classification methods (a decision-tree, a discriminant function or an instance-based method). In order to select the classification method, MCS uses the characteristics of the underlined training-set, and a collection of expert rules. Brodley's expert-rules were based on empirical comparisons of the methods' performance (i.e. on prior knowledge).

The NeC4.5 algorithm, which integrates decision tree with neural networks [Zhou and Jiang (2004)], first trains a neural network ensemble.

Then, the trained ensemble is employed to generate a new training set by replacing the desired class labels of the original training examples with the output from the trained ensemble. Some extra training examples are also generated from the trained ensemble and added to the new training set. Finally, a C4.5 decision tree is grown from the new training set. Since its learning results are decision trees, the comprehensibility of NeC4.5 is better than that of neural network ensembles.

Using several inducers can solve the dilemma which arises from the "no free lunch" theorem. This theorem implies that a certain inducer will be successful only insofar its bias matches the characteristics of the application domain [Brazdil *et al.* (1994)]. Thus, given a certain application, the practitioner need to decide which inducer should be used. Using the multi-inducer obviate the need to try each one and simplifying the entire process.

9.5.6 *Measuring the Diversity*

As stated above, it is usually assumed that increasing diversity may decrease ensemble error [Zenobi and Cunningham (2001)]. For regression problems, *variance* is usually used to measure diversity [Krogh and Vedelsby (1995)]. In such cases it can be easily shown that the ensemble error can be reduced by increasing ensemble diversity while maintaining the average error of a single model.

In classification problems, a more complicated measure is required to evaluate the diversity. There have been several attempts to define diversity measure for classification tasks.

In the neural network literature, two measures are presented for examining diversity:

- Classification coverage: An instance is covered by a classifier, if it yields a correct classification.
- Coincident errors: A coincident error amongst the classifiers occurs when more than one member misclassifies a given instance.

Based on these two measures, Sharkey (1997) defined four diversity levels:

- Level 1 — No coincident errors and the classification function is completely covered by a majority vote of the members.
- Level 2 — Coincident errors may occur, but the classification function is completely covered by a majority vote.

- Level 3 — A majority vote will not always correctly classify a given instance, but at least one ensemble member always correctly classifies it.
- Level 4 — The function is not always covered by the members of the ensemble.

Brown *et al.* (2005) claim that the above four-level scheme provides no indication of how typical the error behavior described by the assigned diversity level is. This claim, especially, holds when the ensemble exhibits different diversity levels on different subsets of instance space.

There are other more quantitative measures which categorize these measures into two types [Brown *et al.* (2005)]: pairwise and non-pairwise. Pairwise measures calculate the average of a particular distance metric between all possible pairings of members in the ensemble, such as Q-statistic [Brown *et al.* (2005)] or kappa-statistic [Margineantu and Dietterich (1997)]. The non-pairwise measures either use the idea of entropy (such as [Cunningham and Carney (2000)]) or calculate a correlation of each ensemble member with the averaged output. The comparison of several measures of diversity has resulted in the conclusion that most of them are correlated [Kuncheva and Whitaker (2003)].

9.6 Ensemble Size

9.6.1 *Selecting the Ensemble Size*

An important aspect of ensemble methods is to define how many component classifiers should be used. There are several factors that may determine this size:

- Desired accuracy — In most cases, ensembles containing 10 classifiers are sufficient for reducing the error rate [Hansen and Salamon (1990)]. Nevertheless, there is empirical evidence indicating that: when AdaBoost uses decision trees, error reduction is observed in even relatively large ensembles containing 25 classifiers [Opitz and Maclin (1999)]. In disjoint partitioning approaches, there may be a trade-off between the number of subsets and the final accuracy. The size of each subset cannot be too small because sufficient data must be available for each learning process to produce an effective classifier.
- Computational cost — Increasing the number of classifiers usually increases computational cost and decreases their comprehensibility. For that reason, users may set their preferences by predefining the ensemble size limit.

- The nature of the classification problem — In some ensemble methods, the nature of the classification problem that is to be solved, determines the number of classifiers. For instance, in the ECOC algorithm the number of classes determine the ensemble size.
- Number of processors available — In independent methods, the number of processors available for parallel learning could be put as an upper bound on the number of classifiers that are treated in paralleled process.

There three methods that are used to determine the ensemble size, as described by the following subsections.

9.6.2 *Pre-selection of the Ensemble Size*

This is the most simple way to determine the ensemble size. Many ensemble algorithms have a controlling parameter such as "number of iterations", which can be set by the user. Algorithms such as Bagging belong to this category. In other cases, the nature of the classification problem determine the number of members (such as in the case of ECOC).

9.6.3 *Selection of the Ensemble Size while Training*

There are ensemble algorithms that try to determine the best ensemble size while training. Usually as new classifiers are added to the ensemble these algorithms check if the contribution of the last classifier to the ensemble performance is still significant. If it is not, the ensemble algorithm stops. Usually these algorithms also have a controlling parameter which bounds the maximum size of the ensemble.

An algorithm that decides when a sufficient number of classification trees have been created was recently proposed [Banfield *et al.* (2007)]. The algorithm uses the out-of-bag error estimate, and is shown to result in an accurate ensemble for those methods that incorporate bagging into the construction of the ensemble. Specifically, the algorithm works by first smoothing the out-of-bag error graph with a sliding window in order to reduce the variance. After the smoothing has been completed, the algorithm takes a larger window on the smoothed data points and determines the maximum accuracy within that window. It continues to process windows until the maximum accuracy within a particular window no longer increases. At this point, the stopping criterion has been reached and the algorithm returns the ensemble with the maximum raw accuracy from within that window.

9.6.4   *Pruning — Post Selection of the Ensemble Size*

As in decision tree induction, it is sometimes useful to let the ensemble grow freely and then prune the ensemble in order to get more effective and compact ensembles. Post selection of the ensemble size allows ensemble optimization for such performance metrics as accuracy, cross entropy, mean precision, or the ROC area. Empirical examinations indicate that pruned ensembles may obtain a similar accuracy performance as the original ensemble [Margineantu and Dietterich (1997)]. In another empirical study that was conducted in order to understand the affect of ensemble sizes on ensemble accuracy and diversity, it has been shown that it is feasible to keep a small ensemble while maintaining accuracy and diversity similar to those of a full ensemble [Liu *et al.* (2004)].

The pruning methods can be divided into two groups: pre-combining pruning methods and post-combining pruning methods.

9.6.4.1   *Pre-combining Pruning*

Pre-combining pruning is performed before combining the classifiers. Classifiers that seem to perform well are included in the ensemble. Prodromidis *et al.* (1999) present three methods for pre-combining pruning: based on an individual classification performance on a separate validation set, diversity metrics, the ability of classifiers to classify correctly specific classes.

In attribute bagging, classification accuracy of randomly selected m-attribute subsets is evaluated by using the wrapper approach and only the classifiers constructed on the highest ranking subsets participate in the ensemble voting.

9.6.4.2   *Post-combining Pruning*

In post-combining pruning methods, we remove classifiers based on their contribution to the collective.

Prodromidis examines two methods for post-combining pruning assuming that the classifiers are combined using meta-combination method: Based on decision tree pruning and the correlation of the base classifier to the unpruned meta-classifier.

A forward stepwise selection procedure can be used in order to select the most relevant classifiers (that maximize the ensemble's performance) among thousands of classifiers [Caruana *et al.* (2004)]. It has been shown that for this purpose one can use feature selection algorithms. However, instead of selecting features one should select the ensemble's members [Liu *et al.* (2004)].

One can also rank the classifiers according to their ROC performance. Then, they suggest to plot a graph where the Y-axis displays a performance measure of the integrated classification. The X-axis presents the number of classifiers that participated in the combination. i.e. the first best classifiers from the list are combined by voting (assuming equal weights for now) with the rest getting zero weights. The ensemble size is chosen when there are several sequential points with no improvement.

The GASEN algorithm was developed for selecting the most appropriate classifiers in a given ensemble [Zhou *et al.* (2002)]. In the initialization phase, GASEN assigns a random weight to each of the classifiers. Consequently, it uses genetic algorithms to evolve those weights so that they can characterize to some extent the fitness of the classifiers in joining the ensemble. Finally, it removes from the ensemble those classifiers whose weight is less than a predefined threshold value.

Recently, a revised version of the GASEN algorithm called GASEN-b has been suggested [Zhou and Tang (2003)]. In this algorithm, instead of assigning a weight to each classifier, a bit is assigned to each classifier indicating whether it will be used in the final ensemble. In an experimental study, the researchers showed that ensembles generated by a selective ensemble algorithm, which selects some of the trained C4.5 decision trees to make up an ensemble, may be not only smaller in size but also stronger in the generalization than ensembles generated by non-selective algorithms.

A comparative study of pre-combining and post-combining methods when meta-combining methods are used has been performed in [Prodromidis *et al.* (1999)]. The results indicate that the post-combining pruning methods tend to perform better in this case.

9.7   Cross-Inducer

This property indicates the relation between the ensemble technique and the inducer used.

Some implementations are considered as an inducer-dependent type, namely these ensemble generators which use intrinsic inducer, have been developed specifically for a certain inducer. They can neither work nor guarantee effectiveness in any other induction method. For instance, the works of [Hansen (1990); Lu and Ito (1999); Sharkey (1996)] were developed specifically for neural networks. The works of [Breiman (2001); Rokach and Maimon (2005b)] were developed specifically for decision trees.

Other implementations are considered to be the inducer-independent type. These implementations can be performed on any given inducer and are not limited to a specific inducer like the inducer-dependent.

9.8   Multistrategy Ensemble Learning

Multistrategy ensemble learning combines several ensemble strategies. It has been shown that this hybrid approach increases the diversity of ensemble members.

MultiBoosting, an extension to AdaBoost expressed by adding wagging-like features [Webb (2000)], can harness both AdaBoost's high bias and variance reduction with wagging's superior variance reduction. Using C4.5 as the base learning algorithm, MultiBoosting, significantly more often than the reverse, produces decision committees with lower error than either AdaBoost or wagging. It also offers the further advantage over AdaBoost of suiting parallel execution. MultiBoosting has been further extended by adding the stochastic attribute selection committee learning strategy to boosting and wagging [Webb and Zheng (2004)]. The latter's research has shown that combining ensemble strategies would increase diversity at the cost of a small increase in individual test error resulting in a trade-off that reduced overall ensemble test error.

Another multistrategy method suggests to create the ensemble by decomposing the original classification problem into several smaller and more manageable sub-problems. This multistrategy uses an elementary decomposition framework that consists of five different elementary decompositions: Concept Aggregation, Function, Sample, Space and Feature Set. The concept of elementary decomposition can be used to obtain a complicated decomposition by using the elementary decomposition concept recursively. Given a certain problem, the procedure selects the most appropriate elementary decomposition (if any) to that problem. A suitable decomposer then decomposes the problem and provides a set of sub-problems. A similar procedure is performed on each sub-problem until no beneficial decomposition is anticipated. The selection of the best elementary decomposition for a given problem is performed by using a meta-learning approach.

9.9   Which Ensemble Method Should be Used?

Recent research has experimentally evaluated bagging and seven other randomization-based approaches for creating an ensemble of decision tree classifiers [Banfield *et al.* (2007)]. Statistical tests were performed on experimental results from 57 publicly available datasets. When cross-validation comparisons were tested for statistical significance, the best method was statistically more accurate than bagging on only eight of the 57 datasets. Alternatively, examining the average ranks of the algorithms across the group of datasets, Banfield found that boosting, random forests, and randomized trees is statistically significantly better than bagging.

9.10 Open Source for Decision Trees Forests

There are two open source software packages which can be used for creating decision trees forests. Both systems, which are free, are distributed under the terms of the GNU General Public License.

- The OpenDT [Banfield (2005)] package has the ability to output trees very similar to C4.5, but has added functionality for ensemble creation. In the event that the attribute set randomly chosen provides a negative information gain, the OpenDT approach is to randomly rechoose attributes until a positive information gain is obtained, or no further split is possible. This enables each test to improve the purity of the resultant leaves. The system is written in Java.
- The Weka package [Frank *et al.* (2005)] is an organized collection of state-of-the-art machine learning algorithms and data preprocessing tools. The basic way of interacting with these methods is by invoking them from the command line. However, convenient interactive graphical user interfaces are provided for data exploration, for setting up large-scale experiments on distributed computing platforms, and for designing configurations for streamed data processing. These interfaces constitute an advanced environment for experimental data mining. Weka includes many decision tree learners: decision stumps, ID3, a C4.5 clone called "J48", trees generated by reduced error pruning, alternating decision trees, and random trees and forests thereof, including random forests, bagging, boosting, and stacking.

## Chapter 10

A Walk-through-guide for Using Decision Trees Software

10.1 Introduction

There are several decision trees software packages available over the internet. In the following section, we will review some of the most popular softwares. We will focus on open-source solutions that are freely available.

For illustrative purposes we will use the Iris dataset. This is one of the best known datasets in pattern recognition literature. It was first introduced by R. A. Fisher (1936). The goal in this case is to classify flowers into the Iris subgeni (such as Iris Setosa, Iris Versicolour and Iris Virginica) according to their characteristics.

The dataset consists of 150 instances. Each instance refers to one of the flowers and obtains the flowers' features, such as the length and the width of the sepal and petal. The label of every instance will be one of the strings *Iris Setosa*, *Iris Versicolour* and *Iris Virginica*. The task is to induce a classifier which will be able to predict the class to which a flower belongs to using its four attributes: sepal length in cm, sepal width in cm, petal length in cm and petal width in cm.

Table 10.1 illustrates a segment of the Iris dataset. The dataset contains three classes that correspond to three types of iris flowers: $dom\,(y) = \{IrisSetosa, IrisVersicolor, IrisVirginica\}$. Each instance is characterized by four numeric features (measured in centimeters): $A = \{sepallength, sepalwidth, petallength, petalwidth\}$.

Table 10.1   The Iris dataset consists of four numeric features and three possible classes.

Sepal Length	Sepal Width	Petal Length	Petal Width	Class (Iris Type)
5.1	3.5	1.4	0.2	Iris-setosa
4.9	3.0	1.4	0.2	Iris-setosa
6.0	2.7	5.1	1.6	Iris-versicolor
5.8	2.7	5.1	1.9	Iris-virginica
5.0	3.3	1.4	0.2	Iris-setosa
5.7	2.8	4.5	1.3	Iris-versicolor
5.1	3.8	1.6	0.2	Iris-setosa
⋮				

10.2   Weka

Weka is a popular machine learning suit developed at the University of Waikato. Weka is an open source software written in Java and available under the GNU General Public License.

The latest version and installation instructions can be downloaded from: `http://www.cs.waikato.ac.nz/~ml/weka/downloading. html`. Note that from version 3.7.2, Weka is installed with only the most popular learning algorithms. In order to install other algorithms one should use the package manager to select which additional component is to be installed. The Inventors of Weka have written a book that provides a detailed description of the Weka suite [Witten *et al.* (2011)]. The book is very popular and it is highly cited (more than 20,000 citations until 2013 according to Google Scholar). In this section, we only provide a brief step-by-step description on how to use Weka for training classification trees.

We begin by initiating the main Weka application. A window with Weka GUI Chooser is opened. For our walk-through-guide we choose the Explorer application. After clicking the Explorer button, the explorer window is opened. At the top of the new window, one can find a tab that corresponds to various tasks (see Figure 10.1) such as: preprocess, classification, clustering etc. At this stage, since no data has been loaded yet, the only task that is available is the preprocess task.

In the preprocess tab, please click the open file and using the windows explorer load the Iris dataset. The Iris dataset is distributed as part of the Weka installation in the `$WEKAHOME/data` directory, where `$WEKAHOME` is the directory of your Weka installation (in Windows the default location is `C:/ProgramFiles/Weka-3-X`, where x stands for the installed version).

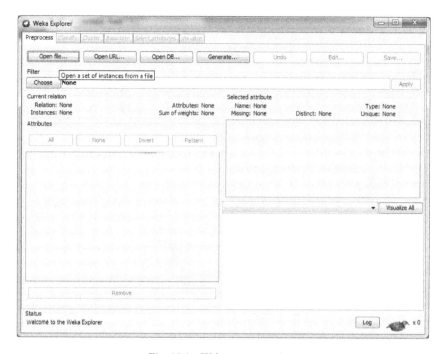

Fig. 10.1   Weka preprocessing.

Figure 10.2 illustrates the preprocess windows after loading the Iris dataset. Note that on the left part of the screen, we can see the list of attributes in the Iris dataset is presented. The right side shows the properties of the selected attribute and how the selected attribute and the target attribute are co-distributed. In the preprocess, it is possible to edit the dataset by clicking the Edit button or run a filtering procedure (such as feature selection) on the raw dataset. This is done by choosing a filter and clicking on Apply.

10.2.1   *Training a Classification Tree*

Weka implements several decision tree induction algorithms. The most frequently used algorithm is the J48 which is a variation of the well-known C4.5 algorithm development. While many consider J48 identical to C45, it should be noted that there are some differences. A comparison study performed by Moore *et al.* (2009) reveals that J48 consistently performs worse than C4.5 on the datasets that were evaluated.

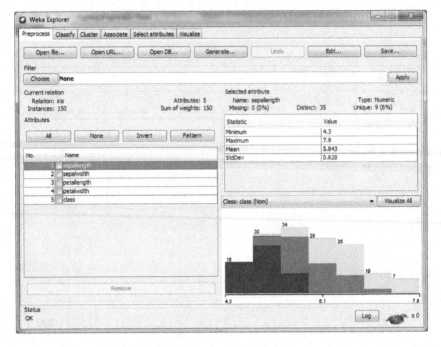

Fig. 10.2   Data view in Weka.

To train the J48 classifier, first go classifier tab (the second tab right to the preprocess tab). Figure 10.3 presents the resulted user interface. In this window, you can select the learning algorithm (with the Choose button), set the algorithm's parameters, select the evaluation procedure (the default is 10 folds cross-validation) and change the target attribute (by default the last attribute is considered as the target attribute).

Click the choose button and select the J48 algorithm under the trees folder as illustrated in Figure 10.4.

It is possible to set the algorithm's parameters by clicking the white text box that contains the algorithm's title along with its current list of parameters' values. Clicking this box opens up a window that lists all the parameters of J48 algorithm that can be set by the user, including:

(1) minNumObj — A numeric parameter that indicates the minimum number of instances that a leaf should have.
(2) binarySplits — A binary parameter that indicates whether nominal attributes should be partitioned using binary splits.

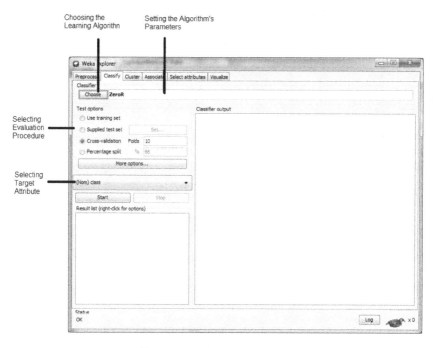

Fig. 10.3   Weka classifier panel.

(3) unpruned — A binary parameter that indicates whether the second step of pruning is disabled.
(4) useLaplace — A binary parameter that indicates whether the posterior probabilities in the leaves are smoothed based on Laplace correction.

In order to train the classifier, click start button (located in the right side of the classifier window). Weka will run the training algorithm 11 times. First it trains a classification tree using the entire dataset. This tree is presented to the user. Then it performs the 10 folds cross-validation procedure to evaluate the predictive performance of the classification tree. Note that in the 10 folds cross-validation procedure the training set is randomly partitioned into 10 disjoint instance subsets. Each subset is utilized once in a test set and nine times in a training set. Figure 10.5 presents the resulted window. The output sub-window presents various predictive performance measures such as: accuracy, AUC and confusion matrix.

Scrolling up through the output sub-windows shows that the tree classifier is presented as a text (see Figure 10.6). Indentation is used to convey the tree topology. The information for each internal node

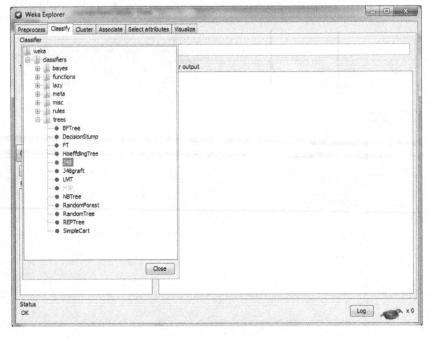

Fig. 10.4   Selecting the J48 classifier.

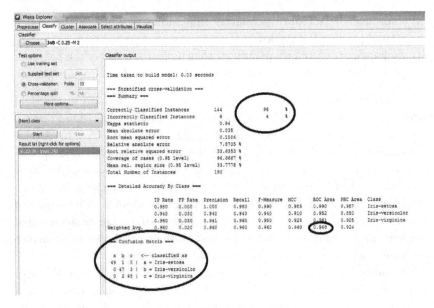

Fig. 10.5   Weka classifier results.

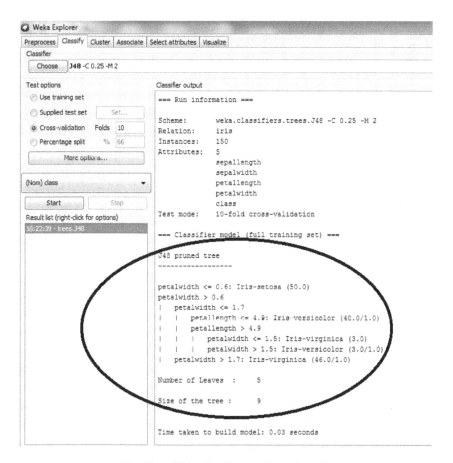

Fig. 10.6   Weka classifier results — Part B.

includes the split condition. The information for each leaf node includes the suggested class (most frequent class) and the number of instances belonging to this leaf. In case there are instances that do not belong to the suggested class, their number would appear. For example, the numbers 48.0/1.0 presented in Figure 10.6 indicate that there are 48 instances in the training set that fit the path: `petalwidth>0.6 -> petalwidth<=1.7 -> petallength<=4.9`. From which 47 are classified as Iris-versicolor whereas one is classified differently (i.e. not Iris-versicolor).

It is possible to produce the tree in a graphics mode. For this purpose right click the J48 classifier that is listed in the "resulted list" (located to the left of the output sub-window) and select Visualize tree as illustrated

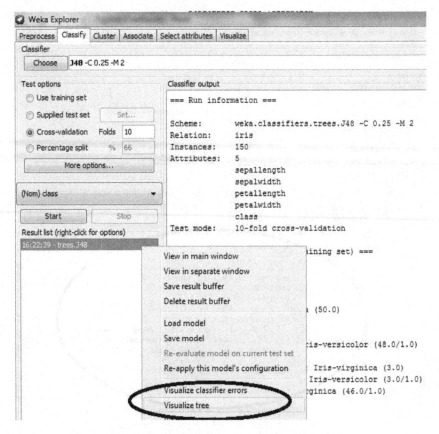

Fig. 10.7   Opening the J48 tree visualization.

in Figure 10.7. Following the last action, a graphical visualization of the J47 is presented (see Figure 10.8).

10.2.2   *Building a Forest*

Weka has a very rich list of ensemble algorithms that can be used to build a decision forest. Ensemble algorithms that were specifically designed for decision trees, such as random forest, are located in the trees section of the hierarchical menu. Other ensemble methods such as bagging, AdaBoost and rotation forest can be applied to any classification algorithm and therefore are located in the meta section. Most meta learning algorithms include one parameter for specifying the base classifier and one parameter for

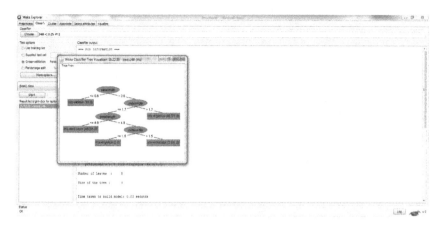

Fig. 10.8   J48 tree visualization.

indicating the ensemble size (i.e. the number of iterations). Figure 10.9 presents the properties list of the Rotation Forest algorithm. Note that a classifier property should refer to a decision tree algorithm (such as J48) in order to actually build a forest. In many cases altering the number of iterations by a trial-and-error procedure is very helpful for improving the predictive performance.

10.3   R

R is a free software programming language that is widely used among data scientists to develop data mining algorithms. Most of the data scientist's tasks can be accomplished in R with a short script code thanks to the diversity and richness of the contributed packages in CRAN (comprehensive R archive network). In this section, we review the packages: `party`, `rpart` and `randomForest` which are used to train decision trees and decision forests.

10.3.1   *Party Package*

The party package provides a set of tools for training classification and regression trees [Hothorn *et al.* (2006)]. At the core of the party package there is the `ctree()` function which implements a conditional inference procedure to train the tree. The following R script illustrates the usage of the ctree function for training a classification tree.

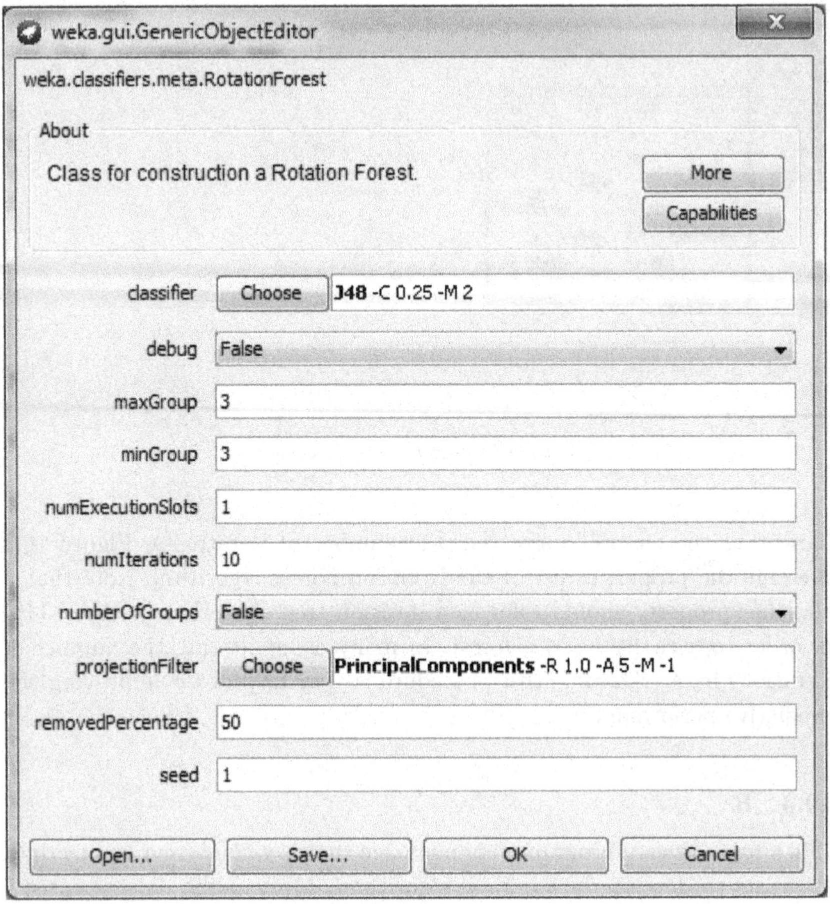

Fig. 10.9   Weka rotation forest.

```
library (''party'')

IrisClassifcationTree<-ctree (Species ~ ., data = iris)

plot (irisct)
```

The above R script first loads the party package (assuming it has been
already installed, see Section Installing packages in your "R Installation and

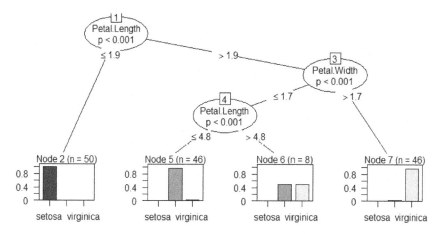

Fig. 10.10   The classifier tree is obtained for Iris dataset.

Administration" for instructions how to install a package). Then it trains a classification tree for the Iris dataset where Species is the target attribute and all other attributes are used as input attributes. Then in the third line the plot function is used to visualize c the tree as illustrated in Figure 10.10. The nodes are numbered. Each leaf node contains a histogram that shows the probability of an instance to be labeled with each one of the classes.

The tree induction algorithm can be configured using the `ctree_control()` function. In particular, the following parameters can be set:

(1) mincriterion — The threshold value of the splitting criterion that must be exceeded in order to implement a split.
(2) minsplit — The minimum number of instances in a node in order to be considered for splitting.
(3) minbucket — The minimum number of instances in a terminal node.
(4) stump — A Boolean parameter that indicates whether a decision stump should be built.
(5) maxdepth — The maximum depth of the tree.

The following script illustrates a more complicated learning process. It begins by splitting the Iris data into train (2/3 of the instances) and test (the remaining instances). Then it trains a classification tree for the Species target attribute by using only the train data with the following input attributes: Sepal.Length, Petal.Length and Sepal.Width. The training algorithm's parameters are set to the following values: `minsplit=3` and `maxdepth=3`.

After training the tree, we plot it using a simple style (instead of showing the histogram, it shows the class distribution). Finally, we classify the instances in the test data and evaluate the predictive performance of the tree by presenting the confusion matrix.

```
library(``party'')

# split the data into train and test
trainIndex<-sample(nrow(iris), 2/3*nrow(iris))
trainData <- iris[trainIndex,]
testData <- iris[-trainIndex,]

# train the classification tree
irisClassifcationTree <- ctree(Species ~ Sepal.Length+
                         Petal.Length + Sepal.Width,
                         data = trainData, control =
                         ctree_control(minsplit=3,
                                       maxdepth=3))
# plot a simple tree
plot(irisClassifcationTree,type=``simple'')

# predict on test data
testPrediction <- predict(irisClassifcationTree,
                          newdata = testData)

# show the confusion matrix
table(testPrediction, testData$Species)
```

10.3.2 *Forest*

The party package provides an implementation of the random forest and bagging ensemble algorithms utilizing ctree algorithm as a base inducer. The following script illustrates the creation and evaluation of a random forest with 10 trees (`ntree=10`). The number of randomly preselected attributes is set by `mtry` parameter.

```
irisForest <- cforest(Species ~ ., data=trainData,
              control = cforest_unbiased(ntree =
                        10, mtry = 2))

testPrediction <- predict(irisForest,
                          newdata = testData)

table(testPrediction, testData$Species)
```

10.3.3 *Other Types of Trees*

With party package, it is possible to train different types of trees other than classification trees using the Model-based Recursive Partitioning functionality. The `mob()` function provides a specific implementation of recursive partitioning based on parametric models for building linear regression trees, logistic regression trees or survival trees.

With `mob()` function [Zeileis *et al.* (2008)] some input attributes are used for fitting the model while others are used for partitioning. For example, the following script trains a tree using the attributes Sepal.Width, Species and Petal.Width as partitioning attributes. Each leaf tries to predict the value of Sepal.Length by fitting a simple linear regression with Petal.Length serving as an explanatory variable. Figure 10.11 presents the resulting regression tree. The regression coefficients for each leaf node can be obtained by the function coef(SepalLengthRegression).

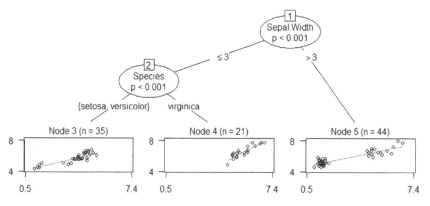

Fig. 10.11   Regression tree.

```
SepalLengthRegression<—mob( Sepal . Length~Petal . Length |
                            Sepal . Width+Species+
                            Petal . Width , control =
                            mob_control( minsplit = 10) .
                            data=trainData ,
                            model = linearModel )

plot ( SepalLengthRegression )
```

In addition to linear regression, it is possible to train other parametric models such as logistic regression (`model = glinearModel`, `family = binomial()`) and survival regression (`model=survReg`).

10.3.4 *The Rpart Package*

The package rpart [Therneau and Atkinson (1997)] is another implementation for training classification and regression trees using recursive partitioning and a two-stage procedure. In the first stage, the tree is built recursively until no sufficient data is left or until no improvement can be noticed. The second stage of the procedure consists of using cross-validation to prune the tree.

The following script trains a classification tree for the Iris dataset using the rpart package and plots the resulted model as presented in Figure 10.12. Note that the leaf nodes include the class frequency and the most frequent class.

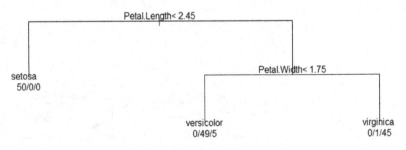

Fig. 10.12   RPart output.

```
library ( rpart )
fit <- rpart ( Species ~ ., data = iris )
plot ( fit )
text ( fit , use.n = TRUE ) )
```

The function rpart() is capable to induce not only classification trees but also regression trees, survival tree and Poisson tree. This is done by setting the method argument to the following values: anova (for regression tree), class (for classification tree), exp (for survival tree) or poisson (for Poisson Regression tree). If the method argument is not set then the function makes an intelligent guess. Note that Poisson regression is a type of regression that aims to model event rate that follows a Poisson distribution. For example, in a manufacturing scenario the target attribute may refer to defective rate. Poisson regression assumes that the logarithm of the target attribute's expected value can be represented as a linear combination of the input attributes.

The function rpart() lets the user select the splitting criterion: gini index or information gain. This is done by setting the split parameter to either split = ''information'' or split=''gini''. In addition, similarly to ctree(), a control object can be included to set various parameters such as minsplit, minbucket and maxdepth. The following script illustrates this tuning capability by indicating that splitting criterion is information gain and that the number of instances should exceed 5 in order to consider splitting a certain node.

```
fit <- rpart ( Species ~ ., data = iris ,
          split = ''information '' ,
          control = rpart . control ( minsplit = 5 )
```

10.3.5 *RandomForest*

In the previous section, we have seen how the function cfores() can be used to build an ensemble of classification trees. An alternative way to build a random forest is to use the RandomForest package [Liaw and Wiener (2002)].

```
library (''randomForest'')

# split the data into to train and test
trainIndex<-sample(nrow(iris), 2/3*nrow(iris))
trainData <- iris[trainIndex,]
testData <- iris[-trainIndex,]

# build the forest
irisRandomForest <- randomForest(Species ~ .,
                          data = trainData)

# predict on test data
testPrediction <- predict(irisRandomForest,
                          newdata = testData)

# show the confusion matrix
table(testPrediction, testData$Species)
```

The function randomForest() has several arguments that control the execution of the algorithm, such as: ntree (Number of trees to grow), mtry (Number of attributes randomly sampled as candidates at each split), replace- (whether sampling of cases can be done with or without a replacement), sampsize (the sizes of the samples to draw) and nodesize (Minimum size of terminal nodes). Finally, the random Forest package provides additional useful functions such as the function getTree() for extracting a certain single tree from a forest and the function grow() for adding additional trees to an existing forest.

Chapter 11

Advanced Decision Trees

11.1 Oblivious Decision Trees

Oblivious decision trees are those in which all nodes at the same level test the same feature. Despite its restriction, oblivious decision trees are effective for feature selection. Almuallim and Dietterich (1994) as well as Schlimmer (1993) have proposed a forward feature selection procedure by constructing oblivious decision trees, whereas Langley and Sage (1994) suggested backward selection using the same means. Kohavi and Sommerfield (1998) have shown that oblivious decision trees can be converted to a decision table.

Figure 11.1 illustrates a typical oblivious decision tree with four input features: Glucose level (G), Age (A), Hypertension (H) and Pregnant (P) and the Boolean target feature representing whether that patient suffers from diabetes. Each layer is uniquely associated with an input feature by representing the interaction of that feature and the input features of the previous layers. The number that appears in the terminal nodes indicates the number of instances that fit this path. For example, regarding patients whose glucose level is less than 107 and whose age is greater than 50, 10 are positively diagnosed with diabetes while 2 are not diagnosed with diabetes.

The principal difference between the oblivious decision tree and a regular decision tree structure is the constant ordering of input attributes at every terminal node of the oblivious decision tree. This latter property is necessary for minimizing the overall subset of input attributes (resulting in dimensionality reduction). The arcs that connect the terminal nodes and the nodes of the target layer are labeled with the number of records that fit this path.

An oblivious decision tree is usually built by a greedy algorithm, which tries to maximize the mutual information measure in every layer. The

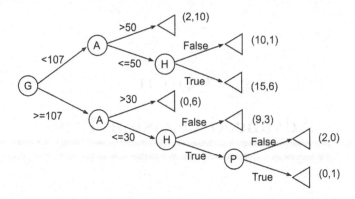

Fig. 11.1   Illustration of oblivious decision tree.

recursive search for explaining attributes is terminated when there is no attribute that explains the target with statistical significance.

11.2   Online Adaptive Decision Trees

A classification scheme called online adaptive decision trees (OADT) was proposed by Basak (2004). As with the decision trees, OADT is a tree-structured network which is capable of online learning like neural networks. This leads to better generalization scores.

The fact that OADT can only handle two-class classification tasks with a given structure is a major drawback. The ExOADT algorithm [Basak (2006)] can handle multiclass classification tasks and is able to perform function approximation. ExOADT is structurally similar to OADT extended with a regression layer.

11.3   Lazy Tree

In lazy tree algorithms learning is delayed until the query point is observed [Friedman *et al.* (1996)]. An *ad hoc* decision tree (actually a rule) is constructed just to classify a certain instance. The LazyDT algorithm constructs the best decision tree for each test instance. In practice, only a path needs to be constructed. A caching scheme makes the algorithm run fast.

With the LazyDT algorithm, a single decision tree built from the training set offers a compromise: the test at the root of each subtree is chosen to be the best split on average. This "average" approach can lead to many irrelevant splits for a given test instance, thus fragmenting the data

Require: x (an unlabelled instance I to classify), S (training set)
Ensure: A label for instance x

1: If all instances in S have label l, then return l.
2: if all instances in S have the same feature values, return the majority Class in S.
3: select a test A and let v be the value of the test on the instance x. Recursively apply the algorithm to the set of instances in S with $A = v$.

Fig. 11.2 The LazyDT algorithm.

unnecessarily. Such fragmentation reduces the significance of tests at lower levels since they are based on fewer instances. Classification paths, built for a specific instance may be much shorter and hence may provide a better explanation.

A generic pseudo-code of the LazyDT algorithm is described in Figure 11.2. The lazy decision tree algorithm, which gets the test instance as part of the input, follows a separate-and-classify methodology: a test is selected and the sub-problem containing the instances with the same test outcome as the given instance is then solved recursively.

11.4 Option Tree

Regular decision trees make a single test at each node and trace a single path corresponding to test outcomes until a leaf is reached and a prediction is made. Option decision trees (also known as and–or trees), first introduced by Buntine (1992), generalize regular decision trees by allowing option nodes in addition to decision nodes; such nodes make it possible to conduct several possible tests instead of the commonly used single test. Classification is similar to regular decision trees, except that a rule is applied to option nodes to combine the predictions of the children nodes.

There are several reasons for using option trees. Option decision trees can reduce the error of decision trees in handling real-world problems by combining multiple options. This is similar to what we find when implementing ensemble methods that learn multiple models and combine the predictions. However, unlike ensemble methods, an option decision tree yields a single tree, which is a compact representation of many possible trees and which can be easily interpreted by humans. The myopic nature of top-down classification tree inducers and the stability of the classifiers are the reasons for the option decision trees improved performance compared to regular decision trees.

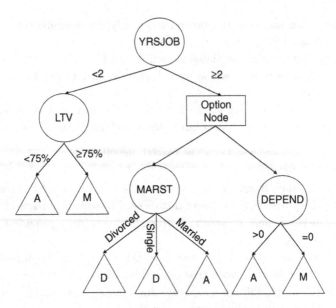

Fig. 11.3   Illustration of option tree.

Figure 11.3 illustrates an option tree. Recall that the task is to classify mortgage applications into: approved ("A"), denied ("D") or manual underwriting ("M"). The tree looks like any other decision tree with a supplement of an option node, which is denoted as a rectangle. If years at current job (YRSJOB) is greater than or equals two years, then there are two options to choose from. Each option leads to a different subtree that separately solve the problem and make a classification.

In order to classify a new instance with an option tree, it is required to weight the labels predicted by all children of the option node. For example, in order to classify an instance with YRSJOB=3, MARST="Married" and DEPEND=3, we need to combine the fifth leaf and the sixth leaf (from left to right), resulting in the class "A" (since both are associated with class "A"). On the other hand, in order to classify an instance with YRSJOB=3, MARST="Single" and DEPEND=3, then we need to combine the fourth leaf and sixth leaf, resulting in either class "A" or "D". Since in simple majority voting, the final class is selected arbitrarily, it never makes sense to create an option node with two children. Consequently the minimum number of choices for an option node is three. Nevertheless, assuming that a probability vector is associated with each leaf, it is possible to use a Bayesian combination to obtain a non-arbitrary selection. In fact, the model

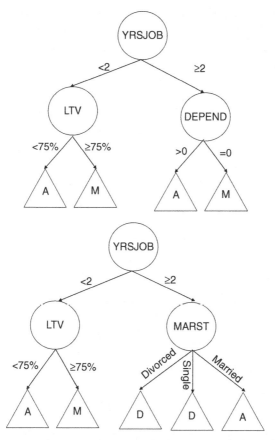

Fig. 11.4   Illustration of two regular trees which are equivalent to the option tree presented in Figure 11.3.

presented in Figure 11.3 can be seen as combining the two regular decision trees presented in Figure 11.4.

TDDTOP is a Top-Down Decision-Tree (TDDT) inducer which is quite similar to C4.5 but with the additional ability to create option nodes [Kohavi and Kunz (1997)]. The principal modication to the basic TDDT algorithm is that instead of always selecting a single test, when several tests evaluate close to the best test, the TDDTOP algorithm creates an option node. All the data is sent to each child of an option node, which then splits the data according to its predetermined test. As for the pruning phase, the C4.5 pruning algorithm was modified so that the pessimistic error of an option node was the average of the pessimistic errors of its children.

Require: S — training set, $f(a)$ — a function of the input attributes values, $SimpleSplitCriterion$ — a splitting criterion function, $Depth$ — the lookahead depth.

Ensure: The lookahead criterion value

1: **if** $Depth = 1$ **then**
2:    return SimpleSplitCriterion(S,f(A))
3: **end if**
4: Split S into subsets $S_1,...,S_k$ according to the values of f(A).
5: **for all** subset S_i **do**
6:    Find a function $g(A)$ of the input attributes values which gets the best value v_i of $LookAhead(S_i, g(A), SimpleSplitCriterion, Depth - 1)$
7: **end for**
8: Return weighted average of v_i

Fig. 11.5   Algorithm for calculating lookahead splitting criterion.

11.5   Lookahead

The splitting criteria in regular top-down decision tree inducers is usually greedy and local. Fixed-depth lookahead search is a standard technique for improving greedy algorithms. More extensive search quickly leads to intolerable time consumption. Moreover, limited lookahead search does not produce significantly better decision trees [Murthy and Salzberg (1995)]. On average, it produces trees with approximately the same generalization error and size as greedy induction. In fact, pruning methods are usually at least as beneficial as limited lookahead.

Figure 11.5 specifies an algorithm of lookahead splitting criterion by wrapping a regular splitting criterion (denoted as SimpleSplitCriterion). Note that the proposed algorithm performs a lookahead of *Depth* levels.

LSID3 [Esmeir and Markovitch (2004)], a variation of the well-known ID3 algorithm, invests more resources for making better split decisions. For every possible candidate split, LSID3 estimates the size of the resulting subtree, and prefers the one with the smallest expected size. For this purpose, it uses a sample of the space of trees rooted at the evaluated attribute. The sample is obtained by selecting attributes with a probability proportional to its information gain.

11.6   Oblique Decision Trees

Regular top-down decision trees inducers, such as C4.5, use only a single attribute in each node. Consequently these algorithms are partitioning the instance space using only axis-parallel separating surfaces (typically, hyperplanes). Several cases presented in the literature use multivariate splitting criteria.

In multivariate splitting criteria, several attributes may participate in a single node split test. Obviously, finding the best multivariate criteria is more complicated than finding the best univariate split. Furthermore, although this type of criteria may dramatically improve the trees performance, these criteria are much less popular than the univariate criteria.

Figure 11.6 presents a typical algorithmic framework for top-down inducing of oblique decision trees. Note that this algorithm is very similar

---

TreeGrowing (S, A, y) Where: S - Training Set
A - Input Feature Set y - Target Feature

Create a new tree T with a single root node.

IF One of the Stopping Criteria is fulfilled THEN
 Mark T as a leaf with the most
 common value of y in S as a label.
ELSE
 Find a discrete function $f(A)$ of the input
  attributes values such that splitting S
  according to $f(A)$'s outcomes $(v_1, \ldots, v_n)$ gains
  the best splitting metric.
 IF best splitting metric > threshold THEN
  Label t with $f(A)$
  FOR each outcome v_i of $f(A)$:
   Set $Subtree_i$= TreeGrowing $(\sigma_{f(A)=v_i} S, A, y)$.
   Connect the root node of t_T to $Subtree_i$ with
    an edge that is labelled as v_i
  END FOR
 ELSE
  Mark the root node in T as a leaf with the most
   common value of y in S as a label.
 END IF
END IF RETURN T

Fig. 11.6 Top-down algorithmic framework for oblique decision trees induction.

to that presented in Figure 3.1. But, instead of looking for a split with a single attribute, it looks for the best function of the input attributes. In each iteration, the algorithm considers the partition of the training set using the outcome of a discrete function of the input attributes. The selection of the most appropriate function is made according to some splitting measures. After the selection of an appropriate split, each node further subdivides the training set into smaller subsets, until no split gains sufficient splitting measures or a stopping criterion is satisfied. Because there are endless functions, the main challenge is to decide on which functions the algorithm should concentrate.

Most of the multivariate splitting criteria are based on the linear combination of the input attributes. In this case the algorithm constructs hyperplanes that are oblique, that is, not parallel to a coordinate axis. Figure 11.7 illustrates an Oblique Decision Tree. The left node in the second level tests a linear combination of the two input attributes $3 \cdot YRSJOB - 2 \cdot DEPEND$. It is reasonable to assume that oblique decision trees would require several less planes then a regular decision tree, resulting in a smaller tree.

Finding the best linear combination can be performed using greedy search ([Breiman *et al.* (1984)], [Murthy (1998)]); linear programming ([Duda and Hart (1973)]; [Bennett and Mangasarian (1994)]); linear discriminant analysis ([Duda and Hart (1973)]; [Friedman (1977)]; [Sklansky and Wassel (1981)]; [Lin and Fu (1983)]; [Loh and Vanichsetakul (1988)];

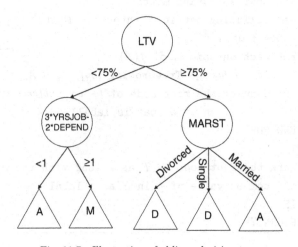

Fig. 11.7   Illustration of oblique decision tree.

[John (1996)] and others ([Utgoff (1989a)]; [Lubinsky (1993)]; [Sethi and Yoo (1994)]).

Growing of oblique decision trees was first proposed as a linear combination extension to the CART algorithm. This extension is known as the CART-LC [Biermann *et al.* (1982)]. oblique classifier 1 (OC1) is an inducer of oblique decision trees designed for training sets with numeric instances [Murthy *et al.* (1994)]. OC1 builds the oblique hyperplanes by using a linear combinations of one or more numeric attributes at each internal node; these trees then partition the space of examples with both oblique and axis-parallel hyperplanes.

11.7 Incremental Learning of Decision Trees

To reflect new data that has become available, most decision trees inducers must be rebuilt from scratch. This is time-consuming and expensive and several researchers have addressed the issue of updating decision trees incrementally. Utgoff [Utgoff (1989b); Utgoff (1997)], for example, presents several methods for incrementally updating decision trees while Crawford (1989) describes an extension to the CART algorithm that is capable of inducing incremental changes.

11.7.1 *The Motives for Incremental Learning*

In the ever-changing world of information technology there are two fundamental problems to be addressed:

- Vast quantities of digital data continue to grow at staggering rates. In organizations such as e-commerce sites, large retailers and telecommunication corporations, data increases of gigabytes per day are not uncommon. While this data could be extremely valuable to these organizations, the tremendous volume makes it virtually impossible to extract useful information. This is due to the fact that KDD systems in general, and traditional data mining algorithms in particular, are limited by several crippling factors. These factors, referred to as computational resources, are the size of the sample to be processed, running time and memory. As a result, most of the available data is unused which leads to underfitting. While there is enough data to model a compound phenomenon, there is no capability for fully utilizing this data and unsatisfactorily simple models are produced.

- Most machine learning algorithms, among them those underlying the data mining process assume that the data, which needs to be learned (training data), serves as a random sample drawn from a stationary distribution. The assumption is unfortunately violated by the majority of databases and data streams available for mining today. These databases accumulate over large periods of time, with the underlying processes generating them changing respectively and at times quite drastically. This occurrence is known as concept drift. According to Hulten *et al.* (2001), "in many cases... it is more accurate to assume that data was generated by... a concept function with time-varying parameters." Incorrect models are learned by the traditional data mining algorithms when these mistakenly assume that the underlying concept is stationary, when it is, in fact, drifting. This may serve to degrade the predictive performance of the models.

A prime example of systems which may have to deal with the aforementioned problems are on-line learning systems, which use continuous incoming batches of training examples to induce rules for a classification task. Two instances in which these systems are currently utilized are credit card fraud detection and real-time monitoring of manufacturing processes.

As a result of the above-mentioned problems it is now common practice to mine a sub-sample of the available data or to mine for a model drastically simpler than the data could support. Ideally, the KDD systems will function continuously, constantly processing data received so that potentially valuable information is never lost. In order to achieve this goal, many methods have been developed. Termed incremental (online) learning methods, these methods aim to extract patterns from changing streams of data.

11.7.2   *The Inefficiency Challenge*

According to Hulten *et al.* (2001), incremental learning algorithms suffer from numerous inadequacies from the KDD point of view. Whereas some of these algorithms are relatively efficient, they do not guarantee that the model that emerges will be similar to the one obtained by learning on the same data in the non-incremental (batch) methods. Other incremental learning algorithms produce the same model as the batch version, but at a higher cost in efficiency, which may mean longer training times.

In order to overcome this trade-off, Domingos and Hulten (2000) proposed VFDT a decision-tree learning method which is aimed at learning online from high-volume data streams by using sub-sampling of the entire data stream generated by a stationary process. This method uses constant time per example and constant memory and can incorporate tens of thousands of examples per second using off-the-shelf hardware. This method involves learning by seeing each example only once; there is no necessity for storing them. As a result it is possible to directly mine online data sources. The sample size is determined in VFDT from distribution-free Hoeffding bounds to guarantee that its output is asymptotically nearly identical to that of a conventional learner.

11.7.3 *The Concept Drift Challenge*

The second problem, centered around concept drift, is also addressed by incremental learning methods that have been adapted to work effectively with continuous, time-changing data streams. Black and Hickey (1999) identified several important sub-tasks involved in handling drift within incremental learning methods. The two most fundamental sub-tasks are identifying that drift is occurring and updating classification rules in the light of this drift.

Time-windowing is one of the most known and acceptable approaches for dealing with these tasks. The basic concept of this approach is the repeated application of a learning algorithm to a sliding window, which contains a certain amount (either constant or changing) of examples. As new examples arrive, they are placed into the beginning of the window. A corresponding number of examples are removed from the end of the window. The latest model is the one used for future prediction of incoming instances until concept drift is detected. At this point the learner is reapplied on the last window of instances and a new model is built.

FLORA, the time-windowing approach developed by Widmer and Kubat (1996) describes a family of incremental algorithms for learning in the presence of drift. This method uses a currently trusted window of examples as well as stored, old concept hypothesis description sets which are reactivated if they seem to be valid again. The first realization of this framework of this family of incremental algorithms is FLORA2, which maintains a dynamically adjustable window of the latest training examples. The method of adjusting the size of the window is known as window adjustment heuristic (WAH). Whenever a concept drift is suspected as a result of a drop in predictive accuracy, the size of the window is decreased by disposing of the oldest examples. The window size is left unchanged if the concept appears to be stable. If concept drift remains uncertain, none of the examples are forgotten, and thus the window size is gradually increased until a stable concept description can be formed. As long as a relatively low rate of concept drift is preserved this strategy of window adjustment can detect radical changes in the underlying concept efficiently.

FLORA3 stores concepts for later use and reassesses their utility when a context change is perceived. FLORA4 is designed to be exceptionally robust with respect to noise in the training data since it is very difficult in incremental learning to distinguish between slight irregularities due to noise and actual concept drift. Both of these algorithms serve as an extension of FLORA2.

According to Hulten *et al.* (2001), as long as the window size is small relative to the rate of concept drift, the time-windowing procedure assures availability of a model reflecting the current concept generating the data. However, if the window is too small, this may result in insufficient examples to satisfactorily learn the concept. Furthermore, the computational cost of reapplying a learner may be prohibitively high, especially if examples arrive at a rapid rate and the concept changes quickly.

To meet these challenges, Domingos and Hulten (2001) proposed an efficient algorithm for mining decision trees from continuously changing data streams. Called CVFDT (concept-adapting very fast decision trees learner), the algorithm is based on the ultra-fast VFDT decision tree learner. CVFDT, a VFDTn extension, maintains VFDTs speed and accuracy advantages but adds the ability to detect and respond to changes in the example-generating process.

Like other systems with this capability, CVFDT works by keeping its model consistent with a sliding window of examples. However, it does not need to learn a new model from scratch every time a new example arrives; instead, it updates the sufficient statistics at its nodes by incrementing the counts corresponding to the new example and by decrementing the counts corresponding to the oldest example in the window (which now must be forgotten). This will statistically have no effect if the underlying concept is stationary. If the concept is changing, however, some splits that previously passed the Hoeffding test will no longer do so because an alternative attribute now has higher gain. In this case, CVFDT begins to grow an alternative sub-tree with the new best attribute at its root. When this alternate sub-tree becomes more accurate on new data than the old one, the new one replaces the old sub-tree. CVFDT learns a model which is similar in accuracy to the one that would be learned by reapplying VFDT to a moving window of examples every time a new example arrives, but with $O(1)$ complexity per example, as opposed to $O(w)$, where w is the size of the window.

Black and Hickey (1999) offer a new approach to handling the aforementioned sub-tasks dealing with drift within incremental learning methods. Instead of utilizing the time-windowing approach presented thus far, they employ a new purging mechanism to remove examples that are no longer valid while retaining valid examples, regardless of age. As a result, the example base grows, thus assisting good classification. Black and Hickey describe an algorithm called CD3, which utilizes ID3 with post-pruning, based on the time-stamp attribute relevance or TSAR approach.

In this approach, the time-stamp is treated as an attribute, and its value is added as an additional input attribute to the examples description, later to be used in the induction process. Consequently, if the time-stamp attribute appears in the decision tree, the implication is that it is relevant to classification. This, in turn, means that drift has occurred. Routes where the value of the time-stamp attribute refers to the old period (or periods) represent invalid rules. When the process is stable for a sufficiently long period, the time-stamp attribute should not appear in any path of the tree.

The CD3 algorithm sustains a set of examples regarded as valid. This set, referred to as the current example base, must be updated before another round of learning can take place. Using invalid rules extracted from the CD3 tree, any example whose description matches (i.e. is covered by) that of an invalid rule can be removed from the current example set. This process of deletion is referred to as purging the current example set.

11.8 Decision Trees Inducers for Large Datasets

While the computaitonal complexity of decision tree induction algorithms is considered to be relatively low, it can still come across difficulties when the datasets are big and in particular if we are interested in building a forest. With the recent growth in the amount of data collected by information systems there is a need for decision trees that can handle large datasets. Big data is a term coined recently to refer large datasets that are too difficult to process using existing methods. Several improvements to decision tree induction algorithms have been suggested to address big data. In this chapter, we will review the main methods.

11.8.1 *Accelerating Tree Induction*

Catlett (1991) has examined two methods for efficiently growing decision trees from a large database by reducing the computation complexity required for induction. However, the Catlett method requires that all data will be loaded into the main memory before induction. Namely, the largest dataset that can be induced is bounded by the memory size. Fifield (1992) suggests parallel implementation of the ID3 Algorithm. However, like Catlett it assumes that all dataset can fit in the main memory. Chan and Stolfo (1997) suggest to partition the datasets into several disjointed datasets, such that each dataset is loaded separately into the memory and used to induce a decision tree. The decision trees are then combined to create a single classifier. However, the experimental results indicate that partition may reduce the classification performance, meaning that the classification accuracy of the combined decision trees is not as good as the accuracy of a single decision tree induced from the entire dataset.

There are several decision tree algorithms which implement disk-based approaches that remove the requirement of loading the entire dataset to the main memory. These algorithms optimize the number of reads and writes to secondary storage during tree construction.

The SLIQ algorithm [Mehta *et al.* (1996)] does not require loading the entire dataset into the main memory, instead it uses a secondary memory (disk) namely a certain instance is not necessarily resident in the main memory all the time. SLIQ creates a single decision tree from the entire dataset. However, this method also has an upper limit for the largest dataset that can be processed, because it uses a data structure that scales with the dataset size and this data structure is required to be resident in main memory all the time.

The SPRINT algorithm uses a similar approach [Shafer *et al.* (1996)]. This algorithm induces decision trees relatively quickly and removes all of the memory restrictions from decision tree induction. SPRINT scales any impurity based split criteria for large datasets. Gehrke *et al.* (2000) introduced RainForest; a unifying framework for decision tree classifiers that are capable to scale any specific algorithms from the literature (including C4.5, CART and CHAID). In addition to its generality, RainForest improves SPRINT on a factor of three. In contrast to SPRINT, however, RainForest requires a certain minimum amount of main memory, proportional to the set of distinct values in a column of the input relation. However, this requirement is considered modest and reasonable.

Other decision tree inducers for large datasets can be found in the works of [Alsabti *et al.* (1998)], [Freitas and Lavington (1998)] and [Gehrke *et al.* (1999)].

Ping *et al.* (2007) introduced the Fast C4.5 (FC4.5) algorithm. This new C4.5 implementation relaxes the memory restriction that the original C4.5 implementation had. The original C4.5 implementation was developed on the early nineties when main-memory was still scarce and therefore it was designed to use as little space as possible. However, nowadays the main memory are plentiful. Therefore by trading memory with speed it is possible to greatly accelerate the tree growing of the C4.5 algorithm. One well-known bottleneck in the induction of decision trees is the fact that the training instances are unordered. However, for finding the best split for continues attributes the instances should be sorted. Moreover, the need for sorting the instances is repeated for every new tree node that is explored and as indicated by Mehta *et al.* (1996), "for numeric attributes, sorting time is the dominant factor when finding the best split at a decision tree node".

By adding a preprocessing step that is executed just before the tree growing one can extract the order information of all the instances on every attribute in advance. Specifically, every continuous attribute column is ordered and the instance rank in the column is attached to the attribute value. Then during the actual tree building, whenever we need to sort the values instead of using quick-sort we can use indirect bucket-sort instead. Finally when a certain numeric attributes is selected, FC4.5 searches for the cutoff using the binary-search within the narrowest range.

Moreover, the sort order for the descendant nodes can be derived from the sort order of the parent by a simple procedure with time complexity of $O(n)$ instead of the complexity of $O(nlogn)$. However, for doing that we will need to store an array of sorted indices for each numeric attribute.

In fact, the idea of presorting the instances for accelerating the induction of a classification tree is being around since the second half of the nineties. Mehta *et al.* (1996) suggest using a dedicated data structure which holds a separate list for each input attribute. In addition, a class list holds the class labels that are assigned to the training instances. An entry in an attribute list has two values: the first value contains the actual attribute value, the second value contains the corresponding index in the class list. Similarly, an entry in the class list refers to a certain instance in the training set and also has two values: one contains the class label, the second value identifies the leaf node in the tree to which an instance belongs. Initially, all instances are referenced to the root node. The attribute lists for the numeric features are then sorted independently.

11.8.2 *Parallel Induction of Tree*

PLANET is a recent classification and regression tree algorithm from Google based on MapReduce. The basic idea of the parallel algorithm is to iteratively build the regression tree in a breadth first manner, one complete level at a time in a distributed environment, until the data partitions are small enough to fit in memory and a "leaf" sub-tree can be constructed locally on a single machine

Panda *et al.* (2009) proposed a parallel implemention of tree induction with MapReduce framework. MapReduce is one of the most popular parallel programming frameworks for data mining. In this framework, programmers need to specify a map function which processes key/value pairs to emit a set of intermediate key/value pairs and a reduce function that aggregates all intermediate values associated with the same intermediate key. The MapReduce framework was pioneered by Google and then popularized by open-source Apache Hadoop project. While there are other parallel programming frameworks (such as CUDA and MPI), MapReduce has become the industry standard and implemented on cloud computing services such as Amazon EC2 and various companies such as Cloudera provide services to ease Hadoop deployment.

The greedy nature of tree induction algorithm does not scale well to a large dataset. For example to find the best split in the root node, it is required to go over all instances in the dataset. And when the entire dataset does not fit in main memory, this full scan becomes a bottleneck because of the cost of scanning data from secondary storage. The basic idea of PLANET is to iteratively grow the decision tree, one layer at a time, until the data partitions are small enough to fit the main memory and the remaining sub-tree can be grown locally on a single machine. For the higher levels the key idea of PLANET is that the splitting criterion at a certain node does not need the entire dataset but a compact data structure of sufficient statistics which in most cases can be fit-in-memory. These statistics are calculated on the mappers.

Most recently, Yin *et al.* (2012) presented OpenPlanet, an open implementation of a scalable regression tree machine learning algorithm on Hadoop.

Chapter 12

Cost-sensitive Active and Proactive Learning of Decision Trees

12.1 Overview

Although the inductive learning models are accurate, they suffer the disadvantage of excessive complexity and are therefore incomprehensible to experts pursuing high accuracy achievement, which may suffice in cases when accuracy is the most important criterion or when there is no background or domain knowledge available. However in real world problems it is rarely the case. In many practical problems there is an abundance of background information that can be incorporated to achieve better and simpler solutions. The use of background knowledge in induction processes produces trees that are easier to understand [Nunez (1991)]. The use of background knowledge is necessary when the features attached to individual examples do not capture abstractions and general distinctions that relate many examples of a concept. The knowledge principle is defined as "a system exhibits intelligent understanding and action at a high level of competence primarily because of the *specific* knowledge that it contains about its domain of endeavor"[Feigenbaum (1988)]. The main conclusion from this principle is that reasoning processes of an intelligent system, being general and therefore weak, are not the source of power that leads to high levels of competence in behavior. The knowledge principle simply says that if a program is to perform well, it must know a great deal about the world in which it operates. In the absence of knowledge, reasoning won't help.

One major form of background knowledge is 'cost' which needs to be incorporated in any potential solution to make it more applicable.

In previous chapters we review a wide variety of algorithms for decision tree induction. However, all of these algorithms assume that all errors have the same cost, which is seldom the case in real world problems. For instance, when an expert in brain tumors receives a patient who suffers a headache, he does not recommend the Scanner as a first diagnostic test, although it is the most effective and accurate one, because the expert has the economic criteria in mind. Therefore the expert asks simple questions and orders other more economic tests in order to isolate the simplest cases, and only recommends such an expensive test for the complex ones.

Effective learning algorithms should also take into consideration *cost* in the concept learning process. Most of the currently available algorithms for classification are designed to minimize zero-one loss or error rate: the number of incorrect predictions made or, equivalently, the probability of making an incorrect prediction. This implicitly assumes that all errors are equally costly. But in most KDD applications this is far from the case. According to Provost [Provost and Fawcett (1997)] *"it is hard to imagine a domain in which a learning system may be indifferent to whether it makes a false positive or a false negative error."* Rarely are mistakes evenly weighted in their cost. In such cases, accuracy maximization should be replaced with cost minimization. In real-world applications of concept learning, there are many different types of costs involved [Turney (1995)]. The majority of the learning literature ignores all types of costs. The literature provides even less guidance in situations where class distributions are imprecise or can be changed [Provost and Fawcett (1997)].

Countless research results have been published based on comparisons of classifier accuracy over benchmark data sets. Comparing accuracies on benchmark data sets say little, if anything, about classifier performance on real-world tasks [Provost and Fawcett (1998)]. Many learning programs create procedures whose goal is to minimize the number of errors made when predicting the classification of unseen examples. Few papers have investigated the cost of misclassification errors [Provost (1994)] and very few papers have examined the many other types of costs.

12.2 Type of Costs

A detailed bibliography of the different types of costs can be found in [Turney (2000)]. The term cost is interpreted in its broadest meaning. Cost may be measured in many different units, such as monetary units (dollars), temporal units (seconds), or abstract units of utility. A benefit can be considered as negative cost. A taxonomy for costs is presented in [Turney (2000)], and it consists of the following types:

- Cost of Misclassification Errors — specifies the cost of assigning a case to class i, when it actually belongs in class j.
- Cost of Tests — specifies the cost of using a certain attribute. For instance, in medical application, doing an X-Ray has a cost.
- Cost of Teacher — the cost associated with providing classified examples (training set) to the inducer.
- Cost of Intervention — This is the cost required to change the value of an attribute in order to gain more profits.
- Cost of Computation — The cost associated with using computers for training a classifier or testing it.
- Human-Computer Interaction Cost — specifies the cost of a user to employ a learning algorithm.

12.3 Learning with Costs

Individually making each classification learner cost-sensitive is laborious, and often non-trivial. A framework that can be used to configure new decision tree models based on a combination of several factors (e.g. accuracy, measurement cost, misclassification cost, achievement cost) is presented in [Someren *et al.* (1997)]. On the other hand there are general methods for making accuracy based classifiers cost-sensitive. [Domingos (1999); Zadrozny and Elkan (2001)]. Nonetheless, these cost sensitive methods where inseparable and inherent to the concept learning models. Almost all such (accuracy-based and cost-based) learning models assume the *passive* role of predicting class membership by producing accurate classifiers.

Few papers investigated different approaches to learning or revising classification procedures that attempt to reduce the cost of misclassification. The cost of misclassifying an example is a function of the predicted class and actual class represented as the cost matrix C [Pazzani *et al.* (1994)]:

$$C(predictedClass, actualClass) \tag{12.1}$$

where $C(P, N)$ is the cost of a false positive, and $C(N, P)$ is the cost of a false negative misclassification, then the misclassification cost can be calculated as:

$$Cost = FP \cdot C(P, N) + FN \cdot C(N, P) \tag{12.2}$$

The cost matrix is an additional input to the learning procedure and can also be used to evaluate the ability of the learning program to reduce misclassification costs. Cost may have any units; the cost matrix reflects the intuition that it is more costly to underestimate how ill someone is than overestimate, and that it is less costly to be slightly wrong than very wrong. Cost matrix is different for cost vector, which has been used in some previous learning research [Provost (1994)]. With a cost vector, the cost of misclassifying an example depends on either the actual cost or the predicted cost but not both. Any cost matrix C can be transformed to an equivalent matrix C' with zeroes along the diagonal [Margineantu (2001)].

To reduce the cost of misclassification errors, some have incorporated an average misclassification cost metric in the learning algorithm [Pazzani *et al.* (1994)]:

$$averageCost = \frac{\sum\limits_{i}^{N} C(actualClass(i), predictedClass(i))}{N} \qquad (12.3)$$

Several decision trees inducers, such as C4.5 and CART can be provided with a cost matrix which consists of numeric penalties for classifying an item into one class when it really belongs in another.

Few algorithms are based on a hybrid of accuracy and classification error cost [Pazzani *et al.* (1994)] replacing the information gain measurement with a combination of accuracy and cost. For example, Information Cost Function (ICF) selects attributes based on both their information gain and their cost [Turney (1995)]. *ICF* for the *i-th* attribute, ICF_i, is defined as follows:

$$ICF_i = \frac{2^{\Delta I_i} - 1}{(C_i + 1)^w} \qquad (12.4)$$

where $0 \leq w \leq 1$, ΔI_i is the information gain associated with the *i-th* attribute at a given stage in the construction of the decision tree, and C_i is the cost of measuring the *i-th* attribute. The parameter w adjusts the strength of the bias towards lower cost attributes. When $w = 0$, cost is ignored and selection by ICF_i is equivalent to selection by ΔI_i (i.e., selection based on the information gain measure). When $w = 1$, ICF_i is strongly biased by cost.

The altered prior method [Biermann *et al.* (1982)], which works with any number of classes, operates by replacing the term for the prior probability, $\pi(j)$, that an example belongs to class j with an altered probability $\pi'(j)$:

$$\pi'(j) = \frac{C(j)\pi(j)}{\sum\limits_{i} C(i)\pi(i)} \qquad (12.5)$$

where $C(j) = \sum\limits_{i} cost(j, i)$

The altered prior requires converting a cost matrix $cost(j, i)$ to cost vector $C(j)$ resulting in a single quantity to represent the importance of avoiding a particular type of error. Accurately performing this conversion is non-trivial since it depends both on the frequency of examples of each class as well as the frequency that an example of one class might be mistaken for another. There are different ways to overcome the difficulties of estimating the class probability. Bayesian classifiers estimate the probability that an example belongs to each class. Similarly, a decision tree can also produce an estimate of the probability that an example belongs to each class given that it is classified by a particular leaf.

$$p(y = i) = \frac{N_i + 1}{k + \sum_{j}^{k} N_j} \tag{12.6}$$

The above equations are a few of the existing main methods for dealing with cost. In general these methods can be divided into three main categories: The first category is a group of methods that *replace* the *accuracy-based* criterion (i.e., information gain) with another cost-based or with a combination of accuracy and cost criterion. However, methods in this category sacrifice accuracy for cost. It also requires the user to select a particular classifier with characteristics that may not suite his domain. The second group is *stratifying* methods [Provost and Fawcett (1998)], which change the frequency of classes in the training data in proportion to their cost. However, this approach has several shortcomings. It distorts the distribution of examples, which may seriously affect the performance of some algorithms. It reduces the data available for learning if stratifying is carried out by under-sampling. It increases the learning time if it is done by over-sampling. The third category is a group of *wrapping* methods, which converts error-based classifiers into cost-sensitive ones. These methods minimize cost while seeking to minimize zero-one loss. It also assumes that the user has chosen a particular classifier because its characteristics are well suited to the domain. The vast majority of the methods (of all three categories) fail to incorporate the widely available domain knowledge in their algorithms, which leaves many of them in the theoretical realm. The few that do consider domain knowledge and deals with cost, take into considerations only the *misclassification* cost.

The MetaCost algorithm [Domingos (1999)] is a wrapper method that can be used to make any inducer, in particular decision tree inducers, to be cost-sensitive. Specifically, MetaCost forms multiple bootstrap replicates of the training set and learning a classifier on each; estimating each class's probability for each example by the fraction of votes that it receives from the ensemble. It then relabels each training example with the estimated optimal class, and reapplies the classifier to the relabeled training set.

12.4 Induction of Cost Sensitive Decision Trees

In this section we present the algorithm proposed in [Ling *et al.* (2006)]. The proposed algorithm takes into account the misclassification costs, and the attribute costs. It selects attributes according to the expected reduction in the total misclassification cost. If the largest expected cost reduction is greater than 0, then the attribute is chosen as the split (otherwise, it is not worth building the tree further, and a leaf is returned). Figure 12.1 presents the algorithm.

For the sake of simplicity we assume that there are only two classes. The notations CP and CN represent the total misclassification cost of being a positive leaf or a negative leaf respectively. If $C(P, N)$ is the cost of false positive misclassification, and $C(N, P)$ is the cost of false negative misclassification, then $CP = C(P, N) \cdot FP$ and $CN = C(N, P) \cdot FN$ is the total misclassification cost of being a negative leaf, and the probability of

Require: S - training set

   A - a set of input attributes

   C - Cost matrix.

Ensure: T - a tree

1: Create a new tree T with a single root node.
2: **if** all instances are positive/negative or maximum expected cost reduction is less than 0 **then**
3:    Mark T as a leaf with the most common class in S as a label.
4: **end if**
5: $\forall a_i \in A$ find a with maximum expected cost reduction
6: root $\leftarrow a$
7: **for all** possible value v_i of the attribute a **do**
8:    $Subtree_i = \text{CSDT}(\sigma_{a=v_i}S, A - a, C)$ to build subtree
9:    Connect the root node of T to $Subtree_i$ with an edge that is labelled as v_i
10: **end for**
11: Return tree

Fig. 12.1   Algorithm for inducing cost sensitive decision trees.

being positive is estimated by the relative cost of CP and CN; the smaller the cost, the larger the probability (as minimum cost is sought). Thus, the probability of being a positive leaf is: $PP = 1 - \frac{CP}{CP+CN}$ and the expected misclassification cost of being positive is: $EP = PP \cdot CP$. Similarly, the expected misclassification cost of being negative is: $EN = (1 - PP) \cdot CN$. Therefore, without splitting, the expected total misclassification cost of a given set of examples is: $E = EP + EN$. Thus, we calculate the expected total misclassification cost before (E) and after (E_i) performing a certain split using attribute a_i. The total expected cost reduction is $E - E_i - TC_i$, where TC_i is the cost of testing examples on attribute A_i. Note that the above algorithm can be easily adjusted to the case in which the cost of obtaining values of a group of attributes is lower than obtaining the value of each attribute independently.

12.5   Active Learning

When marketing a service or a product, firms increasingly use predictive models to estimate the customer interest in their offer. A predictive model estimates the response probability of potential customers and helps the decision maker assess the profitability of the various customers. Predictive models assist in formulating a target marketing strategy: offering the right product to the right customer at the right time using the proper distribution channel. The firm can subsequently approach those customers estimated to be the most interested in the company's product and propose a marketing offer. A customer that accepts the offer and conducts a purchase increases the firms profits. This strategy is more efficient than a mass marketing strategy, in which a firm offers a product to all known potential customers, usually resulting in low positive response rates. For example, a mail marketing response rate of 2% predictive models can be built using data mining methods. These methods are applied to detect useful patterns in the information available about the customer's purchasing behaviors. Data for the models is available, as firms typically maintain databases that contain massive amounts of information about their existing and potential customer's such as the customer's demographic characteristics and past purchase history.

Active learning refers to data mining policies which actively select unlabeled instances for labeling. Active learning has been previously used for facilitating direct marketing campaigns. In such campaigns there is an exploration phase in which several potential customers are approached with a marketing offer. Based on their response, the learner actively selects the next customers to be approached and so forth. Exploration does not come without a cost. Direct costs might involve hiring special personnel for calling customers and gathering their characteristics and responses to the campaign. Indirect costs may be incurred from contacting potential customers who would normally not be approached due to their low buying power or low interest in the product or service offer.

A well-known concept of marketing campaigns is the exploration/exploitation trade-off. Exploration strategies are directed towards customers as a means of exploring their behavior; exploitation strategies operate on a firm's existing marketing model. In the exploration phase, a concentrated effort is made to build an accurate model. In this phase, the firm will try, for example, to acquire any available information which characterizes the customer. During this phase, the results are analysed in depth and the best modus operandi is chosen. In the exploitation phase the firm simply applies the induced model with no intention of improving the model to classify new potential customers and identify the best ones. Thus, the model evolves during the exploration phase and is fixed during the exploitation phase. Given the tension between these two objectives, research has indicated that firms first explore customer behavior and then follow with an exploitation strategy. The result of the exploration phase is a marketing model that is then used in the exploitation phase.

Let consider the following challenge. Which potential customers should a firm approach with a new product offer in order to maximize its net profit? Specifically, our objective is not only to minimize the net acquisition cost during the exploration phase, but also to maximize the net profit obtained during the exploitation phase. Our problem formulation takes into consideration the direct cost of offering a product to the customer, the utility associated with the customer's response, and the alternative utility of inaction. This is a binary discrete choice problem, where the customer's response is binary, such as the acceptance or rejection of a marketing offer. Discrete choice tasks may involve several specific problems, such as unbalanced class distribution. Typically, most customers considered for the exploration phase reject the offer, leading to a low positive response rate. However, a simple classifier may predict that all customers in questions will reject the offer.

It should be noted that the predictive accuracy of a classifier alone is insufficient as an evaluation criterion. One reason is that different classification errors must be dealt with differently: mistaking acceptance for rejection is particularly undesirable. Moreover, predictive accuracy alone does not provide enough flexibility when selecting a target for a marketing offer or when choosing how an offer should be promoted. For example, the marketing personnel may want to approach 30% of the available potential customers, but the model predicts only 6.

Active learning merely aims to minimize the cost of acquisition, and does not consider the exploration/exploitation tradeoff. Active learning techniques do not aim to improve online exploitation. Nevertheless, occasional income is a byproduct of the acquisition process. We propose that the calculation of the acquisition cost performed in active learning algorithms should take this into consideration.

Several active learning frameworks are presented in the literature. In pool-based active learning the learner has access to a pool of unlabeled data and can request the true class label for a certain number of instances in the pool. Other approaches focus on the expected improvement of class entropy, or minimizing both labeling and misclassification costs. It is possible to examine a variation in which instead of having the correct label for each training example, there is one possible label (not necessarily the correct one) and the utility associated with that label. Most active learning methods aim to reduce the generalization accuracy of the model learned from the labeled data. They assume uniform error costs and do not consider benefits that may accrue from correct classifications. They also do not consider the benefits that may be accrued from label acquisition.

Rather than trying to reduce the error or the costs, Saar-Tsechansky and Provost (2007) introduced the GOAL (Goal-Oriented Active Learning) method that focuses on acquisitions that are more likely to affect decision making. GOAL acquires instances which are related to decisions for which a relatively small change in the estimation can change the preferred order of choice. In each iteration, GOAL selects a batch of instances based on their effectiveness score. The score is inversely proportional to the minimum absolute change in the probability estimation that would result in a decision different from the decision implied by the current estimation. Instead of selecting the instances with the highest scores, GOAL uses a sampling distribution in which the selection probability of a certain instance is proportional to its score.

To better understand the idea of active learning we consider a concrete scenario. When marketing a service or a product, firms increasingly use predictive models to estimate the customers' interest in their offer. A predictive model estimates the response probability of the potential customers in question, and helps the decision-maker assess the profitability of the different customers. Predictive models assist a target marketing strategy: offering the right product to the right customer at the right time using the proper distribution channel. The firm approaches the customers estimated as the most interested and proposes a marketing offer. A customer that accepts the offer and conducts a purchase adds to the firms' profits. This strategy affords better efficiency than a mass marketing strategy, in which a firm offers a product to all known potential customers, usually resulting in low positive response rates. For example, a mail marketing response rate of 2% or a phone marketing response of 10% are considered good.

The main objective of a marketing campaign is to select which potential customers a firm should approach with a new product offer, in order to maximize the net profit. In the marketing problem presented in this paper, we assume that the firm holds an initial dataset of potential customers that can be used during the exploration phase. This initial dataset does not, however, cover all potential customers. We also assume that, while acquiring the customers' response is costly, some of the courted customers will respond positively to the offer and the income from their purchase will offset the cost. We propose to refer to the net acquisition cost, which is the total cost of acquiring customer response, less the income generated if the courted customers purchase the products.

We also assume that during a marketing campaign, a firm will not approach its customers one by one, but it will rather approach a batch of customers simultaneously, so that the firm can concentrate its exploitation of resources, such as marketing personnel and equipment. After a campaign session is over and a batch of customers has been courted, the firm can analyze the results and proceed to the next stage of the campaign. We assume a fixed batch size.

In our targeted marketing context, an instance $x_i \in X$ is defined as the set of attributes, such as age and gender, of a unique potential customer i. For the sake of clarity, we will assume a binary outcome for the target attribute y, specifically $y = \{$"accept", "reject"$\}$. Unlabeled instances are defined as instances with an unknown target attribute. A set S of M unlabeled instances from the set X is obtained. The instances in S are independent and behave according to some fixed and unknown joint probability distribution D of X and Y. The cost of approaching customer i with an offer is denoted as $C_i \in \Re$. The probability that customer i will respond positively to the offer is denoted as p_i. If customer i with some unknown probability p_i agrees to the offer, the utility obtained from this customer is denoted as $U_i^S \in \Re$. If the customer rejects the offer, the utility is denoted as $U_i^F \in \Re$. Thus, the net acquisition cost of customer i is defined as:

$$NAC_i = \begin{cases} C_i - U_i^S & \text{if customer } i \text{ accepts the offer} \\ C_i - U_i^F & \text{if customer } i \text{ rejects the offer} \end{cases} \tag{12.7}$$

Note that all utility values are a function of the customer's attribute vector $(\boldsymbol{x}_i)$.

Let the corresponding utility of inaction with respect to customer i be denoted as Ψ_i. In order to maximize the expected profit, the decision-maker should court customer i if the probability of a positive response is higher than the cost of approach (Saar-Tsechansky and Provost, 2007). This is represented in the following equivalent equations:

$$\hat{p}_i \cdot U_i^S + (1 - \hat{p}_i) \cdot U_i^F - C_i > \Psi_i \tag{12.8}$$

or:

$$\hat{p}_i > \frac{C_i + \Psi_i - U_i^F}{U_i^S - U_i^F} \equiv \frac{o_i}{r_i} \tag{12.9}$$

where o_i and r_i are merely shorthand for the numerator and denominator of the decision threshold ratio. The notation $\hat{p}_i$ represents the classifier's estimation for p_i.

A pseudo code for the active learning framework used for the target marketing process is presented in Figure 12.1. The received input includes: a pool of unlabeled instances (S), an inducer (I), and a stopping criterion $(CRIT)$. The first step is to initiate the labeled pool. An initial set of labeled examples is selected. Once the potential customers are selected, they are approached with a product offer. According to the customers' response, the newly labeled examples are added to the labeled pool. The labeled pool is then used for building the classifier. Based on the classifier, the next subset from the unlabeled pool is selected. This process is repeated until triggering some sort of stopping criteria, such as running out of budget. The final classifier (the output) is used to estimate the probability of positive response $\hat{p}_i$ of new customers. Customers with an estimated probability that exceeds the threshold in Eq. (12.9) are contacted.

Require: S - training set
   A - An induction algorithm
   $CRIT$ - A stopping criterion.
Ensure: CL – Classifier for predicting customer response.
 1: Create a new tree T with a single root node.
 2: $L \leftarrow \emptyset$
 3: $i \leftarrow 1$
 4: $S_1 \leftarrow$ Select initial set of instances from S
 5: **while** $CRIT$ is not met **do**
 6:    Remove S_i from S
 7:    Acquire labels for examples in S_i
 8:    Add S_i to L
 9:    Apply I to L, resulting in a classifier CL
10:    $i \leftarrow i + 1$
11:    Select subset S_i from S using CL
12: **end while**
13: Return CL

Fig. 12.2   Pseudo code for the active learning framework.

Based on the active learning framework presented in Figure 12.2, the marketing learning problem can be defined as follows:

While keeping the total net acquisition cost to minimum, the goal is to actively acquire from S mutually exclusive subsets $S_1, S_2, \ldots, S_k$ of a given batch size M, such that the final classifier induced from $\bigcup_{i=1}^{k} S_i$ maximizes the profitability of the campaign. The subsets are acquired sequentially.

This is a Multiple Criteria Decision-Making (MCDM) problem. The first criterion is to improve the decisions of the campaign manager. The positive reaction rate can be used to assess the profitability during the exploitation phase. Higher rates indicate higher gross profit margins and return of investments (ROI). The second criterion is to acquire labeled instances with minimal net acquisition cost during the exploration phase. Both criteria deal with financial utilities. Still, the two criteria cannot be summed. We cannot represent the first criterion as total income during the exploitation phase, since we do not know in advance how many customers are going to be evaluated using the model. The only assumption we make is that the instances in the unlabeled instances set used during the training phase (S) and the instances examined during the operational phase are both distributed according to a fixed and unknown distribution D. In this paper, we consider the first criterion as primary and the second as secondary. Prioritization of these criteria agrees with the assumption that the exploitation phase is longer than the exploration phase.

Assuming that we use a decision tree as the classifier, we are able to estimate the probability p_i by locating the appropriate leaf k in the tree that refers to the current instance x_i. The frequency vector of each leaf node captures the number of instances from each possible class. In the usual case of target marketing, the frequency vector has the form: $(m_{k,accept}, m_{k,reject})$ where $m_{k,c}$ denotes the number of instances in the labeled pool that reach leaf k and satisfy $y = c$. According to Laplace's law of succession, the probability p_i is estimated as:

$$\hat{p}_i = p(m_{k,accept}, m_{k,reject}) = \frac{m_{k,accept} + 1}{m_{k,accept} + m_{k,reject} + 2}. \qquad (12.10)$$

Besides estimating the point probability $\hat{p}_i$, we are interested in estimating a confidence interval for this probability. An approach to a customer can be considered as a Bernoulli trial. For the sake of simplicity, we approximate the confidence interval of the Bernoulli parameter with the normal approximation to the binomial distribution:

$$\hat{p}_i - z_{1-\alpha/2}\hat{\sigma}_i < p_i < \hat{p}_i + z_{1-\alpha/2}\hat{\sigma}_i$$

$$\hat{\sigma}_i = \sigma(m_{k,accept}, m_{k,reject}) = \sqrt{\frac{\hat{p}_i(1 - \hat{p}_i)}{m_{k,accept} + m_{k,reject}}} \qquad (12.11)$$

where $\hat{\sigma}_i$ represents the estimated standard deviation and $z_{1-\alpha/2}$ denotes the value in the standard normal distribution table corresponding to the $1-\alpha/2$ percentile. For a small n we can use the actual binomial distribution to estimate the interval.

To demonstrate the importance of a confidence level, consider two leaves: leaf A and leaf B in a classification tree. Each leaf holds the customers in the labeled pool that fits its path. These customers are labeled as either "accept" or "reject". If the "accept"/"reject" proportions are the same, then according to Eq. (12.10), both leaves have the same estimated probability. Given this, if leaf A has more customers than leaf B, then according to Eq. (12.11), leaf B has a larger confidence interval. Thus, acquiring an instance to leaf B will have a greater impact on the class distribution than adding an example to leaf A. In the initial iterations, when the data are limited and the confidence intervals are large, obtaining an additional instance to the correct leaf is especially important. Moreover, the potential contribution of labeling the ith instance in the same leaf and adding it to the labeled pool decreases in i. Thus, the calculation of the potential contribution of each instance in the new batch depends on the other instances that are selected to this batch.

Rokach *et al.* (2008) introduce Pessimistic Active Learning (PAL). PAL employs a novel pessimistic measure, which relies on confidence intervals and is used to balance the exploration/exploitation trade-off. In order to acquire an initial sample of labeled data, PAL applies orthogonal arrays of fractional factorial design. PAL is particularly advantageous when the estimation confidence intervals are relatively large. Once the decision tree obtains sufficient evidence for each leaf, the relative advantage of PAL is diminished.

12.6 Proactive Data Mining

Data mining algorithms are used as part of the broader process of knowledge-discovery. The role of the data-mining algorithm, in this process, is to extract patterns hidden in a dataset. The extracted patterns are then evaluated and deployed. The objectives of the evaluation and deployment phases include decisions regarding the interest of the patterns and the way they should be used.

While data mining algorithms, particularly those dedicated to supervised learning, extract patterns almost automatically (often with the user making only minor parameter settings), humans typically evaluate and deploy the patterns manually. In regard to the algorithms, the best practice in data mining is to focus on description and prediction and not on action. That is to say, the algorithms operate as *passive* "observers" on the underlying dataset while analyzing a phenomenon. These algorithms neither affect nor recommend ways of affecting the real world. The algorithms only report to the user on the findings. As a result, if the user chooses not to act in response to the findings, then nothing will change. The responsibility for action is in the hands of humans. This responsibility is often overly complex to be handled manually, and the data mining literature often stops short of assisting humans in meeting this responsibility.

Consider the following scenario. In marketing and customer relationship management (CRM), data mining is often used for predicting customer lifetime value (LTV). Customer LTV is defined as the net present value of the sum of the profits that a company will gain from a certain customer, starting from a certain point in time and continuing through the remaining lifecycle of that customer. Since the exact LTV of a customer is revealed only after the customer stops being a customer, managing existing LTVs requires some sort of prediction capability. While data mining algorithms can assist in deriving useful predictions, the CRM decisions that result from these predictions (for example, investing in customer retention or customer-service actions that will maximize her or his LTV) are left in the hands of humans.

In *proactive* data mining, we seek automatic methods that will not only describe a phenomenon, but also recommend actions that affect the real world. In data mining, the world is reflected by a set of observations. In supervised learning tasks, which are the focal point of this book, each observation presents an instance of the explaining attributes and the corresponding target results. In order to affect the real world and to assess the impact of actions on the world, the data observations must encompass certain changes. We discuss these changes in the following section.

12.6.1 *Changing the Input Data*

We consider the training record, $< x_{1,n}, x_{2,n}, \ldots, x_{k,n}; y_n >$ for some specific n. This record is based on a specific object in the real world. For example, $x_{1,n}, x_{2,n}, \ldots, x_{k,n}$ may be the explaining attributes of a client, and y_n, the target attribute, might describe a result that interests the company, whether the client has left or not.

It is obvious that some results are more beneficial to the company than others, such as a profitable client remaining with the company rather than leaving it or that clients with high LTV are more beneficial than those with low LTV. In proactive data mining, our motivation is to search for means of actions that lead to desired results (i.e., desired target values).

The underlying assumption in supervised learning is that the target attribute is a dependent variable whose values depend on those of the explaining attributes. Therefore, in order to affect the target attribute towards the desired, more beneficial, values, we need to change the explaining attributes in such a way that target attributes will receive the desired values.

Consider the supervised learning scenario of churn prediction, where a company observes its database of clients and tries to predict which clients will leave and which will remain loyal. Assuming that most of the clients are profitable to the company, the motivation in this scenario is churn prevention. However, the decision of a client about whether to leave or not may depend on other considerations, such as her or his price plan. The client's price plan, hardcoded in the company's database, is often part of the churn-prediction models. Moreover, if the company seeks for ways to prevent a client from leaving, it can consider changing the price plan of the client as a churn-prevention action. Such action, if taken, might affect the value of an explaining attribute towards a desired direction.

When we refer to "changing the input data", we mean that in proactive data mining we seek to implement actions that will change the values of the explaining attributes and consequently lead to a desired target value. We not consider any other sort of action because it is external to the domain of the supervised learning task. To look at the matter in a slightly different light, the objective in proactive data mining is *optimization*, and not prediction. In the following section we focus on the required domain knowledge that results from the shift to optimization, and we define an *attribute changing cost* function and a *benefit* function as crucial aspects of the required domain knowledge.

12.6.2   *Attribute Changing Cost and Benefit Functions*

The shift from supervised learning to optimization requires us to consider additional knowledge about the business domain, which is exogenous to the actual training records. In general, the additional knowledge may cover various underlying business issues behind the supervised learning task, such as: What is the objective function that needs to be optimized? What changes in the explaining attributes can and cannot be achieved? At what cost? What are the success probabilities of attempts to change the explaining attributes? What are the external conditions, under which these changes are possible? The exact form of the additional knowledge may differ, depending on the exact business context of the task. Specifically, in this book we consider a certain form of additional knowledge that consists of attribute changing costs and benefit functions. Although we describe these functions below as reasonable and crucial considerations for many scenarios, nevertheless, one might have to consider additional aspects of domain knowledge, or maybe even different aspects, depending on the particular business scenario being examined.

The attribute changing cost function, $C: D \times D \to R$, assigns a real value cost for each possible change in the values of the explaining attributes. If a particular change cannot be achieved (e.g., changing the gender of a client, or making changes that conflict with laws or regulations), the associated costs are infinite. If for some reason the cost of an action depends on attributes that are not included in the set of explaining attributes, we include these attributes in D, and call them *silent attributes* — attributes that are not used by the supervised learning algorithms, but are included in the domain of the proactive data mining task.

The benefit function $B : D \times D(T) \to R$ assigns a real value benefit (or outcome) that represents the company's benefit from any possible record. The benefit from a specific record depends not only on the value of the target attribute, but also on the values of the explaining attributes. For example, benefit from a loyal client depends not only on the target value of churning $= 0$, but also on the explaining attributes of the client, such as his or her revenue. As in the case of the attribute changing cost function, the domain D may include silent attributes. In the following section we combine the benefit and the attribute changing functions and formally define the objective of the proactive data mining task.

12.6.3 *Maximizing Utility*

The objective in proactive data mining is to find the *optimal decision making policy*. A policy is a mapping $O : D \to D$ that defines the impact of some actions on the values of the explaining attributes. In order for a policy to be optimal, it should maximize the expected value of a utility function. The utility function that we consider in this book results from the benefit and attribute changing cost functions in the following manner: the addition to the benefit due to the move minus the attribute changing cost that is associated with that move.

It should be noted that the stated objective is to find an optimal policy. The optimal policy may depend on the probability distribution of the explaining attributes which is considered unknown. We use the training set as the empirical distribution, and search for the optimal actions with regard to that dataset. That is, we search for the policy that, if followed, will maximize the sum of the utilities that are gained from the N training observations.

It should also be noted that the cost, which is associated to O, can be calculated directly from the function C. The cost of a *move* — that is, changing the values of the explaining attributes from $x_i = < x_{1,i}, x_{2,i}, \ldots, x_{k,i} >$ to $x_j = < x_{1,j}, x_{2,j}, \ldots, x_{k,j} >$ is simply $C(x_i, x_j)$. However, in order to evaluate the benefit that is associated with the move, we must also know the impact of the change on the target attribute. This observation leads to our algorithmic framework for proactive data mining which we present in the following section.

12.6.4 *An Algorithmic Framework for Proactive Data Mining*

In order to evaluate the benefit of a move, we must know the impact of a change on the value of the target attribute. Fortunately, the problem of evaluating the impact of the values of the explaining attributes on the target attribute is well-known in data mining and is solved by supervised learning algorithms. Similarly our algorithmic framework for proactive data mining also uses a supervised learning algorithm for evaluating impact. Our framework consists of the following phases:

(1) Define the explaining attributes and the target result as in the case of any supervised-learning task.
(2) Define the benefit and the attribute changing cost functions.
(3) Extract patterns that model the dependency of the target attribute on the explaining attributes by using a supervised learning algorithm.
(4) Using the results of phase 3, optimize by finding the changes in values of the explaining attributes that maximize the utility function.

The main question regarding phase 3 is what supervised algorithm to use. One alternative is to use an existing algorithm, such as a decision tree (which we use in the following chapter). Most of the existing supervised learning algorithms are built in order to maximize the accuracy of their output model. This desire to obtain maximum accuracy, which in the classification case often takes the form minimizing the 0-1 loss, does not necessarily serve the maximal-utility objective that we defined in the previous section.

Consider a supervised learning scenario in which a decision tree is being used to solve a question of churn prediction. Let us consider two possible splits: (a) according to client gender, and (b) according to the client price plan. It might be the case (although typically this is not the case) that splitting according to client gender results in more homogeneous sub-populations of clients than splitting according to the client price plan. Although contributing to the overall accuracy of the output decision tree, splitting according to client gender provides no opportunity for evaluating the consequences of actions, since the company cannot act to change that gender. On the other hand, splitting according to the client price plan, even if inferior in terms of accuracy, allows us to evaluate the consequences of an important action: changing a price plan.

Another alternative for a supervised learning algorithm is to design an algorithm that will enable us to find better changes in the second phase, that is, to design an algorithm that is sensitive to the utility function and not to accuracy. Dahan Dahan *et al.* (2014) introduce a full implementation of proactive data mining for decision trees. We refer the readers to [Dahan *et al.* (2014)] for all the details.

Chapter 13

Feature Selection

13.1 Overview

Dimensionality (i.e. the number of dataset attributes or groups of attributes) constitutes a serious obstacle to the efficiency of most induction algorithms, primarily because induction algorithms are computationally intensive. Feature selection is an effective way to deal with dimensionality.

The objective of feature selection is to identify those features in the dataset which are important, and discard others as irrelevant and redundant. Since feature selection reduces the dimensionality of the data, data mining algorithms can be operated faster and more effectively by using feature selection. The reason for the improved performance is mainly due to a more compact, easily interpreted representation of the target concept [George and Foster (2000)]. We differentiate between three main strategies for feature selection: filter, wrapper and embedded [Blum and Langley (1997)].

13.2 The "Curse of Dimensionality"

High dimensionality of the input (that is, the number of attributes) increases the size of the search space in an exponential manner and thus increases the chance that the inducer will find spurious classifiers that are not valid in general. It is well known that the required number of labeled samples for supervised classification increases as a function of dimensionality [Jimenez and Landgrebe (1998)]. Fukunaga (1990) showed that the required number of training samples is linearly related to the dimensionality for a linear classifier and to the square of the dimensionality for a quadratic classifier. In terms of non-parametric classifiers like decision trees, the situation is even more severe. It has been estimated that as the number of dimensions increases, the sample size needs to increase exponentially in order to have an effective estimate of multivariate densities [Hwang *et al.* (1994)].

This phenomenon is usually referred to as the "curse of dimensionality". Bellman (1961) was the first to coin this term, while working on complicated signal processing issues. Techniques like decision trees inducers that are efficient in low dimensions fail to provide meaningful results when the number of dimensions increases beyond a "modest" size. Furthermore, smaller classifiers, involving fewer features (probably less than 10), are much more understandable by humans. Smaller classifiers are also more appropriate for user-driven data mining techniques such as visualization.

Most methods for dealing with high dimensionality focus on Feature Selection techniques, i.e. selecting a single subset of features upon which the inducer (induction algorithm) will run, while ignoring the rest. The selection of the subset can be done manually by using prior knowledge to identify irrelevant variables or by using proper algorithms.

In the last decade, many researchers have become increasingly interested in feature selection. Consequently, many feature selection algorithms have been proposed, some of which have been reported as displaying remarkable improvements in accuracy. Since the subject is too broad to survey here, readers seeking further information about recent developments should see: ([Langley (1994)]; [Liu and Motoda (1998)]).

A number of linear dimension reducers have been developed over the years. The linear methods of dimensionality reduction include projection pursuit [Friedman and Tukey (1973)]; factor analysis [Kim and Mueller (1978)]; and principal components analysis [Dunteman (1989)]. These methods are not aimed directly at eliminating irrelevant and redundant features, but are rather concerned with transforming the observed variables into a small number of "projections" or "dimensions". The underlying assumptions are that the variables are numeric and the dimensions can be expressed as linear combinations of the observed variables (and vice versa). Each discovered dimension is assumed to represent an unobserved factor and thus provide a new way of understanding the data (similar to the curve equation in the regression models).

The linear dimension reducers have been enhanced by constructive induction systems that use a set of existing features and a set of predefined constructive operators to derive new features [Pfahringer (1994)]; [Ragavan and Rendell (1993)]. These methods are effective for high dimensionality applications only if the original domain size of the input feature can be decreased dramatically.

On the one hand, feature selection can be used as a preprocessing step before building a decision tree. On the other hand, the decision tree can be used as a feature selector for other induction methods.

At first glance, it seems redundant to use feature selection as a preprocess phase for the training phase. Decision trees inducers, as opposed to other induction methods, incorporate in their training phase a built-in feature selection mechanism. Indeed, all criteria described in Section 5.1 are criteria for feature selection.

Still, it is well known that correlated and irrelevant features may degrade the performance of decision trees inducers. This phenomenon can be explained by the fact that feature selection in decision trees is performed on one attribute at a time and only at the root node over the entire decision space. In subsequent nodes, the training set is divided into several sub-sets and the features are selected according to their local predictive power [Perner (2001)]. Geometrically, it means that the selection of features is done in orthogonal decision sub-spaces, which do not necessarily represent the distribution of the entire instance space. It has been shown that the predictive performance of decision trees could be improved with an appropriate feature pre-selection phase. Moreover, using feature selection can reduce the number of nodes in the tree making it more compact.

Formally, the problem of feature subset selection can be defined as follows [Jain *et al.* (1997)]: Let A be the original set of features, with cardinality n. Let d represent the desired number of features in the selected subset B, $B \subseteq A$. Let the feature selection criterion function for the set B be represented by $J(B)$. Without any loss of generality, a lower value of J is considered to be a better feature subset (for instance, if J represents the generalization error). The problem of feature selection is to find an optimal subset B that solves the following optimization problem:

$$\min J(Z)$$
$$s.t.$$
$$Z \subseteq A \tag{13.1}$$
$$|Z| = d.$$

An exhaustive search would require examining all $\frac{n!}{d! \cdot (n-d)!}$ possible d-subsets of the feature set A.

13.3 Techniques for Feature Selection

Feature selection techniques can be used in many applications — from choosing the most important socio-economic parameters for determining what a person can return on a bank loan to selecting the best set of ingredients relating to a chemical process.

The filter approach operates independently of the data mining method employed subsequently — undesirable features are filtered out of the data before the learning of a filtering threshold begins. These fileterning algorithms use heuristics based on general characteristics of the data to evaluate the merit of feature subsets. A sub-category of filter methods, referred to as rankers, includes methods that employ some criterion to score each feature and provide a ranking. From this ordering, several feature subsets can be chosen manually.

The wrapper approach [Kohavi and John (2003)] uses a learning algorithm as a black box along with a statistical re-sampling technique such as cross-validation to select the best feature subset according to some predictive measure.

The *embedded* approach [Guyon and Elisseeff (2003)] is similar to the wrapper approach in the sense that the features are specifically selected for a certain learning algorithm. However, in the embedded approach the features are selected in the process of learning.

While most of the feature selection methods have been applied to supervised methods (such as classification and regression) there are important works that deals with unsupervised methods [Wolf and Shashua (2005)].

Feature selection algorithms search through the space of feature subsets in order to find the best subset. This subset search has four major properties [Langley (1994)]:

- Starting Point — Selecting a point in the feature subset space from which to begin the search can affect the direction of the search.
- Search Organization — A comprehensive search of the feature sub-space is prohibitive for all but a small initial number of features.
- Evaluation Strategy — How feature subsets are evaluated (filter, wrapper and ensemble).
- Stopping Criterion — A feature selector must decide when to stop searching through the space of feature subsets.

The next sections provide detailed description of feature selection techniques for each property described above.

13.3.1 *Feature Filters*

Filter methods, the earliest approaches for feature selection, use general properties of the data in order to evaluate the merit of feature subsets. As a result, filter methods are generally much faster and practical than wrapper methods, especially for use on data of high dimensionality.

13.3.1.1 *FOCUS*

The FOCUS algorithm is originally designed for attributes with Boolean domains [Almuallim and Dietterich (1994)]. FOCUS exhaustively searches the space of feature subsets until every combination of feature values is associated with one value of the class. After selecting the subset, it is passed to the $ID3$ algorithm which constructs a decision tree.

13.3.1.2 *LVF*

The LVF algorithm [Liu and Setiono (1996)] is consistency-driven and can handle noisy domains if the approximate noise level is known *a priori*. During every round of implementation, LVF generates a random subset from the feature subset space. If the chosen subset is smaller than the current best subset, the inconsistency rate of the dimensionally reduced data described by the subset is compared with the inconsistency rate of the best subset. If the subset is at least as consistent as the best subset, the subset replaces the best subset.

13.3.1.3 *Using a Learning Algorithm as a Filter*

Some works have explored the possibility of using a learning algorithm as a pre-processor to discover useful feature subsets for a primary learning algorithm. Cardie (1995) describes the application of decision tree algorithms for selecting feature subsets for use by instance-based learners. In [Provan and Singh (1996)], a greedy oblivious decision tree algorithm is used to select features to construct a Bayesian network. Holmes and Nevill- Manning (1995) apply Holte's (1993) 1R system in order to estimate the predictive accuracy of individual features. A program for inducing decision table majority classifiers used for selecting features is presented in [Pfahringer (1995)].

Decision table majority (DTM) classifiers are restricted to returning stored instances that are exact matches with the instance to be classified. When no instances are returned, the most prevalent class in the training data is used as the predicted class; otherwise, the majority class of all matching instances is used. In such cases, the minimum description length (MDL) principle guides the search by estimating the cost of encoding a decision table and the training examples it misclassifies with respect to a given feature subset. The features in the final decision table are then used with other learning algorithms.

13.3.1.4   *An Information Theoretic Feature Filter*

There are many filters techniques that are based on information theory and probabilistic reasoning [Koller and Sahami (1996)]. The rationale behind this approach is that, since the goal of an induction algorithm is to estimate the probability distributions over the class values, given the original feature set, feature subset selection should attempt to remain as close to these original distributions as possible.

13.3.1.5   *RELIEF Algorithm*

RELIEF [Kira and Rendell (1992)] uses instance-based learning to assign a relevance weight to each feature. The weight for each feature reflects its ability to single out the class values. The features are ranked by its weights and chosen by using a user-specified threshold. RELIEF randomly chooses instances from the training data. For every instance, RELIEF samples the nearest instance of the same class (nearest hit) and finds the opposite class (nearest miss). The weight for each feature is updated according to how well its values differentiate the sampled instance from its nearest hit and nearest miss. A feature will gain a high weight if it differentiates between instances from different classes and has the same value for instances of the same class.

13.3.1.6   *Simba and G-flip*

The SIMBA (iterative search margin-based algorithm) technique introduces the idea of measuring the quality of a set of features by the margin it induces. To overcome the drawback of iterative search, a greedy feature flip algorithm G-flip is used [Gilad-Bachrach *et al.* (2004)] for maximizing the margin function of a subset. The algorithm constantly iterates over the feature set and updates the set of chosen features. During each iteration, G-flip decides to eliminate or include the current feature to the selected subset by evaluating the margin with and without this feature.

13.3.1.7 *Contextual Merit (CM) Algorithm*

The CM algorithm [Hong (1997)] uses a merit function based upon weighted distances between examples which takes into account complete feature correlation's to the instance class. This approach assumes that features should be weighted according to their discrimination power regarding instances that are close to each other (based on the Euclidean distance) but which are associated with different classes. The CM approach has been used to select features for decision trees and an experimental study shows that feature subset selection can help to improve the prediction accuracy of the induced classifier [Perner (2001)].

The notation $d_{r,s}^i$ represents the distance between the value of feature i in the instances r and s (i.e. the distance between $x_{r,i}$ and $x_{s,i}$). For numerical attributes, the distance is $min(1, \frac{x_{r,i} - x_{s,i}}{t_i})$ where t_i is usually 0.5 of the value range of the attribute i. For nominal attributes, the distance is 0 if $x_{r,i} = x_{s,i}$, and 1 otherwise. The contextual merit for attribute i is calculated as $M_i = \sum_{r=1}^m \sum_{s \in \{(x,y) \in S | y_i \neq y_r\}} w_{r,s}^i d_{r,s}^i$ where m is the training set size, $\{(x,y) \in S | y_i \neq y_r\}$ is the set of instances associated with a different class than the instance r, and $w_{r,s}^i$ is a weighting factor.

13.3.2 *Using Traditional Statistics for Filtering*

13.3.2.1 *Mallows Cp*

This method minimizes the mean square error of prediction [Mallows (1973)]:

$$C_p = \frac{RSS_\gamma}{\hat{\sigma}_{FULL}^2} + 2q_\gamma - nC_p = \frac{RSS_\gamma}{\hat{\sigma}_{FULL}^2} + 2q_\gamma - n, \qquad (13.2)$$

where, RSS_γ is the residual sum of squares for the γth model and σ_{FULL}^2 is the usual unbiased estimate of σ^2 based on the full model.

The goal is to find the subset which has minimum Cp.

13.3.2.2 *AIC, BIC and F-ratio*

Akaike Information Criterion (AIC) and Bayesian Information Criterion (BIC) are criteria for choosing a subset of features. Letting $\hat{l}_\gamma$ denote the maximum log likelihood of the γth model, AIC selects the model which maximizes $(\hat{l}_\gamma - q_\gamma)$ whereas BIC selects the model which maximizes $(\hat{l}_\gamma - (\log n)q_\gamma 2)$.

For the linear model, many of the popular selection criteria are a penalized sum of squares criterion that can provide a unified framework for comparisons. This criterion selects the subset model that minimizes:

$$RSS_\gamma/\hat{\sigma}^2 + Fq_\gamma, \qquad (13.3)$$

where F is a preset "dimensionality penalty". The above penalizes $RSS\gamma/\sigma$ 2 by F times $q\gamma$, the dimension of the γth model. AIC and minimum Cp are equivalent, corresponding to $F = 2$, and BIC is obtained by $F = \log n$. Using a smaller penalty, AIC and minimum Cp will select larger models than BIC (unless n is very small).

13.3.2.3   *Principal Component Analysis (PCA)*

PCA is linear dimension reduction technique [Jackson (1991)]. PCA based on the covariance matrix of the variables, is a second-order method. PCA seeks to reduce the dimension of the data by finding a few orthogonal linear combinations (the PCs) of the original features with the largest variance. The first PC, s_1, is the linear combination with the largest variance. We have $s_1 = x^T w_1$, where the p-dimensional coefficient vector $w_1 = (w_{1,1}, \ldots, w_{1,p})^T$ solves:

$$w_1 = \arg \max_{\|w=1\|} Var\{x^T w\}. \qquad (13.4)$$

The second PC is the linear combination with the second largest variance and orthogonal to the first PC, and so on. There are as many PCs as the number of original features. For many datasets, the first several PCs explain most of the variance, so that the rest can be ignored with minimal loss of information.

13.3.2.4   *Factor Analysis (FA)*

FA, a linear method based on the second-order data summaries, assumes that the measured features depend on some unknown factors. Typical examples include features defined as various test scores of individuals that might to be related to a common intelligence factor. The goal of FA is to find out such relations, and thus it can be used to reduce the dimension of datasets following the factor model.

13.3.2.5   *Projection Pursuit (PP)*

PP is a linear method which is more computationally intensive than second-order methods. Given a projection index that defines the merit of a direction, the algorithm looks for the directions that optimize that index. As the Gaussian distribution is the least interesting distribution, projection indices usually measure some aspect of non-Gaussianity.

13.3.3 *Wrappers*

The wrapper strategy for feature selection uses an induction algorithm to evaluate feature subsets. The motivation for this strategy is that the induction method that will eventually use the feature subset should provide a better predictor of accuracy than a separate measure that has an entirely different inductive bias [Langley (1994)].

Feature wrappers are often better than filters since they are tuned to the specific interaction between an induction algorithm and its training data. Nevertheless, they tend to be much slower than feature filters because they must repeatedly perform the induction algorithm.

13.3.3.1 *Wrappers for Decision Tree Learners*

The wrapper general framework for feature selection, has two degrees of feature relevance definitions that are used by the wrapper to discover relevant features [John *et al.* (1994)]. A feature X_i is said to be strongly relevant to the target concept(s) if the probability distribution of the class values, given the full feature set, changes when X_i is eliminated. A feature X_i is said to be weakly relevant if it is not strongly relevant and the probability distribution of the class values, given some subset which contains X_i, changes when X_i is removed. All features that are not strongly or weakly relevant are irrelevant.

Vafaie and De Jong (1995) and Cherkauer and Shavlik (1996) have both applied genetic search strategies in a wrapper framework in order to improve the performance of decision tree learners. Vafaie and De Jong (1995) present a system that has two genetic algorithm driven modules. The first performs feature selection while the second module performs constructive induction, which is the process of creating new attributes by applying logical and mathematical operators to the original features.

13.4 Feature Selection as a means of Creating Ensembles

The main idea of ensemble methodology is to combine a set of models, each of which solves the same original task, in order to obtain a better composite global model, with more accurate and reliable estimates or decisions than can be obtained from using a single model. Some of the drawbacks of wrappers and filters can be solved by using an ensemble. As mentioned above, filters perform less than wrappers. Due to the voting process, noisy results are filtered. Secondly, the drawback of wrappers which "cost" computing time is solved by operating a group of filters. The idea of building a predictive model by integrating multiple models has been under investigation for a long time.

Ensemble feature selection methods [Opitz (1999)] extend traditional feature selection methods by looking for a set of feature subsets that will promote disagreement among the base classifiers. Simple random selection of feature subsets may be an effective technique for ensemble feature selection because the lack of accuracy in the ensemble members is compensated for by their diversity [Ho (1998)]. Tsymbal and Puuronen (2002) presented a technique for building ensembles of simple Bayes classifiers in random feature subsets.

The hill-climbing ensemble feature selection strategy randomly constructs the initial ensemble [Cunningham and Carney (2000)]. Then, an iterative refinement is performed based on hill-climbing search in order to improve the accuracy and diversity of the base classifiers. For all the feature subsets, an attempt is made to switch (include or delete) each feature. If the resulting feature subset produces better performance on the validation set, that change is kept. This process is continued until no further improvements are obtained.

Genetic Ensemble Feature Selection (GEFS) [Opitz (1999)] uses genetic search for ensemble feature selection. This strategy begins with creating an initial population of classifiers where each classifier is generated by randomly selecting a different subset of features. Then, new candidate classifiers are continually produced by using the genetic operators of crossover and mutation on the feature subsets. The final ensemble is composed of the most fitted classifiers.

Another method for creating a set of feature selection solutions using a genetic algorithm was proposed by Oliveira *et al.* (2003). They create a Pareto-optimal front in relation to two different objectives: accuracy on a validation set and number of features. Following that, they select the best feature selection solution.

In the statistics literature, the most well-known feature-oriented ensemble algorithm is the MARS algorithm [Friedman (1991)]. In this algorithm, a multiple regression function is approximated using linear splines and their tensor products.

Tuv and Torkkola (2005) examined the idea of using ensemble of classifiers such as decision trees in order to create a better feature ranker. They showed that this ensemble can be very effective in variable ranking for problems with up to a 100,000 input attributes. Note that this approach uses inducers for obtaining the ensemble by concentrating on wrapper feature selectors.

13.5 Ensemble Methodology for Improving Feature Selection

The ensemble methodology can be employed as a filter feature selector. More specifically, the selected subset is a weighted average of subsets obtained from various filter methods [Rokach *et al.* (2007)].

The problem of feature selection ensemble is that of finding the best feature subset by combining a given set of feature selectors such that if a specific inducer is run on it, the generated classifier will have the highest possible accuracy. Formally, the optimal feature subset with respect to a particular inducer [Kohavi (1996)] is defined as:

Definition 13.1. *Given an inducer I, a training set S with input feature set $A = \{a_1, a_2, \ldots, a_n\}$ and target feature y from a fixed and unknown distribution D over the labeled instance space, the subset $B \subseteq A$ is said to be optimal if the expected generalization error of the induced classifier $I(\pi_{B \cup y} S)$ will be minimized over the distribution D, where $\pi_{B \cup y} S$ represents the corresponding projection of S and $I(\pi_{B \cup y} S)$ represents a classifier which was induced by activating the induction method I onto dataset $\pi_{B \cup y} S$.*

Definition 13.2. *Given an inducer I, a training set S with input feature set $A = \{a_1, a_2, \ldots, a_n\}$ and target feature y from a fixed and unknown distribution D over the labeled instance space, and an optimal subset B, a Feature Selector FS is said to be consistent if it selects an attribute $a_i \in B$ with probability $p > \frac{1}{2}$ and it selects an attribute $a_j \notin B$ with probability $q < \frac{1}{2}$.*

Definition 13.3. *Given a set of feature subsets $B_1, \ldots, B_\omega$ the majority combination of features subsets is a single feature subset that contains any attribute a_i such that $f_c(a_i, B_1, ..., B_\omega) > \frac{\omega}{2}$ where $f_c(a_i, B_1, ..., B_\omega) = \sum_{j=1}^{\omega} g(a_i, B_j)$ and $g(a_i, B_j) = \begin{cases} 1 & a_i \in B_j \\ 0 & otherwise \end{cases}$.*

The last definition refers to a simple majority voting, in which attribute a_i is included in the combined feature subset if it appears in at least half of the base feature subsets $B_1, \ldots, B_\omega$, where ω is the number of base feature subsets. Note that $f_c(a_i, B_1, \ldots, B_\omega)$ counts the number of base feature subsets in which a_i is included.

Lemma 13.1. *A majority combination of feature subsets obtained from a given a set of independent and consistent feature selectors $FS_1, \ldots, FS_\omega$ (where ω is the number of feature selectors) converges to the optimal feature subset when $\omega \to \infty$.*

Proof. For ensuring that for attributes for which $a_i \in B$ are actually selected, we need to show that:

$$\lim_{\omega \to \infty, p > 1/2} p\left(f_c(a_i) > \frac{\omega}{2}\right) = 1. \tag{13.5}$$

We denote by $p_{j,i} > 1$ the probability of FS_j to select a_i. We denote by $p_i = \min(p_{j,i})$. Note that $p_i > \frac{1}{2}$. Because the feature selectors are independent, we can use approximation binomial distribution, i.e.:

$$\lim_{\omega \to \infty} p\left(f_c(a_i) > \frac{\omega}{2}\right) \leq \lim_{\omega \to \infty, p_i > 1/2} \sum_{k=0}^{\frac{\omega}{2}} \binom{\omega}{k} p_i^k (1-p_i)^{\omega-k}. \tag{13.6}$$

Due to the fact that $\omega \to \infty$ we can use the central limit theorem in which, $\mu = \omega p_i, \sigma = \sqrt{\omega p_i(1-p_i)}$:

$$\lim_{\omega \to \infty, p_i > 1/2} p\left(Z > \frac{\sqrt{\omega}(1/2 - p_i)}{\sqrt{p_i(1-p_i)}}\right) = p(Z > -\infty) = 1. \tag{13.7}$$

For ensuring that for attributes for which $a_i \notin B$ are actually selected we need to show that:

$$\lim_{\omega \to \infty} p\left(f_c(a_i) < \frac{\omega}{2}\right) = 0. \tag{13.8}$$

We denote by $q_{j,i} < 1/2$ the probability of FS_j to select a_i. We denote by $q_i = \max(q_{j,i})$. Note that $q_i < \frac{1}{2}$. Because the feature selectors are independent, we can use approximation binomial distribution, i.e.:

$$\lim_{\omega \to \infty} p\left(f_c(a_i) < \frac{\omega}{2}\right) \geq \lim_{\omega \to \infty, q_i < 1/2} \sum_{k=0}^{\frac{\omega}{2}} \binom{\omega}{k} q_i^k (1-q_i)^{\omega-k}. \tag{13.9}$$

Due to the fact that $\omega \to \infty$ we can use the central limit theorem again this time: $\mu = \omega q_i, \sigma = \sqrt{\omega q_i(1 - q_i)}$:

$$\lim_{\omega \to \infty, q_i < 1/2} \sum_{k=0}^{\frac{\omega}{2}} \binom{\omega}{k} q_i^k (1 - q_i)^{\omega - k} = \lim_{\omega \to \infty, q_i < 1/2} p \left(Z > \frac{\frac{\omega}{2} - q_i\omega}{\sqrt{\omega q_i(1 - q_i)}} \right)$$

$$= \lim_{\omega \to \infty, q_i < 1/2} p \left(Z > \frac{\sqrt{\omega}(1/2 - q_i)}{\sqrt{q_i(1 - q_i)}} \right)$$

$$= p(Z > \infty) = 0. \tag{13.10}$$

$\square$

13.5.1   *Independent Algorithmic Framework*

Roughly speaking, the feature selectors in the ensemble can be created dependently or independently. In the dependent framework, the outcome of a certain feature selector affects the creation of the next feature selector. Alternatively, each feature selector is built independently; the resulted features subsets are then combined in some fashion. Here, we concentrate on an independent framework. Figure 13.1 presents the proposed algorithmic framework. This simple framework receives as an input the following arguments:

(1) A Training set (S) — A labeled dataset used for feature selectors.
(2) A set of feature selection algorithms $\{FS_1, \ldots, FS_\xi\}$ — A feature selection algorithm is an algorithm that obtains a training set and outputs a subset of relevant features. Recall that we employ non-wrapper and non-ranker feature selectors.
(3) Ensemble Size (ω).
(4) Ensemble generator (G) — This component is responsible for generating a set of ω pairs of feature selection algorithms and their corresponding training sets. We refer to G as a class that implements a method called "genrateEnsemble".
(5) Combiner (C) — The combiner is responsible for creating the subsets and combining them into a single subset. We refer to C as a class that implements the method "combine".

The proposed algorithm simply uses the ensemble generator to create a set of feature selection algorithm pairs and their corresponding training sets. Then it calls the combine method in C to execute the feature selection

Require: S, $\{FS_1, \ldots, FS_\xi\}$, G, C
Ensure: A combined feature subset.
1: $(S_1, FS_1), \ldots, (S_\omega, FS_\omega)$ =G.genrateEnsemble(S, $(FS_1, \ldots, FS_\xi)$, ω)
2: Return C.combine ($\{(S_1, FS_1), \ldots, (S_\omega, FS_\omega)\}$)

Fig. 13.1   Pseudo-code of independent algorithmic framework for feature selection.

algorithm on its corresponding dataset. The various feature subsets are then combined into a single subset.

13.5.2   Combining Procedure

We begin by describing two implementations for the combiner component. In the literature, there are two ways of combining the results of the ensemble members: weighting methods and meta-learning methods. Here, we concentrate on weighting methods. The weighting methods are best suited for problems where the individual members have comparable success or when we would like to avoid problems associated with added learning (such as over-fitting or long training time).

13.5.2.1   Simple Weighted Voting

Figure 13.2 presents an algorithm for selecting a feature subset based on the weighted voting of feature subsets. As this is an implementation of the abstract combiner used in Figure 13.1, the input of the algorithm is a set of pairs; every pair is built from one feature selector and a training set. After executing the feature selector on its associated training set to obtain a feature subset, the algorithm employs some weighting method and attaches a weight to every subset. Finally, it uses a weighted voting to decide which attribute should be included in the final subset. We considered the following methods for weighting the subsets:

(1) **Majority Voting** — In this weighting method, the same weight is attached to every subset such that the total weights is 1, i.e. if there are ω subsets then the weight is simply $1/\omega$. Note that the inclusion of a certain attribute in the final result requires that this attribute will appear in at least $\omega/2$ subsets. This method should have a low false positive rate, because selecting an irrelevant attribute will take place only if at least $\omega/2$ feature selections methods will decide to select this attribute.

Require: $\{(S_1, FS_1), \ldots, (S_\omega, FS_\omega)\}$
Ensure: A Combined feature subset
1: **for all** $(S_i, FS_i) \in F$ **do**
2:     $B_i = FS_i.\text{getSelectedFeatures}(S_i)$
3: **end for**
4: $\{w_1, \ldots, w_\omega\} = getWeight\left(\{B_1, \ldots, B_\omega\}\right)$
5: $B \leftarrow \emptyset$
6: **for all** $a_j \in A$ **do**
7:     totalWeight=0
8:     **for** $i = 1$ **to** ω **do**
9:         **if** $a_j \in B_i$ **then**
10:             totalWeight $\leftarrow$ totalWeight+W_i
11:         **end if**
12:     **end for**
13:     **if** totalWeight > 0.5 **then**
14:         B $\leftarrow B \cup a_j$
15:     **end if**
16: **end for**
17: Return B

Fig. 13.2   Pseudo-code of combining procedure.

(2) **"Take-It-All"** — In this weighting method, all subsets obtain a weight that is greater than 0.5. This leads to the situation in which any attribute that has been in at least one of the subsets will be included in the final result. This method should have a low false negative rate, because losing a relevant attribute will take place only if all feature selections methods will decide to filter out this attribute.

(3) **"Smaller is Heavier"** — The weight for each selector is defined by its bias to the smallest subset. Selectors that tend to provide small subsets will gain more weight than selectors that tend to provide large subsets. This approach is inspired by the fact that the precision rate of selectors tend to decrease as the size of the subset increases. This approach can be used to avoid noise caused by feature selectors that tend to select most of the possible attributes. More specifically, the weights are defined as:

$$w_i = \frac{|B_i|}{\sum_{j=1}^{\omega} |B_j|} \Bigg/ \sum_{k=1}^{\omega} \frac{|B_k|}{\sum_{j=1}^{\omega} |B_j|}. \tag{13.11}$$

13.5.2.2 *Using Artificial Contrasts*

Using the Bayesian approach, a certain attribute should be filtered out if: $P(a_i \notin B|B_1,\ldots,B_\omega) > 0.5$ or $P(a_i \notin B|B_1,\ldots,B_\omega) > P(a_i \in B|B_1,\ldots,B_\omega)$ where $B \subseteq A$ denote the set of relevant features. By using the Bayes Theorem, we obtain:

$$P(a_i \notin B|B_1,\ldots,B_\omega) = \frac{P(B_1,\ldots,B_\omega|a_i \notin B)P(a_i \notin B)}{P(B_1,\ldots,B_\omega)}. \quad (13.12)$$

However, since calculating the above probability might be difficult, we use the naive Bayes combination. This is a well-known combining method due to its simplicity and its relatively outstanding results. According to the naive Bayes assumption, the results of the feature selectors are independent given the fact that the attribute a_i is not relevant. Thus, using this assumption, we obtain:

$$\frac{P(B_1,\ldots,B_\omega|a_i \notin B)P(a_i \notin B)}{P(B_1,\ldots,B_\omega)} = \frac{P(a_i \notin B)\prod\limits_{j=1}^{\omega} P(B_j|a_i \notin B)}{P(B_1,\ldots,B_\omega)}. \quad (13.13)$$

Using Bayes theorem again:

$$\frac{P(a_i \notin B)\prod\limits_{j=1}^{\omega} P(B_j|a_i \notin B)}{P(B_1,\ldots,B_\omega)} = \frac{P(a_i \notin B)\prod\limits_{j=1}^{\omega} \frac{P(a_i \notin B|B_j)}{P(a_i \notin B)}P(B_j)}{P(B_1,\ldots,B_\omega)}$$

$$= \frac{\prod\limits_{j=1}^{\omega} P(B_j)\prod\limits_{j=1}^{\omega} P(a_i \notin B|B_j)}{P(B_1,\ldots,B_\omega)\cdot P^{\omega-1}(a_i \notin B)}. \quad (13.14)$$

Thus, a certain attribute should be filtered out if:

$$\frac{\prod\limits_{j=1}^{\omega} P(B_j)\prod\limits_{j=1}^{\omega} P(a_i \notin B|B_j)}{P(B_1,\ldots,B_\omega)\cdot P^{\omega-1}(a_i \notin B)} > \frac{\prod\limits_{j=1}^{\omega} P(B_j)\prod\limits_{j=1}^{\omega} P(a_i \in B|B_j)}{P(B_1,\ldots,B_\omega)\cdot P^{\omega-1}(a_i \in B)}. \quad (13.15)$$

or after omitting the common term from both sides:

$$\frac{\prod\limits_{j=1}^{\omega} P(a_i \notin B|B_j)}{P^{\omega-1}(a_i \notin B)} > \frac{\prod\limits_{j=1}^{\omega} P(a_i \in B|B_j)}{P^{\omega-1}(a_i \in B)}. \quad (13.16)$$

Assuming that the *a priori* probability for a_i to be relevant is equal to that of not being relevant:

$$\prod_{j=1}^{\omega} P(a_i \notin B\,|B_j\,) > \prod_{j=1}^{\omega} P(a_i \in B\,|B_j\,). \qquad (13.17)$$

Using the complete probability theorem:

$$\prod_{j=1}^{\omega} P(a_i \notin B\,|B_j\,) > \prod_{j=1}^{\omega} (1 - P(a_i \notin B\,|B_j\,)). \qquad (13.18)$$

Because we are using non-ranker feature selectors the above probability is estimated using:

$$P(a_i \notin B\,|B_j\,) \approx \begin{cases} P(a \notin B|a \in B_j) & if\ a_i \in B_j \\ P(a \notin B|a \notin B_j) & if\ a_i \notin B_j \end{cases}. \qquad (13.19)$$

Note that $P(a \notin B|a \in B_j)$ does not refer to a specific attribute, but to the general bias of the feature selector j. In order to estimate the remaining probabilities, we are adding to the dataset a set of ϕ contrast attributes that are known to be truly irrelevant and analyzing the number of artificial features ϕ_j included in the subset B_j obtained by the feature selector j:

$$P(a \in B_j\,|a \notin B\,) = \frac{\phi_j}{\phi}; \quad P(a \notin B_j\,|a \notin B\,) = 1 - \frac{\phi_j}{\phi}. \qquad (13.20)$$

The artificial contrast variables are obtained by randomly permuting the values of the original n attributes across m instances. Generating just random attributes from some simple distribution, such as Normal Distribution, is not sufficient, because the values of original attributes may exhibit some special structure. Using Bayes theorem:

$$P(a \notin B\,|a \in B_j\,) = \frac{P(a \notin B)P(a \in B_j\,|a \notin B\,)}{P(a \in B_j\,)}$$

$$= \frac{P(a \notin B)}{P(a \in B_j\,)} \frac{\phi_j}{\phi} \qquad (13.21)$$

$$P(a \notin B\,|a \notin B_j\,) = \frac{P(a \notin B)P(a \notin B_j\,|a \notin B\,)}{P(a \notin B_j\,)}$$

$$= \frac{P(a \notin B)}{1 - P(a \in B_j\,)} \left(1 - \frac{\phi_j}{\phi}\right), \qquad (13.22)$$

where $P(a \in B_j\,) = \frac{|B_j|}{n+\phi}$

13.5.3   *Feature Ensemble Generator*

In order to make the ensemble more effective, there should be some sort of diversity between the feature subsets. Diversity may be obtained through different presentations of the input data or variations in feature selector design. The following sections describe each one of the different approaches.

13.5.3.1   *Multiple Feature Selectors*

In this approach, we simply use a set of different feature selection algorithms. The basic assumption is that since different algorithms have different inductive biases, they will create different feature subsets.

The proposed method can be employed with the correlation-based feature subset selection (CFS) as a subset evaluator [Hall (1999)]. CFS evaluates the worth of a subset of attributes by considering the individual predictive ability of each feature along with the degree of redundancy between them. Subsets of features that are highly correlated with the class while having low inter-correlation are preferred.

At the heart of the CFS algorithm is a heuristic for evaluating the worth or merit of a subset of features. This heuristic takes into account the usefulness of individual features for predicting the class label along with the level of inter-correlation among them. The heuristic is based on the following hypothesis: a good features subset contains features that are highly correlated with the class, but which are uncorrelated with each other.

Equation (13.23) formalizes the feature selection heuristics:

$$M_B = \frac{k\overline{r_{c_f}}}{\sqrt{k + k(k-1)\overline{r_{f_f}}}}, \tag{13.23}$$

where M_B is the heuristic "merit" of a feature subset B containing k features; $\overline{r_{c_f}}$ is the average feature-class correlation; and $\overline{r_{f_f}}$ is the average feature-feature correlation.

In order to apply Equation (13.23) to estimate the merit of a feature subset, it is necessary to compute the correlation (dependence) between attributes. For discrete class problems, CFS first discretises numeric features then uses symmetrical uncertainty (a modified information gain measure) to calculates feature–class and feature–feature correlations:

$$SU = \frac{\text{InformationGain}(a_i, a_j, S)}{Entropy(a_i, S) + Entropy(a_j, S)}. \tag{13.24}$$

Recall from Section 5.1.3:

$$\text{InformationGain}(a_i, a_j, S) = Entropy(a_j, S) - \sum_{v_{i,k} \in dom(a_i)} \frac{|\sigma_{a_i = v_{i,k}} S|}{|S|}$$

$$\cdot Entropy(a_j, \sigma_{a_i = v_{i,k}} S), \tag{13.25}$$

$$Entropy(a_i, S) = \sum_{v_{i,k} \in dom(a_i)} -\frac{|\sigma_{a_i = v_{i,k}} S|}{|S|} \cdot \log_2 \frac{|\sigma_{a_i = v_{i,k}} S|}{|S|}. \tag{13.26}$$

Symmetrical uncertainty is used (rather than simple gain ratio) because it is a symmetric measure and can therefore be used to measure feature–feature correlations where there is no notion of one attribute being the "class" as such.

As for the search organization the following methods can be used: Best First Search; Forward Selection Search; Gain Ratio; Chi-Square; OneR classifier; and Information Gain.

Beside the CFS, other evaluation methods can be considered including, consistency subset evaluator and the wrapper subset evaluator with simple classifiers (K-nearest neighbors, logistic regression and naïve bayes).

13.5.3.2 *Bagging*

The most well-known independent method is bagging (bootstrap aggregating). In this case, each feature selector is executed on a sample of instances taken with replacement from the training set. Usually, each sample size is equal to the size of the original training set. Note that since sampling with a replacement is used, some of the instances may appear more than once in the same sample and some may not be included at all. Although the training samples are different from each other, they are certainly not independent from a statistical point of view.

13.6 Using Decision Trees for Feature Selection

Using decision trees for feature selection has one important advantage known as "anytime". However, for highly dimensional datasets, the feature selection process becomes computationally intensive.

Decision trees can be used to implement a trade-off between the performance of the selected features and the computation time which is required to find a subset. Top-down inducers of decision trees can be considered as anytime algorithms for feature selection, because they gradually improve the performance and can be stopped at any time and provide sub-optimal feature subsets.

Decision trees have been used as an evaluation means for directing the feature selection search. For instance, a hybrid learning methodology that integrates genetic algorithms (GAs) and decision tree inducers in order to find the best feature subset was proposed in [Bala *et al.* (1995)]. A GA is used to search the space of all possible subsets of a large set of candidate discrimination features. In order to evaluate a certain feature subset, a decision tree is trained and its accuracy is used as a measure of fitness for the given feature set, which, in turn, is used by the GA to evolve better feature sets.

13.7 Limitation of Feature Selection Methods

Despite its popularity, the usage of feature selection methodologies for overcoming the obstacles of high dimensionality has several drawbacks:

- The assumption that a large set of input features can be reduced to a small subset of relevant features is not always true; in some cases the target feature is actually affected by most of the input features, and removing features will cause a significant loss of important information.
- The outcome (i.e. the subset) of many algorithms for feature selection (for example, almost any of the algorithms that are based upon the wrapper methodology) is strongly dependent on the training set size. That is, if the training set is small, then the size of the reduced subset will also be small. Consequently, relevant features might be lost. Accordingly, the induced classifiers might achieve lower accuracy compared to classifiers that have access to all relevant features.
- In some cases, even after eliminating a set of irrelevant features, the researcher is left with relatively large numbers of relevant features.
- The backward elimination strategy, used by some methods, is extremely inefficient for working with large-scale databases, where the number of original features is more than 100.

One way to deal with the above-mentioned disadvantages is to use a very large training set (which should increase in an exponential manner as the number of input features increases). However, the researcher rarely enjoys this privilege, and even if it does happen, the researcher will probably encounter the aforementioned difficulties derived from a high number of instances.

Practically, most of the training sets are still considered "small" not because of their absolute size but rather due to the fact that they contain too few instances given the nature of the investigated problem, namely the instance space size, the space distribution and the intrinsic noise. Furthermore, even if a sufficient dataset is available, the researcher will probably encounter the aforementioned difficulties derived from a high number of records.

Chapter 14

Fuzzy Decision Trees

14.1 Overview

There are two main types of uncertainty in supervised learning: statistical and cognitive. Statistical uncertainty deals with the random behavior of nature and all techniques described in previous chapters can handle the uncertainty that arises (or is assumed to arise) in the natural world from statistical variations or randomness. While these techniques may be appropriate for measuring the likelihood of a hypothesis, they say nothing about the meaning of the hypothesis.

Cognitive uncertainty, on the other hand, deals with human cognition. Cognitive uncertainty can be further divided into two sub-types: vagueness and ambiguity. Ambiguity arises in situations with two or more alternatives such that the choice between them is left unspecified. Vagueness arises when there is a difficulty in making a precise distinction in the world.

Fuzzy set theory, first introduced by Zadeh in 1965, deals with cognitive uncertainty and seeks to overcome many of the problems found in classical set theory. For example, a major problem in the early days of control theory is that a small change in input results in a major change in output. This throws the whole control system into an unstable state. In addition, there was also the problem that the representation of subjective knowledge was artificial and inaccurate.

Fuzzy set theory is an attempt to confront these difficulties and in this chapter we present some of its basic concepts. The main focus, however, is on those concepts used in the induction process when dealing with fuzzy decision trees. Since fuzzy set theory and fuzzy logic are much broader than the narrow perspective presented here, the interested reader is encouraged to read [Zimmermann (2005)].

14.2 Membership Function

In classical set theory, a certain element either belongs or does not belong to a set. Fuzzy set theory, on the other hand, permits the gradual assessment of the membership of elements in relation to a set.

Definition 14.1. Let U be a universe of discourse, representing a collection of objects denoted generically by u. A fuzzy set A in a universe of discourse U is characterized by a membership function μ_A which takes values in the interval $[0, 1]$, where $\mu_A(u) = 0$ means that u is definitely not a member of A and $\mu_A(u) = 1$ means that u is definitely a member of A.

The above definition can be illustrated on a vague set, that we will label as *young*. In this case, the set U is the set of people. To each person in U, we define the degree of membership to the fuzzy set *young*. The membership function answers the question: "To what degree is person u young?". The easiest way to do this is with a membership function based on the person's age. For example, Figure 14.1 presents the following membership function:

$$\mu_{Young}(u) = \begin{cases} 0 & age(u) > 32 \\ 1 & age(u) < 16 \\ \dfrac{32 - age(u)}{16} & otherwise \end{cases}. \tag{14.1}$$

Given this definition, John, who is 18 years old, has degree of youth of 0.875. Philip, 20 years old, has degree of youth of 0.75. Unlike probability theory, degrees of membership do not have to add up to 1 across all

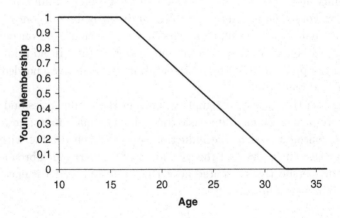

Fig. 14.1   Membership function for the young set.

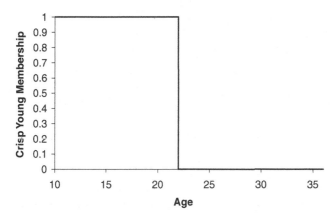

Fig. 14.2   Membership function for the crisp young set.

objects and therefore either many or few objects in the set may have high membership. However, an objects membership in a set (such as "young") and the sets complement ("not young") must still sum to 1.

The main difference between classical set theory and fuzzy set theory is that the latter admits to partial set membership. A classical or crisp set, then, is a fuzzy set that restricts its membership values to $\{0,1\}$, the endpoints of the unit interval. Membership functions can be used to represent a crisp set. For example, Figure 14.2 presents a crisp membership function defined as:

$$\mu_{CrispYoung}(u) = \begin{cases} 0 & age(u) > 22 \\ 1 & age(u) \le 22 \end{cases}. \tag{14.2}$$

14.3   Fuzzy Classification Problems

All classification problems we have discussed so far in this chapter assume that each instance takes one value for each attribute and that each instance is classified into only one of the mutually exclusive classes [Yuan and Shaw (1995)].

To illustrate the idea, we introduce the problem of modeling the preferences of TV viewers. In this problem, there are three input attributes:

$$A = \{\text{Time of Day, Age Group, Mood}\}$$

and each attribute has the following values:

- $dom(\text{Time of Day}) = \{\text{Morning, Noon, Evening, Night}\}$
- $dom(\text{Age Group}) = \{\text{Young, Adult}\}$
- $dom(\text{Mood}) = \{\text{Happy, Indifferent, Sad, Sour, Grumpy}\}$

The classification can be the movie genre that the viewer would like to watch, such as $C = \{\text{Action, Comedy, Drama}\}$.

All the attributes are vague by definition. For example, people's feelings of happiness, indifference, sadness, sourness and grumpiness are vague without any crisp boundaries between them. Although the vagueness of "Age Group" or "Time of Day" can be avoided by indicating the exact age or exact time, a rule induced with a crisp decision tree may then have an artificial crisp boundary, such as "IF Age < 16 THEN action movie". But how about someone who is 17 years of age? Should this viewer definitely not watch an action movie? The viewer preferred genre may still be vague. For example, the viewer may be in a mood for both comedy and drama movies. Moreover, the association of movies into genres may also be vague. For instance, the movie "Lethal Weapon" (starring Mel Gibson and Danny Glover) is considered to be both comedy and action movie.

Fuzzy concept can be introduced into a classical problem if at least one of the input attributes is fuzzy or if the target attribute is fuzzy. In the example described above, both input and target attributes are fuzzy. Formally, the problem is defined as following [Yuan and Shaw (1995)]:

Each class c_j is defined as a fuzzy set on the universe of objects U. The membership function $\mu_{c_j}(u)$ indicates the degree to which object u belongs to class c_j. Each attribute a_i is defined as a linguistic attribute which takes linguistic values from $dom(a_i) = \{v_{i,1}, v_{i,2}, \ldots, v_{i,|dom(a_i)|}\}$. Each linguistic value $v_{i,k}$ is also a fuzzy set defined on U. The membership $\mu_{v_{i,k}}(u)$ specifies the degree to which object u's attribute a_i is $v_{i,k}$. Recall that the membership of a linguistic value can be subjectively assigned or transferred from numerical values by a membership function defined on the range of the numerical value.

14.4   Fuzzy Set Operations

Like classical set theory, fuzzy set theory includes such operations as union, intersection, complement, and inclusion, but also includes operations that have no classical counterpart, such as the modifiers concentration and dilation, and the connective fuzzy aggregation. Definitions of fuzzy set operations are provided in this section.

Definition 14.2. The membership function of the union of two fuzzy sets A and B with membership functions μ_A and μ_B respectively is defined as the maximum of the two individual membership functions $\mu_{A \cup B}(u) = max\{\mu_A(u), \mu_B(u)\}$.

Definition 14.3. The membership function of the intersection of two fuzzy sets A and B with membership functions μ_A and μ_B respectively is defined as the minimum of the two individual membership functions $\mu_{A \cap B}(u) = min\{\mu_A(u), \mu_B(u)\}$.

Definition 14.4. The membership function of the complement of a fuzzy set A with membership function μ_A is defined as the negation of the specified membership function $\mu_{\overline{A}}(u) = 1 - \mu_A(u)$.

To illustrate these fuzzy operations, we elaborate on the previous example. Recall that John has a degree of youth of 0.875. Additionally, John's happiness degree is 0.254. Thus, the membership of John in the set Young ∪ Happy would be $max(0.875, 0.254) = 0.875$, and its membership in Young ∩ Happy would be $min(0.875, 0.254) = 0.254$.

It is possible to chain operators together, thereby constructing quite complicated sets. It is also possible to derive many interesting sets from chains of rules built up from simple operators. For example, John's membership in the set $\overline{Young} \cup$ Happy would be $max(1 - 0.875, 0.254) = 0.254$.

The usage of the max and min operators for defining fuzzy union and fuzzy intersection, respectively is very common. However, it is important to note that these are not the only definitions of union and intersection suited to fuzzy set theory.

14.5 Fuzzy Classification Rules

Definition 14.5. The fuzzy subsethood $S(A, B)$ measures the degree to which A is a subset of B.

$$S(A, B) = \frac{M(A \cap B)}{M(A)}, \qquad (14.3)$$

where $M(A)$ is the *cardinality* measure of a fuzzy set A and is defined as

$$M(A) = \sum_{u \in U} \mu_A(u). \qquad (14.4)$$

The subsethood can be used to measure the truth level of the rule of classification rules. For example, given a classification rule such as "IF Age is Young AND Mood is Happy THEN Comedy" we have to calculate $S(Hot \cap Sunny, Swimming)$ in order to measure the truth level of the classification rule.

14.6 Creating Fuzzy Decision Tree

There are several algorithms for induction of decision trees. In this section, we will focus on the algorithm proposed by Yuan and Shaw (1995). This algorithm can handle the classification problems with both fuzzy attributes and fuzzy classes represented in linguistic fuzzy terms. It can also handle other situations in a uniform way where numerical values can be fuzzified to fuzzy terms and crisp categories can be treated as a special case of fuzzy terms with zero fuzziness. The algorithm uses classification ambiguity as fuzzy entropy. The classification ambiguity, which directly measures the quality of classification rules at the decision node, can be calculated under fuzzy partitioning and multiple fuzzy classes.

The fuzzy decision tree induction consists of the following steps:

- Fuzzifying numeric attributes in the training set.
- Inducing a fuzzy decision tree.
- Simplifying the decision tree.
- Applying fuzzy rules for classification.

14.6.1 *Fuzzifying Numeric Attributes*

When a certain attribute is numerical, it needs to be fuzzified into linguistic terms before it can be used in the algorithm. The fuzzification process can be performed manually by experts or can be derived automatically using some sort of clustering algorithm. Clustering groups the data instances into subsets in such a manner that similar instances are grouped together; different instances belong to different groups. The instances are thereby organized into an efficient representation that characterizes the population being sampled.

Yuan and Shaw (1995) suggest a simple algorithm to generate a set of membership functions on numerical data. Assume attribute a_i has numerical value x from the domain X. We can cluster X to k linguistic terms $v_{i,j}, j = 1, \ldots, k$. The size of k is manually predefined. For the first linguistic term $v_{i,1}$, the following membership function is used:

$$
\mu_{v_{i,1}}(x) = \begin{cases} 1 & x \leq m_1 \\ \dfrac{m_2 - x}{m_2 - m_1} & m_1 < x < m_2 \\ 0 & x \geq m_2 \end{cases} \qquad (14.5)
$$

For each $v_{i,j}$ when $j = 2, \ldots, k-1$ has a triangular membership function as follows:

$$\mu_{v_{i,j}}(x) = \begin{cases} 0 & x \leq m_{j-1} \\ \dfrac{x - m_{j-1}}{m_j - m_{j-1}} & m_{j-1} < x \leq m_j \\ \dfrac{m_{j+1} - x}{m_{j+1} - m_j} & m_j < x < m_{j+1} \\ 0 & x \geq m_{j+1} \end{cases} . \qquad (14.6)$$

Finally, the membership function of the last linguistic term $v_{i,k}$ is:

$$\mu_{v_{i,k}}(x) = \begin{cases} 0 & x \leq m_{k-1} \\ \dfrac{x - m_{k-1}}{m_k - m_{k-1}} & m_{k-1} < x \leq m_k \\ 1 & x \geq m_k \end{cases} . \qquad (14.7)$$

Figure 14.3 illustrates the creation of four groups defined on the age attribute: "young", "early adulthood", "middle-aged" and "old age". Note that the first set ("young") and the last set ("old age") have a trapezoidal form which can be uniquely described by the four corners. For example, the "young" set could be represented as $(0, 0, 16, 32)$. In between, all other sets ("early adulthood" and "middle-aged") have a triangular form which can be uniquely described by the three corners. For example, the set "early adulthood" is represented as $(16, 32, 48)$.

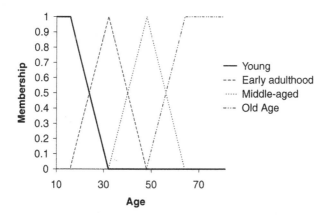

Fig. 14.3   Membership function for various groups in the age attribute.

Require: X — a set of values, $\eta(t)$ — some monotonic decreasing scalar function representing the learning rate.

Ensure: $M = \{m_1, \ldots, m_k\}$

1: Initially set m_i to be evenly distributed on the range of X.

2: $t \leftarrow 1$

3: **repeat**

4:    Randomly draw one sample x from X

5:    Find the closest center m_c to x.

6:    $m_c \leftarrow m_c + \eta(t) \cdot (x - m_c)$

7:    $t \leftarrow t + 1$

8:    $D(X, M) \leftarrow \sum\limits_{x \in X} \min_i \|x - m_i\|$

9: **until** $D(X, M)$ converges

Fig. 14.4   Algorithm for fuzzifying numeric attributes.

The only parameters that need to be determined are the set of k centers $M = \{m_1, \ldots, m_k\}$. The centers can be found using the algorithm presented in Figure 14.4. Note that in order to use the algorithm, a monotonic decreasing learning rate function should be provided.

14.6.2   *Inducing of Fuzzy Decision Tree*

The induction algorithm of fuzzy decision tree is presented in Figure 14.5. The algorithm measures the classification ambiguity associated with each attribute and splits the data using the attribute with the smallest classification ambiguity. The classification ambiguity of attribute a_i with linguistic terms $v_{i,j}, j = 1, \ldots, k$ on fuzzy evidence S, denoted as $G(a_i|S)$, is the weighted average of classification ambiguity calculated as:

$$G(a_i|S) = \sum_{j='1}^{k} w(v_{i,j}|S) \cdot G(v_{i,j}|S), \qquad (14.8)$$

where $w(v_{i,j}|S)$ is the weight which represents the relative size of $v_{i,j}$ and is defined as:

$$w(v_{i,j}|S) = \frac{M(v_{i,j}|S)}{\sum\limits_{k} M(v_{i,k}|S)}. \qquad (14.9)$$

The classification ambiguity of $v_{i,j}$ is defined as $G(v_{i,j}|S) = g(\vec{p}(C|v_{i,j}))$, which is measured based on the possibility distribution vector $\vec{p}(C|v_{i,j}) = (p(c_1|v_{i,j}), \ldots, p(c_{|k|}|v_{i,j}))$.

Require: S — Training Set A — Input Feature Set y — Target Feature
Ensure: Fuzzy Decision Tree
1: Create a new fuzzy tree FT with a single root node.
2: **if** S is empty OR Truth level of one of the classes $\geq \beta$ **then**
3:     Mark FT as a leaf with the most common value of y in S as a label.
4:     Return FT.
5: **end if**
6: $\forall a_i \in A$ find a with the smallest classification ambiguity.
7: **for** each outcome v_i of a **do**
8:     Recursively call procedure with corresponding partition v_i.
9:     Connect the root node to the returned subtree with an edge that is labeled as v_i.
10: **end for**
11: Return FT

Fig. 14.5   Fuzzy decision tree induction.

Given $v_{i,j}$, the possibility of classifying an object to class c_l can be defined as:

$$p\left(c_l \left| v_{i,j}\right.\right) = \frac{S(v_{i,j}, c_l)}{\max_k S(v_{i,j}, c_k)}, \tag{14.10}$$

where $S(A, B)$ is the fuzzy subsethood that was defined in Definition 14.5. The function $g(\vec{p})$ is the possibilistic measure of ambiguity or non-specificity and is defined as:

$$g(\vec{p}) = \sum_{i=1}^{|\vec{p}|} (p_i^* - p_{i+1}^*) \cdot \ln(i), \tag{14.11}$$

where $\vec{p}^* = (p_1^*, \ldots, p_{|\vec{p}|}^*)$ is the permutation of the possibility distribution $\vec{p}$ sorted such that $p_i^* \geq p_{i+1}^*$.

All the above calculations are carried out at a predefined significant level α. An instance will take into consideration of a certain branch $v_{i,j}$ only if its corresponding membership is greater than α. This parameter is used to filter out insignificant branches.

After partitioning the data using the attribute with the smallest classification ambiguity, the algorithm looks for non-empty branches. For each non-empty branch, the algorithm calculates the truth level of classifying all instances within the branch into each class. The truth level is calculated using the fuzzy subsethood measure $S(A, B)$.

If the truth level of one of the classes is above a predefined threshold β then no additional partitioning is needed and the node become a leaf in which all instance will be labeled to the class with the highest truth level. Otherwise the procedure continues in a recursive manner. Note that small values of β will lead to smaller trees with the risk of underfitting. A higher β may lead to a larger tree with higher classification accuracy. However, at a certain point, higher values β may lead to overfitting.

14.7 Simplifying the Decision Tree

Each path of branches from root to leaf can be converted into a rule with the condition part representing the attributes on the passing branches from the root to the leaf and the conclusion part representing the class at the leaf with the highest truth level classification. The corresponding classification rules can be further simplified by removing one input attribute term at a time for each rule we try to simplify. Select the term to remove with the highest truth level of the simplified rule. If the truth level of this new rule is not lower than the threshold β or the truth level of the original rule, the simplification is successful. The process will continue until no further simplification is possible for all the rules.

14.8 Classification of New Instances

In a regular decision tree, only one path (rule) can be applied for every instance. In a fuzzy decision tree, several paths (rules) can be applied for one instance. In order to classify an unlabeled instance, the following steps should be performed [Yuan and Shaw (1995)]:

- Step 1: Calculate the membership of the instance for the condition part of each path (rule). This membership will be associated with the label (class) of the path.
- Step 2: For each class, calculate the maximum membership obtained from all applied rules.
- Step 3: An instance may be classified into several classes with different degrees based on the membership calculated in Step 2.

14.9 Other Fuzzy Decision Tree Inducers

There have been several fuzzy extensions to the ID3 algorithm. The UR-ID3 algorithm [Maher and Clair (1993)] starts by building a strict decision tree, and subsequently fuzzifies the conditions of the tree. Tani and Sakoda

(1992) use the ID3 algorithm to select effective numerical attributes. The obtained splitting intervals are used as fuzzy boundaries. Regression is then used in each sub-space to form fuzzy rules. Cios and Sztandera (1992) use the ID3 algorithm to convert a decision tree into a layer of a feedforward neural network. Each neuron is represented as a hyperplane with a fuzzy boundary. The nodes within the hidden layer are generated until some fuzzy entropy is reduced to zero. New hidden layers are generated until there is only one node at the output layer.

Fuzzy-CART [Jang (1994)] is a method which uses the CART algorithm to build a tree. However, the tree, which is the first step, is only used to propose fuzzy sets of the continuous domains (using the generated thresholds). Then, a layered network algorithm is employed to learn fuzzy rules. This produces more comprehensible fuzzy rules and improves the CART's initial results.

Another complete framework for building a fuzzy tree including several inference procedures based on conflict resolution in rule-based systems and efficient approximate reasoning methods was presented in [Janikow, 1998].

Olaru and Wehenkel (2003) presented a new type of fuzzy decision trees called soft decision trees (SDT). This approach combines tree-growing and pruning, to determine the structure of the soft decision tree. Refitting and backfitting are ised to improve its generalization capabilities. The researchers empirically showed that soft decision trees are significantly more accurate than standard decision trees. Moreover, a global model variance study shows a much lower variance for soft decision trees than for standard trees as a direct cause of the improved accuracy.

Peng (2004) has used FDT to improve the performance of the classical inductive learning approach in manufacturing processes. Peng proposed using soft discretization of continuous-valued attributes. It has been shown that FDT can deal with the noise or uncertainties existing in the data collected in industrial systems.

Chapter 15

Hybridization of Decision Trees with other Techniques

15.1 Introduction

Hybridization in artificial intelligence (AI) involves simultaneously using two or more intelligent techniques in order to handle real world complex problems, involving imprecision, uncertainty and vagueness. Hybridization is frequently practiced in machine learning, to make more powerful and reliable classifiers.

The combination or integration of additional methodologies can be done in any form: by modularly integrating two or more intelligent methodologies, which maintains the identity of each methodology; by fusing one methodology into another; or by transforming the knowledge representation in one methodology into another form of representation characteristic to another methodology.

Hybridization of decision trees with other AI techniques can be performed by using either a decision tree to partition the instance space for other induction techniques or other AI techniques for obtaining a better decision tree.

15.2 A Framework for Instance-Space Decomposition

In the first approach, termed instance-space decomposition (ISD) and involving hybrid decision tree with other inducers, the instance space of the original problem is partitioned into several sub-spaces using a decision tree with a distinct classifier assigned to each sub-space. Subsequently, an unlabeled, previously unseen instance is classified by employing the classifier that was assigned to the sub-space to which the instance belongs.

In an approach, which Cohen *et al.* (2007) term decision tree ISD, the partition of the instance-space is attained by a decision tree. Along with the decision tree, the ISD method employs another classification method, which classifies the tree's leaves (the tree's leaves represent the different sub-spaces). Namely, decision tree ISD methods produce decision tree *s*, in which the leaves are assigned classifiers rather than simple class labels. When a non-decision tree method produces the leaves' classifiers, the composite classifier is sometimes termed a decision tree hybrid classifier.

The term "decision tree hybrid classifier", however, is also used in a broader context, such as in cases where a sub-classification method decides about the growth of the tree and its pruning [Sakar and Mammone (1993)].

There are two basic techniques for implementing decision tree ISD. The first technique is to use some decision tree method to create the tree and then, in a post-growing phase, to attach classifiers to the tree's leaves. The second technique is to consider the classifiers as part of the tree-growing procedure. Potentially, the latter technique can achieve more accurate composite classifiers. On the other hand, it usually requires more computationally intensive procedures.

Carvalho and Freitas. (2004) proposed a hybrid decision-tree genetic-algorithm GA classifier, which grows a decision tree and assigns some of the leaves with class labels and the others with GA classifiers. The leaves with the classifiers are those that have a small number of corresponding instances. A previously unseen instance is subsequently either directly assigned with a class label or is sub-classified by a GA classifier (depending on the leaf to which the instance is sorted). Zhou and Chen (2002) suggested a method, called hybrid decision tree (HDT). HDT uses the binary information gain ratio criterion to grow a binary decision tree in an instance-space that is defined by the nominal explaining-attributes only. A feed-forward neural network, subsequently classifies the leaves, whose diversity exceeds a pre-defined threshold. The network only uses the ordinal explaining-attributes.

In this chapter, we focus on the second decision tree ISD technique, which considers the classifiers as part of the decision tree's growth. NBTree is a method which produces a decision tree naive-Bayes hybrid classifier [Kohavi (1996)]. In order to decide when to stop the recursive partition of the instance-space (i.e. stop growing the tree), NBTree compares two alternatives: partitioning the instance-space further on (i.e. continue splitting the tree) versus stopping the partition and producing a single naive Bayes classifier. The two alternatives are compared in terms of their error estimations, which are calculated by a cross-validation procedure. Naive Bayes classification, by itself, is very efficient in terms of its processing time. However, using cross-validation significantly increases the overall computational complexity. Although Kohavi has used naive Bayes, to produce the classifiers, other classification methods are also applicable. However, due to the cross-validation estimations, NBTree becomes computationally expensive for methods that are more time-consuming than naive Bayes (e.g. neural networks).

We describe a simple framework for decision tree ISD, termed decision tree framework for instance space decomposition (DFID). The framework hierarchically partitions the instance space using a top-down (pruning-free) decision tree procedure. Although various DFID implementations use different stopping rules, split-validation examinations and splitting rules, in this chapter we concentrate on a specific DFID method — contrasted populations miner (CPOM). The splitting rule that this method uses — grouped gain ratio — combines the well-accepted gain ratio criterion with a heuristic grouping procedure. CPOM can reduce the processing time while keeping the composite classifier accurate.

Implementations of DFID consist of a decision-tree (as a wrapper) and another embedded classification method (this method can, in principle, also be a decision tree). The embedded classification method generates the multiple classifiers for the tree's leaves. The DFID sequence is illustrated by the pseudo code in Figure 14.1. DFID inputs are: training instances; a list of attributes (which will be examined as candidates for splitting the decision tree); a classification method; and, optionally (depending on the specific implementation), some additional parameters.

The procedure begins by creating the decision tree's root node. The root represents the entire instance space X. When constructed, each node is attached with a rule which defines the sub-space of X that the node represents. The DFID framework considers rules that can be expressed in a conjunctive normal form. A rule may be, for example: "$(A_1 = 3 \vee A_1 = 4) \wedge A_2 = 1$". DFID then checks whether there should be a split from the root node (i.e. whether X should be partitioned). This check, which uses some stopping rules, is represented, in Figure 14.1 by the general function StoppingCriterion. The function receives some inputs (depending on the specific implementation) and returns a Boolean value that indicates whether the stopping rules are met. If the stopping rules are met, then I is trained using all of the training instances. The classifier that results is attached to the root node and the procedure terminates. If, however, the stopping-rules are not met, then DFID searches for a split, according to some splitting rule, represented in Figure 14.1 by the general function split.

Splits in DFID are based on the values of a certain candidate attribute. We assume that there exists at least a single attribute that can create a split (or otherwise the stopping-rules would have indicated that there should be no more splits).

The function split receives a training set, a set of candidate attributes and optionally some additional inputs. It then returns the attribute upon whose values the split is based and a set of descendents nodes. Recall that upon its creation, each node is attached with a rule, which defines the sub-space of X that the node represents. The rules for the descendent nodes are conjunctions of the root's rule and restrictions on the values of the selected attribute. The split that was found may be then subjected to a validation examination, represented, in Figure 14.1 by the general function validate. If a split is found to be invalid, then DFID will search for another split (another attribute). If there are no more candidate attributes, I will be trained using all the training instances and the classifier that results will be attached to the root node. As soon as a valid split is found, the descendent nodes that were created by the split are recursively considered for further splits. Further splits are achieved by the recurrence of DFID. In the recurrence, only a subset of the training instances is relevant (the instances that are actually sorted to the certain descendent node). In addition, the attribute, which defined the current split, is removed from the list of candidate attributes. The descendents are finally linked to their parent (the root). Different DFID implementations may differ in all or some of the procedures that implement the three main framework components — stopping-rules (the function StoppingCriterion), splitting rules (the function split) and split validation examinations (the function validate).

15.2.1 *Stopping Rules*

Stopping rules are checked by the general function StoppingCriterion (Figure 14.1). However, it should be noticed that a negative answer by this function is not the only condition that stops the DFID recurrence; another, and even more natural, condition, is the lack of any valid split.

According to the simple stopping rule that NBTree uses, no splits are considered when there are 30 instances or less in the examined node. Splitting a node with only a few training instances will hardly affect the final accuracy and will lead, on the other hand, to a complex and less comprehensible decision tree (and hence a complex and less comprehensible composite classifier). Moreover, since the classifiers are required to generalize from the instances in their sub-spaces, they must be trained on samples of sufficient size.

Kohavi's stopping-rule can be revised into a rule that never considers further splits in nodes that correspond to $\beta|S|$ instances or less, where $0 < \beta < 1$ is a proportion and $|S|$ is the number of instances in original training set, S. When using this stopping rule (either in Kohavi's way or in the revised version), a threshold parameter must be provided to DFID as well as to the function StoppingCriterion. Another heuristic stopping rule is never to consider splitting a node, if a single classifier can accurately describe the node's sub-space (i.e. if a single classifier which was trained by all of the training instances, and using the classification method appear to be accurate). Practically, this rule can be checked by comparing an accuracy estimation of the classifier to a predefined threshold (thus, using this rule requires an additional parameter). The motivation for this stopping rule is that if a single classifier is good enough, why replace it with a more complex tree that also has less generalization capabilities? Finally, as mentioned above, another (inherent) stopping-rule of DFID is the lack of even a single candidate attribute.

15.2.2 *Splitting Rules*

The core question of DFID is how to split nodes. The answer to this question lies in the general function split (Figure 14.1). It should be noted that any splitting rule that is used to grow a pure decision tree, is also suitable in DFID.

Kohavi (1996) has suggested a new splitting rule, which selects the attribute with the highest value of a measure, which he refers to as the "utility". Kohavi defines the utility as the fivefold cross-validation accuracy estimation of using a naive-Bayes method for classifying the sub-spaces which will be generated by the considered split.

15.2.3 *Split Validation Examinations*

Since splitting rules, are heuristic, it may be beneficial to regard the splits they produce as recommendations that should be validated. Kohavi (1996) validated a split by estimating the reduction in error, which is gained by the split and comparing it to a predefined threshold of 5% (i.e. if it is estimated that the split will reduce the overall error rate by only 5% or less, the split is regarded as invalid). In an NBTree, it is enough to examine only the first proposed split in order to conclude that there are no valid splits, if the one examined is invalid. This follows since in an NBTree, the attribute according to which the split is done is the one that maximizes the utility measure, which is strictly increasing with the reduction in error. If a split, in accordance with the selected attribute cannot reduce the accuracy by more than 5%, then no other split can.

We suggest a new split validation procedure. In very general terms, a split according to the values of a certain attribute is regarded as invalid if the sub-spaces that result from this split are similar enough to be grouped together.

15.3 The Contrasted Population Miner (CPOM) Algorithm

This section presents the CPOM, which splits nodes according to a novel splitting rule, termed grouped gain ratio. Generally speaking, this splitting rule is based on the gain ratio criterion [Quinlan (1993)], followed by a grouping heuristic. The gain ratio criterion selects a single attribute from the set of candidate attributes, and the grouping heuristic thereafter groups together sub-spaces which correspond to different values of the selected attribute.

15.3.1 *CPOM Outline*

CPOM uses two stopping rules. First, the algorithm compares the number of training instances to a predefined ratio of the number of instances in the original training set. If the subset is too small, CPOM stops (since it is undesirable to learn from too small a training subset). Secondly, CPOM compares the accuracy estimation of a single classifier to a pre-defined threshold. It stops if the accuracy estimation exceeds the threshold (if a single classifier is accurate enough, there is no point in splitting further on). Therefore, in addition to the inputs in Figure 15.1, CPOM must receive two parameters: β, the minimal ratio of the training instances and acc, the maximal accuracy estimation that will still result in split considerations.

CPOM's split validation procedure is directly based on grouped gain ratio. The novel rule is described in detail, in the following subsection; however, in general terms, the rule returns the splitting attribute and a set of descendent nodes. The nodes represent sub-spaces of X that are believed

```
DFID (S, A, I)
Where:
S - Training Set
A - Input Feature Set
I - Inducer

Create a tree with a root node;
IF StoppingCriterion(S, A, I) THEN
    Attach the classifier I(S, A) to the root;
ELSE
    A* ← A;
    valid ← FALSE;
    WHILE A* ≠ ∅ and NOT(valid)
            (SplitAtt, nodes) ← split(S, A*);
            IF validate(nodes, SplitAtt, S)   THEN
                valid ← TRUE;
                A ← A − SplitAtt;
                FOR each node ∈ nodes
                    Generate classifier DFID(NodeInstances, A, I);
                    Attach the classifier to node;
                    Link the node to root;
                END FOR
            ELSE
                A* ← A * −SplitAtt;
    END WHILE
    IF NOT (valid) THEN
        Attach the classifier I(S, A) to the root;
    END IF
END IF
RETURN tree;
```

Fig. 15.1   DFID outline: A DFID implementation recursively partitions the instance space of the training set, according to the values of the candidate attributes. As the recursive partition ends, classifiers are attached to the leaves by employing the embedded classification method.

to be different. If the procedure returns just a single descendent node, the split it has generated is regarded as invalid.

15.3.2 *The Grouped Gain Ratio Splitting Rule*

Grouped gain ratio is based on the gain ratio criterion followed by a grouping heuristic. The gain ratio criterion selects a single attribute from a set of candidate attributes. The instance sub-space, whose partition we are now considering, may, in principle, be partitioned so that each new sub-subspace will correspond to a unique value of the selected attribute. Group gain ratio avoids this alternative, through heuristically grouping sub-subspaces together. By grouping sub-subspaces together, grouped gain ratio increases the generalization capabilities, since there are more instances in a group of sub-subspaces than there are in the individual sub-subspaces.

Clearly, if we separately train I on each subset and obtain the same exact classifier from each subset, then there is no point in the split, since using this single classifier for the entire instance space is as accurate as using the multiple classifiers; it is also much simpler and understandable, and it can generalize better. The other direction of this argument is slightly less straightforward. If the classifiers that were trained over the training subsets are very different from one another, then none of them can classify X as one, and we can believe that the split is beneficial. Based on this observation, the grouped gain ratio splitting rule groups together sub-spaces that have similar classifiers.

The intuition regarding the classifier comparisons raises questions of what is similar, what is different and how to compare classifiers? Although there may be multiple classifiers, all of which must be simultaneously compared to each other, we begin answering these questions with the simpler case of exactly two classifiers, using a comparison heuristic, which we refer to as cross-inspection (see Figure 15.2).

Cross-inspection is based on two mutually-exclusive training subsets and a classification method as inputs. The comparison begins by randomly partitioning each subset into a training sub-subset and a test sub-subset. Then, two classifiers are produced, by training the input method, once over each training sub-subset. After producing the two classifiers, the cross-inspection heuristic calculates the error rates of each classifier over each of the test sub-subsets. If the error rate of the first classifier over the first test sub-subset is significantly (with confidence level alpha) different from the error of the first classifier over the second test sub-subset, or vice versa, then the two classifiers are regarded as different. The errors are compared by testing the hypothesis that the errors are generated by the same binomial random variable [Dietterich (1998)].

The cross-inspection heuristic compares only two distinct classifiers. However, in the DFID framework, more than two classifiers must be compared at a time (if the attribute, which was selected by the gain ratio criterion, has more than two possible values). For example, if it is believed that graduate students from different schools behave differently, one may consider splitting according to the school's name. The attribute school can receive multiple values, all of which will have to be compared simultaneously. A successful split will group similar schools together, while different schools will be in different groups. Since an exhaustive search, over all the possible groupings, is unacceptable in terms of complexity, grouped gain ratio (see Figure 15.4) uses a greedy grouping heuristic, which is based on cross-inspection.

The procedure begins by using cross-inspection, to compare all the distinct pairs of classifiers (if there are q classifiers, there are $q(q\text{-}1)/2$ comparisons). For each instance sub-space, the procedure computes the number of instances that belong to sub-spaces that are similar to it (by definition the similarity by cross-inspection is defined with regard to classifiers rather than sub-spaces; each sub-space, however, is described by a classifier). The classifier that represents the sub-space with the largest such number is regarded as the classifier that covers the maximal number of instances. The sub-spaces of all the instances which are covered by this classifier are grouped together, and the procedure iterates. The heuristic does not explicitly guarantee that any two classifiers in a group are equivalent, but equivalence is assumed to be a transitive relation. The greedy grouping procedure is a simple clustering method and other clustering methods, like graph coloring [Zupan *et al.* (1998)] may also be suitable here. Alternatively one could use the Warshall algorithm [Warshall (1962)] for finding the transitive closure of the comparison matrix, which can be used for calculating $\sup_j$. However, this form of calculation will not be convenient in this case because it will tend to group too much as the following example illustrates.

Cohen *et al.* (2007) demonstrated that CPOM improved the obtained accuracy compared to the examined embedded methods (naive Bayes, backpropagation and C4.5). Not only was CPOM more accurate than other decision tree ISD methods, the grouping heuristic significantly improved the accuracy results, compared to a CPOM variation which does not

```
CrossInspection (S₁,S₂,I,α)

Where:
S₁, S₂ - Mutually-exclusive training sets
I - Inducer
α - Confidence level

S₁₁ ← a random sample from S₁;
S₁₂ ← S₁ − S₁₁;
S₂₁ ← a random sample from S₂;
S₂₂ ← S₂ − S₂₁;
H₁ ← I(S₁₁);
H₂ ← I(S₂₁);
FOR i,j ∈{1,2} DO
      εᵢ,ⱼ ← accuracy estimation of Hᵢ over Sⱼ,₂;
END FOR
IF ε₁,₂ is different from ε₁,₁ with a confidence level α OR
      ε₂,₁ is different from ε₂,₂ with a confidence level α THEN
      return FALSE;
ELSE
      return TRUE;
```

Fig. 15.2   The cross-inspection procedure outline: Searching for statistical significance, the procedure compares the accuracy estimations of two distinct classifiers.

group. Finally, using three synthetic datasets, CPOM distinguished between different populations in an underlined dataset.

15.4   Induction of Decision Trees by an Evolutionary Algorithm (EA)

EAs are stochastic search algorithms inspired by the concept of Darwinian evolution. The motivation for applying EAs to data mining tasks is that they are robust, adaptive search techniques that perform a global search in the solution space [Freitas (2005)]. Since a well-designed EA continually considers new solutions, it can be viewed as an "anytime" learning algorithm capable of quite quickly producing a good-enough solution. It then continues to search the solution space, reporting the new "best" solution whenever one is found.

GroupedGainRatio $(S, A, I, root, \alpha)$

Where:

S - Training Set

A - Input Feature Set

I - Inducer

$root$ - the node from which the split is considered

α confidence level

$A_i \leftarrow$ the attribute from A with the maximal gain ratio;

$S_1, S_2, \ldots, S_{d(i)} \leftarrow$ a partition of S, according to values of A_i;

FOR all $j, k \in \{1, 2, \ldots ,\text{d(i)}\}$ so that $j \leq k$

    $E_{j,k} \leftarrow$ CrossInspection(S_j, S_k, I, α)

    $E_{k,j} \leftarrow E_{j,k}$;

END FOR

FOR all $j \in \{1, 2, \ldots ,\text{d(i)}\}$

    $sup_j \leftarrow$ the number of instances in the

            subsets S_k for which $E_{j,k}$=TRUE;

END FOR

$L \leftarrow$ a list of the subsets indices sorted descending by sup_j;

$nodes \leftarrow$ an empty set of nodes

WHILE L is not empty DO

    Create a new node;

    Attach the rule which is a conjecture of the root's rule

           and a disjoint of the values that correspond to

           S_j the first member of L and the members

           S_k for which $E_{j,k}$=TRUE;

    Remove from L any member that is described by the new

node;

    Add node to nodes;

END WHILE

RETURN $(A_i, nodes)$

Fig. 15.3   The grouped gain ratio procedure outline. The procedure groups together similar values of a candidate attribute. Similarity is based on the cross-inspection heuristic.

GA, a popular type of EA, have been successfully used for feature selection. Figure 14.5 presents a high level pseudo code of GA adapted from [Freitas (2005)].

GA begin by randomly generating a population of L candidate solutions. Given such a population, a GA generates a new candidate solution (population element) by selecting two of the candidate solutions as the parent solutions. This process is termed reproduction. Generally, parents are selected randomly from the population with a bias toward the better candidate solutions. Given two parents, one or more new solutions are generated by taking some characteristics of the solution from the first parent (the "father") and some from the second parent (the "mother"). This process is termed "crossover". For example, in GA that use binary encoding of n bits to represent each possible solution, we might randomly select a crossover bit location denoted as o. Two descendant solutions could then be generated. The first descendant would inherit the first o string characteristics from the father and the remaining $n - o$ characteristics from the mother. The second descendant would inherit the first o string characteristics from the mother and the remaining $n - o$ characteristics from the father. This type of crossover is the most common and it is termed one-point crossover. Crossover is not necessarily applied to all pairs of individuals selected for mating: a $P_{crossover}$ probability is used in order to decide whether crossover will be applied. If crossover is not applied, the offspring are simply duplications of the parents.

Finally, once descendant solutions are generated, GA allow characteristics of the solutions to be changed randomly in a process known as mutation. In the binary encoding representation, according to a certain probability (P_{mut}), each bit is changed from its current value to the opposite value. Once a new population has been generated, it is decoded and evaluated. The process continues until some termination criterion is satisfied. A GA converges when most of the population is identical, or in other words, when the diversity is minimal.

Based on the pseudo code, one should provide the following ingredients when using a GA algorithm for decision trees: crossover operator, mutation operator, fitness function, a method to create the initial population and a stopping criterion.

Several GA-based systems, which learn decision trees in the top-down manner have been proposed, such as BTGA [Chai *et al.* (1996)], OC1-ES [Cantu-Paz and Kamath (2003)] and DDT-EA [Krtowski (2004)]. Generally, they apply an evolutionary approach to the test search, especially in the form of hyper-planes.

The GDT-EA algorithm [Krtowski and Grze (2005)] that we describe here searches for the whole tree at once in contrast to greedy, top-down

```
GA
Create initial population of individuals
      (candidate solutions)
Compute the fitness of each individual
REPEAT
      Select individuals based on fitness
      Apply genetic operators to selected individuals,
            creating new individuals
      Compute fitness of each of the new individuals
      Update the current population
            (new individuals replace old individuals)
UNTIL (stopping criterion)
```

Fig. 15.4   A Pseudo code for GA.

approaches. The initial population is generated by applying a standard top-down decision tree inducers but attributes are selected in a dipolar way. Specifically, two instances from different classes are randomly chosen. Then an attribute which differentiates between the two instances is selected.

The Fitness function is composed of two terms: the classification accuracy on the training set and the tree complexity. Specifically, the fitness function, which must be maximized, has the following form:

$$Fitness = Acc - \alpha \cdot S, \qquad (15.1)$$

where Acc is the classification quality estimated on the learning set; S is the size of the tree (number of nodes); and α — is a parameter which indicate the relative importance of the complexity term. The value of α should be provided by the user by tuning it to the specific problem that is solved.

The algorithm terminates if the fitness of the best individual in the population does not improve during the fixed number of generations. This status indicates, that the algorithm has converged. Additionally, the maximum number of generations is specified, which allows limiting the computation time in case of a slow convergence.

Like many other GAs, the GDT-EA also has two operators: *MutateNode* (for mutation) and *CrossTrees* (for crossover). The first operator MutateN-ode, which is applied with the given probability to every node of the tree, can modify the test or change the node structure. If a non-leaf node is concerned it can be pruned to a leaf or its test can be altered. Specifically, there are four modification options in case of non-leaf node:

• A completely new test is applied with another randomly chosen attribute and threshold.
• A new threshold is randomly chosen without changing the attribute used in the test.
• The current sub-tree is replaced by a sub-tree of an adjacent node.
• The test can be exchanged with another test taken from randomly chosen descendant-nodes.

If a leaf node is to be mutated, then there are two options:

• The leaf node is replaced with a non-leaf node with a new randomly chosen test.
• The leaf node is replaced with a sub-tree generated using an appropriate algorithm.

The CrossTrees operator is equivalent to the standard crossover operator. It alters two solutions by exchanging certain parts of input trees. There are three possible exchange types: two types of sub-tree exchanges and an exchange of only tests. At the beginning, regardless of the type, one node in each tree is randomly chosen. Then the type of exchange between trees is decided.

In the first CrossTree variant, the tests that are associated with the chosen nodes are substituted. This option is valid only when the chosen nodes have the same number of outgoing branches. In the second CrossTree variant, we substitute the sub-trees starting from the chosen nodes. The third CrossTree variant actually combines the first two variants. Branches which start from the chosen nodes are exchanged in random order.

Chapter 16

Decision Trees and Recommender Systems

16.1 Introduction

Recommender Systems (RS) are considered to be a very popular research area as they offer users useful and interesting items that increase both the seller's profit and the buyer's satisfaction. They contribute to the commercial success of many on-line ventures such as Amazon.com and NetFlix. Examples of recommended items include movies, web pages, books, news items and more. Often a RS attempts to predict the rating a user will give to items based on his or her past ratings and the ratings of other (similar) users.

RSs are primarily directed towards individuals who lack sufficient personal experience or competence to evaluate the potentially overwhelming number of alternative items that a Websitemay offer. A case in point is a book recommender system that assists users to select a book to read. In the popular Website, Amazon.com, the site employs an RS to personalize the online store for each customer. Since recommendations are usually personalized, different users or user groups receive dissimilar suggestions. In addition, there are non-personalized recommendations. These are much simpler to generate and are normally featured in magazines or newspapers. Typical examples include the top ten selections of books, CDs etc. While they may be useful and effective in certain situations, these types of non-personalized recommendations are typically not the ones to be addressed by RS research.

In their simplest form, personalized recommendations are offered as ranked lists of items. RSs try to predict the most suitable products or services based on the user's preferences and constraints. In order to complete such a computational task, RSs collect from users their preferences, which are either explicitly expressed, e.g. as products ratings, or are inferred by interpreting the user's actions. For instance, an RS may consider the navigation to a particular product page as an implicit sign of preference for the items shown on that page.

RSs' development has its origins in a rather simple observation: individuals often rely on recommendations provided by others in making mundane decisions. For example, it is common to rely on what one's peers recommend when selecting a book to read; employers count on recommendation letters in their recruiting decisions; and when selecting a movie to watch, individuals tend to trust the movie reviews that a film critic has written and which appear in the newspaper they read.

In seeking to mimic this behavior, the first RSs applied algorithms to leverage recommendations produced by a community of users to deliver recommendations to an active user, i.e. a user looking for suggestions. The recommendations were for items that similar users (those with similar tastes) had liked. This approach is termed collaborative-filtering (CF) and its rationale is that if the active user agreed in the past with some users, then the other recommendations coming from these similar users should be relevant as well and of interest to the active user.

16.2 Using Decision Trees for Recommending Items

Decision Trees are used as a model-based approach for recommender systems. The use of decision trees for building recommendation models offers several benefits, such as: efficiency, interpretability and flexibility in handling a variety of input data types (ratings, demographic, contextual, etc.).

However, simply using existing decision tree induction algorithms for recommendation tasks is not always straightforward. A major weakness in using decision trees as a prediction model in RS is the need to build a huge number of trees (either for each item or for each user). Moreover, the model can only compute the expected rating of a single item at a time. To provide recommendations to the user, we must traverse the tree(s) from root to leaf once for each item in order to compute its predicted rating. Only after computing the predicted rating of all items can the RS provide the recommendations (highest predicted rating items). Thus, decision trees in RS do not scale well with respect to the number of items.

Gershman *et al.* (2010) propose a modification to the decision tree model, to make it of practical use for larger scale RS. Instead of predicting the rating of an item, the decision tree would return a weighted list of recommended items. Thus, with just a single traverse of the tree, recommendations can be constructed and provided to the user. This variation of decision tree based RS is described in Section 16.2.1.

Gershman *et al.* (2010) also introduce a new heuristic criterion for building the decision tree. Instead of picking the split attribute to be the attribute which produces the largest information gain ratio, the proposed heuristic looks at the number of shared items between the divided sets. The split attribute which had the lowest probability of producing its number of shared items, when compared to a random split, was picked as the split attribute. This heuristic is described in further detail in Section 16.2.2. A comparison study shows that the new criterion outperforms the well-known information gain criterion in terms of predictive performance.

16.2.1 *RS-Adapted Decision Tree*

In recommender systems the input set for building the decision tree is composed of *Ratings*. *Ratings* can be described as a relation $<$ *ItemID, UserID, Rating* $>$ (in which $<$ *ItemID, UserID* $>$ is assumed to be a primary key). The users can be described by means of various attributes, such as the user's age, gender, occupation, etc. Other attributes can describe the various items, for example the weight, price, dimensions etc. *Rating* is the target attribute. Based on the training set, the system attempts to predict the *Rating* of items the user does not have a *Rating* for, and recommends to the user the items with the highest predicted *Rating*.

The construction of a decision tree is performed by a recursive process. The process starts at the root node with an input set (training set). At each node an item attribute is picked as the split attribute. For each possible value (or set of values) child-nodes are created and the parent's set is split between child-nodes so that each child-node receives all items that have the appropriate value(s) that correspond to this child-node as input-set. Picking the split-attribute is done heuristically since we cannot know which split will produce the best tree (the tree that produces the best results for future input), for example the popular C4.5 algorithm uses a heuristic that picks the split that produces the largest information gain out of all possible splits. One of the attributes is predefined as the target attribute. The recursive process continues until all the items in the node's set share the same target attribute value or the number of items reaches a certain threshold. Each leaf node is assigned a label (classifying its set of items); this label is the shared target attribute value or the most common value in case there is more than one such value.

Decision trees can be used for different recommender systems approaches:

- Collaborative Filtering (CF) — Decision trees can be used for building a CF system. Each instance in the training set refers to a single customer. The training set attributes refer to the feedback provided by the customer for each item in the system. In this case, a dedicated decision tree is built for each item. For this purpose, the feedback provided for the targeted item (for instance like/dislike) is considered to be the decision that is needed to be predicted, while the feedback provided for all other items is used as the input attributes (decision nodes). Figure 16.1 illustrates an example of such tree, when the item under discussion is a movie.

- Content-Based Approach — Content features can be used to build a decision tree. A separate decision tree is built for each user and is used as a user profile. The features of each item are used to build a model that explains the user's preferences. The information gain of every feature is used as the splitting criteria. Figure 16.2 (right) illustrates Bob's profile.

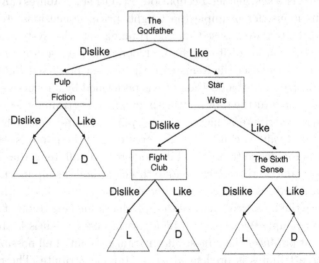

Fig. 16.1 A CF decision tree for whether users like the movie "The Usual Suspects" based on their preferences to other movies such as The Godfather, Pulp Fiction etc. A leaf labeled with "L" or "D" correspondingly indicates that the user likes/dislikes the movie "The Usual Suspects".

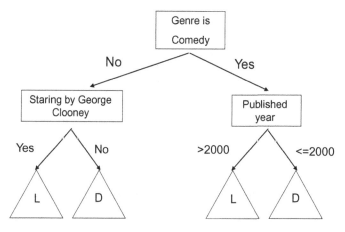

Fig. 16.2   A CB decision tree for Bob.

It should be noted that although this approach is interesting from a theoretical perspective, the precision rate that was reported for this system is not as accurate as that of recommending the average rating.

- Hybrid Approach — A hybrid decision tree can also be constructed. Only a single tree is constructed in this approach. The tree is similar to the collaborative approach in the way it treats the user's attributes as attributes to split by (such as her liking/disliking of a certain movie). But the attributes the tree utilizes are merely general attributes that represent the user's preference for the general case and that are based on the content of the items. The attributes are constructed based on the user's past ratings and the content of the items. For example, a user that rated negatively all movies of the comedy genre is assigned a low value in a "degree of liking comedy movies" attribute. Similarly to the collaborative approach, the constructed tree is applicable to all users. However, it is now also applicable to all items since the new attributes represent the user's preferences for all items and not only for a single given item. Figure 16.3 illustrates such a hybrid tree.

Consider a general case with a dataset containing n users, m items, and an average decision tree of height h. The collaborative filtering based RS requires m trees to be constructed, one for each item. When a user likes to receive a recommendation on what movie to watch, the system traverses all trees, from root to leaf, until it finds an item the user would like to view. The time complexity in this case is therefore $O(h \cdot m)$. This might be too slow for a large system that needs to provide fast and

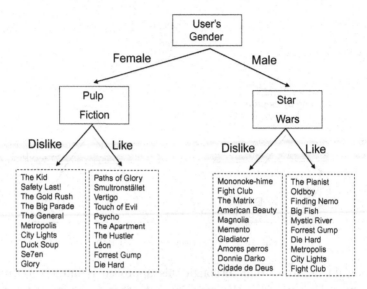

Fig. 16.3   An example CF-CB hybrid decision tree.

on-demand recommendations to users. The content based approach requires n individual trees to be constructed: one for each user. When a user likes to receive a recommendation, the system needs to traverse the user's tree from root to leaf once for each item, until it finds an item the user might like watching. Therefore, the time complexity in this case is $O(h \cdot m)$. Similarly, in the hybrid approach, the tree needs to be traversed once for each item, and here too the time complexity is $O(h \cdot m)$.

In systems that have multiple possible items to recommend and that require fast computation of recommendations, all the above decision tree based RS would be impractical. Therefore, it is required to revise the decision tree to better fit RS, and provide recommendations faster to users. The proposed algorithm is similar to the ID3 algorithm and uses the hybrid approach. Because we employ the hybrid approach, only a single tree is needed, whereas the attributes to split by are user's descriptive attributes. These qualities can be computed based on the user's past ratings and the content of the items, as shown in the example in Figure 16.3, but these can also include user profile attributes aforementioned. The major variation from the ID3 algorithm is in the tree's leaf nodes; instead of creating leaf nodes with a label that predicts the target attribute value (such as rating), each leaf holds a recommendation list. When a user wishes to receive recommendations, the tree is traversed based on the user's attributes until the leaf node is reached. The node contains a pre-computed recommendation list and this list is returned to the user. Thus, the time complexity is reduced to $O(h)$.

Building the recommendation list at the leaf node can be done in various ways. We selected the following solution: to compute the weighted average of the ratings in all tuples at the leaf's *Ratings* set and to prefer the items with the highest weighted average. Consider the rightmost leaf in the example tree in Figure 16.3. For any tuple $< i, u, r >$ in the *Ratings* set (i, u, r denote an item, a user and a rating respectively). At this leaf node we know that u has a degree of liking the comedy genre more than 0.5 and a degree of liking movies with the actor George Clooney more than 0.7. All the items rated by users such as u appear in this *Ratings* set alongside the ratings each user submitted. This leaf therefore contains the ratings of users similar to u. If we now pick the items that were rated the highest by the users similar to u, these would form a good recommendation for this user. Thus, we order all items based on a weighted average (since items can appear more than once, when more than one user rated them) and set this list as the recommendation list for this leaf node. The algorithm is presented in detail in Figure 16.4.

16.2.2   *Least Probable Intersections*

Based on the model constructed with the training set, decision trees seek to provide good results for new unseen cases. To accomplish this, the construction algorithm strives for a small tree (in terms of the number of nodes) that performs well on the training set. It is believed that a small tree generalizes better, avoids over fitting, and forms a simpler representation for users to understand. The C4.5 is a popular algorithm for constructing such decision trees. It employs the criterion of normalized information gain to pick the attribute which is used to split each node. The attribute with the largest normalized information gain is picked, as it provides the largest reduction in entropy. Since this is a heuristic, it does not guarantee the smallest possible tree.

In RS the input set for building the decision tree is composed of *Ratings*. *Ratings* can be described as a relation $< ItemID, UserID, Rating >$ (in which $< ItemID, UserID >$ is assumed to be a primary key). The intuition behind the heuristic proposed in this chapter is as follows. Consider a split into two subsets, A and B. The less *ItemIDs* are shared between the sets A and B, the better the split is since it forms a better distinction between

1: Create Root Node
2: **if** *Ratings.size* < *threshold* **then**
3:     *root.recommendations* ← *recommendation_list(Ratings)*
4:     Return root
5: **else**
6:     Let A be the user attribute that best classifies the input
7:     **for all** value v of A **do**
8:         Add a branch b below root, labeled $(A = v)$
9:         $Ratings_{s_v}$ ← subset of *Ratings* that have the value v for A.
10:        Add RS-Adapted-Decision-Tree($Ratings_{s_v}$) below this new branch b
11:    **end for**
12: **end if**
13: Return Root

Fig. 16.4   A modified decision tree for recommender systems.

the two groups. However, different splits may result in different group sizes. Comparing the size of the intersection between splits of different sub-relation sizes would not be sufficient since an even split for example (half the tuples in group A and half in group B) would probably have a larger intersection than a very uneven split (such as one tuple in group A and all the rest in group B). Instead, we look at the probability of our split's item-intersection size compared to a random (uniform) split of similar group sizes. A split which is very likely to occur even in a random split is considered a bad split (less preferred) since it is similar to a random split and probably does not distinguish the groups from each other. A split that is the least probable to occur is assumed to be a better distinction of the two subgroups and is the split selected by the heuristic.

More formally let us denote:

- $items(S) = \pi_{ItemID}(S)$, where π is the projection operation in relational algebra, the set of all *ItemIDs* that appear in a set S.
- $O_i(S) = |\sigma_{ItemID=i}(S)|$, where σ is the select operation in relation algebra, is the number of occurrences of the *ItemID* i in the set S.

Let S_q (q denotes the number of ratings) be a random binary partition of the tuples in *Ratings* into two sub-relations A and B consisting of k and $q - k$ tuples, respectively. We are interested in the probability distribution of $S_q \equiv |(items(A) \bigcap items(B)|$.

First, let us find the probability of an item belonging to the intersection. The probability of all o_i occurrences of any item i to be in the set A is $\left(\frac{k}{q}\right)^{o_i}$. Similarly, the probability for all o_i occurrences of an item i to be in the set B is $\left(\frac{q-k}{q}\right)^{o_i}$. In all other cases an item i will appear in the intersection, thus the probability P_i that an item i belongs to $items(A) \bigcap items(B)$ is:

$$P_i = 1 - \left(\frac{k}{q}\right)^{o_i} - \left(\frac{q-k}{q}\right)^{o_i}. \tag{16.1}$$

Next, we can construct a random variable x_i which takes the value 1 when an item i belongs to the intersection of A and B, and otherwise the value is 0. Using the above equation, the variable x_i is distributed according to a Bernoulli distribution with a success probability P_i. Thus, S_q is distributed as the sum of $|items(Ratings)|$ non-identically distributed Bernoulli random variables which can be approximated by a Poisson distribution:

$$Pr(S_q = j) = \frac{\lambda^j \cdot e^{-\lambda}}{j!}, \tag{16.2}$$

where

$$\lambda = \sum_{i \in items(Ratings)} P_i. \tag{16.3}$$

The cumulative distribution function (CDF) is therefore given by:

$$Pr(S_q \leq j) = \frac{\Gamma(\lfloor k+1 \rfloor, \lambda)}{\lfloor k \rfloor!}, \tag{16.4}$$

where $\Gamma(x, y)$ is the incomplete gamma function and $\lfloor k \rfloor$ is the floor function.

To summarize, given a binary split of *Ratings* into two sub-relations A and B, of sizes q and $q - k$ respectively. Our proposed heuristic initially computes the size of the item-intersection, $|(items(A) \bigcap items(B)| = j$. Next, we compute the probability of receiving such intersection size in a similar-size random split using the probability $Pr(S_q \leq j)$. Out of all possible splits of *Ratings*, our heuristic picks the one with the lowest probability $Pr(S_q \leq j)$ to be the next split in the tree.

16.3 Using Decision Trees for Preferences Elicitation

Most RS methods, such as collaborative filtering, cannot provide personalized recommendations until a user profile has been created. This is known as the new user cold-start problem. Several systems try to learn the new users' profiles as part of the sign up process by asking them to provide feedback regarding several items. In this section, we present an anytime preferences elicitation method that uses the idea of pairwise comparison between items. Our method uses a lazy decision tree, with pairwise comparisons at the decision nodes. Based on the user's response to a certain co mparison we select on-the-fly what pairwise comparison should next be asked. A comparative field study shows that the proposed pairwise approach provides more accurate recommendations than existing methods and requires less effort when signing up newcomers [Rokach and Kisilevich (2012)].

Most recommendation techniques use some types of a user profile or user model but these techniques cannot provide personalized recommendations until a user profile has been created. As the user interacts with the system, the profile can be incrementally established to eventually provide personalized recommendations. One way to address the challenge is to ask newcomers to fill-in a simple questionnaire that will lead them to an immediately beneficial recommendation.

Methods that ask the user to specify her preferences for item attributes are also known as preference elicitation or preference-based search. Research in the area has mainly focused on using a set of examples (e.g. the number of movies the user likes) or through a form of specifying the user's interests. Such approaches have drawbacks. While rating observed items is a painless process, using only a set of rated items can cause the system to later recommend only items similar to the ones the user rated. Furthermore, asking users to fill in lengthy forms is usually considered a boring chore and users tend to either avoid it or answer questions arbitrarily (e.g. always picking the first answer).

Decision trees can improve the initialization of the profile generation by using a questionnaire. The questionnaire is created as an interactive, easy-to-use process. At each stage the user is presented with two items and is asked to select the preferred item. The items are presented as pictures to make the answering process intuitive. The underlying process is "anytime" in the sense that although the user may choose to abandon the questionnaire at any stage, the system is still able to create a profile. The more answers the user provides, the more specific her profile becomes. It is advisable to perform a pairwise comparison because previous research shows that users are more accurate when making relative indirect judgments than when they directly rank items using a linear scale.

Pairwise comparison is a well-known method in decision making. But there are only a few attempts to use it in RSs and none of them has been used in the context of the collaborative filtering setting.

While pairwise comparison is considered to be accurate, it is time consuming and thus hardly used in real-time applications. Instead of comparing items, we suggest clustering the items, for the purposes of acceleration and simplification of the pairwise comparison. In this way we can trade accuracy with time consumption.

When new users signup to a recommendation service, the system is oblivious to their preferences. Therefore, the initial recommendations the system provides are of relatively low quality. This phenomenon is known as the user cold start problem. A common approach to solve the cold start problem and to learn the user's preferences is to ask her to rate a number of items (known as training points). Preference elicitation is the initial acquisition of this profile for a given user.

It would seem apparent that a user's preferences could be elicited by simply asking her to define her preferences on various aspects (such as film genre in the movie domain). However, this simplistic approach usually does not work, mainly because users have problems in expressing their preferences and may not have the domain knowledge to answer the questions correctly. Thus another approach is to ask the user to provide feedback regarding several items presented to her. Roughly speaking there are two types of item-based methods: static and dynamic methods. With static methods, the system manages a seed set of items to be rated by the newcomer. This set is preselected regardless of the feedback provided by the current during the elicitation process. The methods are described as static because they use the same items for all users. On the other hand, with dynamic methods, the questions are adopted to feedback from the current user.

This is the place to note that several researchers criticize the idea of initial questionnaire. According to these researchers, users may lack the motivation to answer initial elicitation questions prior to any discerned and concrete benefits. Moreover, user preferences are context-dependent and may be constructed gradually as a user develops self-awareness. If the recommender system imposes a prolonged elicitation process just when the user signs up, the preferences obtained in this way are likely to be uncertain and erroneous.

16.3.1 *Static Methods*

Recently, published researches discuss the criteria for selecting the items about which the user should be queried. Among the ideas that have emerged are the use of controversial items that are also indicative of their tendencies. The contention of an item is frequently estimated using the Entropy measure. However, selecting non-popular items may not be helpful because the users might not be able to rate them. On the other hand, selecting items that are too popular, may not provide us with sufficient information regarding the user's taste. Thus, in order to steer a clear course between selecting non-popular items and ones that are too popular, the appropriate way seems to be to query users about popular yet controversial items.

Nevertheless, combining entropy and popularity is not always sufficient for learning about the user's general taste. The queried items should also be indicative to other items.

The use of the three criteria above — popularity, controversiality and predictability — is not sufficient for obtaining a good user profile because of two main reasons. First, the interactions among the items are ignored. Namely, two queried items with high criteria values can also be highly dependent. Thus, querying the user regarding both items will usually contribute relatively little information compared to asking the user about only one item.

16.3.2 *Dynamic Methods and Decision Trees*

There have been very few attempts to dynamically implement the initial profile process, i.e. adopt further queries to the current user feedback. Most of the dynamic methods employ decision trees. Decision trees seem to be more successful for initial profile generation.

The Information Gain through Clustered Neighbors (IGCN) algorithm selects the next item by using the information gain criterion while taking into account only the ratings data of those users who match best the target newcomer's profile so far.

While IGCN is based on a non-tree idea, the inventors of IGCN indicate that the usage of a decision tree can be easily adopted. Users are considered to have labels that correspond to the clusters they belong to and the role of the most informative item is treated as helping the target user most in reaching her representative cluster.

In the next section, we present one of the recent dynamic methods that employ decision trees to guide the user through the elicitation process. Moreover, in all cases each tree node is associated with a group of users. This makes the elicitation process an anytime process. The essence of an anytime process is that the user may answer as many questions as she likes.

Whenever the user terminates the process, we can still formulate a valid profile. The advantages of the anytime approach for preference elicitation have been shown to be important in the past.

16.3.3 *SVD-based CF Method*

CF methods identify similarities between users based on items they have rated and recommend new items that similar users have liked. CF stems from the idea that people who look for recommendations often ask their friends for advice. The main advantage of CF is that it is independent of item specification and can therefore provide recommendations for complex items which are very different but often used together. The major drawback of this approach is the inability to create good recommendations for new users who have not yet rated many items, and for new items that were not rated by many users.

CF algorithms vary according to the method they employ in order to identify similar users. Originally nearest-neighbor approaches, based on the Pearson correlation to compute a similarity between users, were implemented. Later on, matrix factorization techniques became the first choice for implementing CF.

RSs rely on various types of input. Most important of all is the explicit feedback, where users express their interest in items. We consider a set of m users denoted as U and a set of n items denoted as I. We reserve special indexing letters to distinguish users from items: u, v for users and i, j for items. A rating r_{ui} indicates the rating of user u to item i, where high values indicate a stronger preference. For example, the ratings, usually presented in terms of stars accorded the preference, can be integers ranging from 1 star indicating no interest to 5 (stars) indicating a strong interest. Usually the vast majority of ratings are unknown. As the catalog of items may contain millions of items, the user is capable of rating only small portion of the items. This phenomenon is known as the sparse rating data problem.

We denote by μ the overall average rating. The parameters b_u and b_i indicate the observed deviations from the average of user u and item i, respectively. For example, let us say that the average rating over all movies, μ, is 3 stars. Furthermore, Toy Story is better than an average movie, so it tends to be rated 0.7 stars above the average. On the other hand, Alice is a critical user, who tends to rate 0.2 stars lower than the average. Thus, the baseline predictor for Toy Story's rating by Alice would be 3.5 stars by calculating $3 + 0.7 - 0.2$.

The SVD CF methods transform users and items into a joint latent factor space, $\mathbb{R}^f$ where f indicate the number of latent factors. Both users u and items i are represented by corresponding vectors $p_u, q_i \in \mathbb{R}^f$. The cosine similarity

The final rating is created by adding baseline predictors that depend only on the user or item. Thus, a rating is predicted by the rule:

$$\hat{r}_{ui} = \mu + b_i + b_u + q_i^T p_u. \tag{16.5}$$

We distinguish predicted ratings from known ones, by using the hat notation for the predicted value. In order to estimate the model parameters $(b_u, b_i, p_u \text{ and } q_i)$ one can solve the regularized least squares error problem using a stochastic gradient descent procedure:

$$\min_{b_*,q_*,p_*} \sum_{(u,i)\in\mathcal{K}} (r_{ui} - \mu - b_i - b_u - q_i^T p_u)^2 + \lambda_4(b_i^2 + b_u^2 + \|q_i\|^2 + \|p_u\|^2).$$

$$\tag{16.6}$$

16.3.4 *Pairwise Comparisons*

A pairwise comparison is used for eliciting new user profiles. The main idea is to present the user with two items and ask her which of them is preferred. Usually, she has to choose the answer from among several discrete pairwise choices.

It has previously been shown in psychological studies that due to the human capacity, the best number of discrete choices is 7 ± 2, each of which is a linguistic phrase such as "I much prefer item A to item B" or "I equally like item A and item B".

While we are using pairwise comparisons to generate the initial profile, we still assume that the feedback from existing users is provided as a rating of individual items (the rating matrix). As the preferences are expressed in different ways, they are not directly comparable. Mapping from one system to another poses a challenge. Satty explains how a rating scale can be converted into a pairwise comparison and vice versa. We illustrate the mapping process with the following example: we are given four items A,B,C,D rated in the scale $[1,5]$ as following $r_{uA} = 5$, $r_{uB} = 1$, $r_{uC} = 3$, $r_{uD} = 2$. The pairwise comparison value between two items is set to:

$$C_{uij} = r_{ui}/r_{uj}. \tag{16.7}$$

Table 16.1   Illustration of 4×4 judgment matrix corresponding to ratings $r_A = 5$, $r_B = 1$, $r_C = 3$, $r_D = 2$ using Equation (16.7).

	A	B	C	D
A	1	5/1	5/3	5/2
B	1/5	1	1/3	1/2
C	3/5	3/1	1	3/2
D	2/5	2/1	2/3	1

Based on Equation (16.7) we can prepare a square judgment matrix, where every element in the matrix refers to a single, pairwise comparison. Table 16.1 presents the corresponding table.

Once the matrix is obtained, the original rating of the items can be reconstructed by calculating the right principal eigenvector of the judgment matrix. It follows from the fact that, for any completely consistent matrix, any column is essentially (i.e. to within multiplication by a constant) the dominant right eigenvector.

It should be noted that there are other methods for converting a judgment matrix into an affinity vector, including, for example, the least squares method, logarithmic least squares method, weighted least squares method, logarithmic least absolute values method and singular value decomposition. Each of these methods has advantages and weaknesses. In this chapter, we use the eigenvector method due to its popularity. The eigenvector can be approximated by using the geometric mean of each row. That is, the elements in each row are multiplied with each other and then the kth root is taken (where k is the number of items).

Recall that the user selects a linguistic phrase such as "I much prefer item A to item B" or "I equally like item A and item B". In order to map it into a five stars rating scale, we first need to quantify the linguistic phrase by using a scale. Such a scale is a one-to-one mapping between the set of discrete linguistic choices and a discrete set of numbers representing the importance or weight of the choice. Satty suggests matching the linguistic phrases to the set of integers $k = 1, \ldots, 9$ values for representing the degree to which item A is preferred over item B. Here, the value 1 indicates that both of the items are equally preferred. The value 2 shows that item A is slightly preferred over item B, etc.

The value 3 indicates that item A is preferred over item B. The value 4 signifies that item A is much more preferred over item B and so on.

Table 16.2 Illustration of 4×4 judgment matrix corresponding to ratings $r_A = 5$, $r_B = 1$, $r_C = 3$, $r_D = 2$ using Equation (16.8).

	A	B	C	D
A	1	9	2	4
B	1/9	1	1/5	1/3
C	1/2	5	1	2
D	1/4	3	1/2	1

Similarly, the inverse numbers $(1/k)$ are used to represent the degree to which item B is preferred over item A. In order to fit the five stars ratings to Satty's pairwise scores, we need to adjust Equation (16.7) to:

$$C_{uij}^* = \begin{array}{ll} round\left(\dfrac{2r_{ui}}{r_{uj}} - 1\right) & \textbf{if } r_{ui} \geq r_{uj} \\[2ex] 1\backslash round\left(\dfrac{2r_{uj}}{r_{ui}} - 1\right) & \textbf{if } r_{ui} < r_{uj} \end{array} . \tag{16.8}$$

This will generate the judgment matrix presented in Table 16.2. The dominant right eigenvector of the matrix in Table 16.2 is $(3.71; 0.37; 1.90; 1)$. After rounding, we obtain the vector of $(4, 0, 2, 1)$. After scaling we successfully restore the original ratings, i.e.: $(5, 1, 3, 2)$. The rounding of the vector's components is used to show that it is possible to restore the original rating values of the user. However, for obtaining a prediction for a rating, rounding is not required and therefore it is not used from here on. Note that because we are working in a SVD setting, instead of using the original rating provided by the user, we first subtract the baseline predictors (i.e. $r_{ui} - \mu - b_i - b_u$) and then scale it to the selected rating scale.

Our last example assumed that all pairwise comparisons should be performed before the judgment matrix can be converted into the regular rating scale. However, it is possible to approximate the rating using the incomplete pairwise comparison (IPC) algorithm. In fact, if each item is compared at least once, the approximation is quite good.

16.3.5 *Profile Representation*

Since we are working in a SVD setting, the profile of the newcomer should be represented as a vector p_v in the latent factor space, as is the case with existing users. Nevertheless, we still need to fit the p_v of the newcomer to her answers to the pairwise comparisons. There are two options for achieving this. The first option is to convert the pairwise answers into individual ratings using the procedure described below. Once the individual ratings are obtained, we can use an incremental SVD algorithm to update the model and to generate the new user vector. While the resulting model is not a perfect SVD model, the folding-in procedure still provides a fairly good approximation of the new user vector. The second option is to match the newcomer's responses with existing users and to build the newcomer's profile based on the profiles of the corresponding users. We assume that a user will get good recommendations if like-minded users are found. First, we map the ratings of existing users into pairwise comparisons using Equation (16.8). Next, using the Euclidian distance, we find among existing users those who are most similar to the newcomer. Once these users have been identified, the profile of the newcomer is defined as the mean of their vectors.

16.3.6 *Selecting the Next Pairwise Comparison*

We take the greedy approach for selecting the next pairwise comparison, i.e. given the responses of the newcomer to the previous pairwise comparisons, we select the next best pairwise comparison. Figure 16.4 presents the pseudo code of the greedy algorithm. We assume that the algorithm gets $N(v)$, as an input. $N(v)$ represents the set of non-newcomer similar users that was identified based on pairwise questions answered so far by the newcomer v.

In lines 3–15, we iterate over all candidate pairs of items. For each pair, we calculate its score based on its weighted generalized variance. For this purpose, we go over (lines 5–10) all possible outcomes C of the pairwise question. In line 6, we find $N(v, i, j, C)$ which is a subset of $N(v)$ which contains all users in $N(v)$ that have rated items i and j with ratio C, where C_{uij}^* is calculated as in Equation (16.8). Since in a typical recommender system we cannot assume that all users have rated both item i and item j, we treat these users as a separate subset and denote it by $N(v, i, j, \emptyset)$.

In lines 7–9, we update the pair's scores. We search for the pairwise comparison that best refines the set of similar users. Thus, we estimate the dispersion of the p_u vectors by first calculating the covariance matrix (line 7). The covariance matrix Σ is a $f \times f$ matrix where f is the number of latent factors. The covariance matrix gathers all the information about the individual latent factor variabilities. In line 8, we calculate the determinant of Σ which corresponds the generalized variance of the users' profiles. The usefulness of GV as a measure of the overall spread of the distribution is best explained by the geometrical fact that it measures the hypervolume that the distribution of the random variables occupies in the space.

In conclusion, the greedy algorithm selects the next pairwise comparison as the pair of items minimizes the weighted generalized variance:

$$NextPair \equiv \underset{(i,j)}{\operatorname{argmin}} \sum_C |N(v,i,j,C)| \cdot GV(N(v,i,j,C)). \qquad (16.9)$$

Before the first interaction of the newcomer u with the system, we initialize the similar users set as the whole set of existing users, i.e.: $N(v) \leftarrow U$. After selecting the best pair, we present the pairwise comparison to the newcomer and wait for her response. Based on the response, we can update the set of similar users to a corresponding subset. Specifically, if the newcomer responded with C to the comparison between (i,j), then $N(v) \leftarrow N(v,i,j,C)$. Consequently, the process can be recursively repeated with the new set of similar users. If the newcomer is not familiar with one of the items, we continue the process with $N(v) \leftarrow N(v,i,j,\emptyset)$.

Require: v (the newcomer user), $N(v)$ (set of existing users that so far answered the same as v), p_u (the latent profiles of all users), I (set of items).

1: $BestPair \leftarrow \emptyset$
2: $BestPairScore \leftarrow \infty$
3: **for all** pair of items (i,j) such that $i,j \in I$ and $i \neq j$ **do**
4:    $PairScore \leftarrow 0$
5:    **for all** possible outcomes C of the pairwise (i,j) **do**
6:       $N(v,i,j,C) \leftarrow \{u \in N(v)|C^*_{uij} = C\}$
7:       Get covariance matrix Σ from $N(v,i,j,C)$ profiles
8:       $GV \leftarrow det(\Sigma)$
9:       $PairScore \leftarrow PairScore + |N(v,i,j,C)| \cdot GV$
10:    **end for**
11:    **if** $PairScore < BestPairScore$ **then**
12:       $BestPairScore \leftarrow PairScore; BestPair \leftarrow (i,j)$
13:    **end if**
14: **end for**
15: Return $BestPair$

Fig. 16.5   An algorithm for selecting the next pairwise comparison.

16.3.7 *Clustering the Items*

Searching the space of all possible pairs is reasonable only for a small set of items. We can try to reduce running time by various means. First, if the newcomer user v has already commented on some item pairs, then these pairs should be skipped during the search. Moreover, we can skip any item that has not been rated by a sufficiently large number of users in the current set of similar users. Their exclusion from the process can speed execution time. Moreover, the searching can be easily parallelized because each pair can be analyzed independently. Still, since typical RSs include thousands of rated items, it is completely impractical or very expensive to go over all remaining pairs.

A different problem arises due to the sparse rating data problem. In many datasets only a few pairs can provide a sufficiently large set of similar users to each possible comparison outcome. In the remaining pairs, the empty bucket (i.e. $C = \emptyset$) will populate most of the users in $N(v)$.

One way to resolve these drawbacks is to cluster the items. The goal of clustering is to group items so that intra-cluster similarities of the items are maximized and inter-cluster similarities are minimized. We perform the clustering in the latent factor space. Thus, the similarity between two items can be calculated as the cosine similarity between vectors of the two items, q_i and q_j. By clustering the items, we define an abstract item that has general properties similar to a set of actual items.

Instead of searching for the best pair of items, we should search now for the best pair of clusters. We can still use Equation (16.9) for this purpose. However, we need to handle the individual rating of the users differently. Because the same user can rate multiple items in the same cluster, her corresponding pairwise score as obtained from Equation (16.8) is not unequivocal. There are many ways to aggregate all cluster-wise ratings into a single score. Here, we implement a simple approach. We first determine for each cluster l its centroid vector in the factorized space $\dot{q}_l$, then the aggregated rating of user u to cluster l is defined as $\dot{r}_{ul} \equiv \dot{q}_i{}^T \cdot p_u$. Finally, the cluster pairwise score can be determined using Equation (16.9).

After finding the pair of clusters, we need to transform the selected pairs into a simple visual question that the user can easily answer. Because the user has no notion of the item clusters, we propose to represent the pairwise comparison of the two clusters (s,t), by the posters of two popular items that most differentiate between these two clusters. For this purpose, we first sort the items in each cluster by their popularity (number of times it was rated). Popular items are preferred to ensure that the user recognizes the items and can rate them. From the most rated items in each cluster (say the top 10%), we select the item that maximizes the Euclidian distance from the counter cluster. Finally, it should be noted that the same item cannot be used twice (i.e. in two different pairwise comparisons). First, this prevents monotonous visuals that might bore the user. More importantly, we get hold of a better picture of user preferences by obtaining her response from a variety of items from the same cluster. While the above selection of items is ad-hoc, the reader should take into consideration that this is only a secondary criterion that follows pairwise cluster selection. We focus on finding good enough items in an almost instantaneous time.

16.3.8 *Training a Lazy Decision Tree*

We utilize decision trees to initiate a profile for a new user. In particular, we use the top-down lazy decision tree (Lazy decision tree) as the base algorithm. However, we use a different splitting criterion described in Equation (16.9) as the splitting criterion. The pairwise comparisons are located at the decision nodes. Each node in the tree is associated with a set of corresponding users. This allows the user to quit the profile initialization process anytime she wants. If the user does not wish to answer more questions, we take the list of users that are associated with the current node and calculate the mean of their factorized vectors. The more questions the user answers, the more specific her vector becomes. But even with answering only a few questions we can still provide the user a profile vector.

Figure 16.6 illustrates the root of the decision tree. Each inner node represents a different pairwise comparison. Based on the response to the first (root) question, the decision tree is used to select the next pairwise comparison to be asked. Note that one possible outcome is "unknown", this option is selected when the user does not recognize the items. Every path in the decision tree represents a certain set of comparisons with which the user is presented. Assuming that there are k clusters, then the longest possible path contains $\frac{k \cdot (k-1)}{2}$ inner nodes (comparisons).

Note that if there are s possible outcomes in each pairwise comparison and there are k clusters, then the complete decision tree will have $s^{k*(k-1)/2}$ leaves. Even for moderate values of k this becomes impractical. Thus, instead of building the entire decision tree, we take the lazy approach. If the current newcomer has reached a leaf and is willing to answer additional questions, only then do we expand the current node using the suggested splitting criterion. In this way, the tree expands gradually and on-demand. Given a limited memory size, we keep only the most frequent visited nodes.

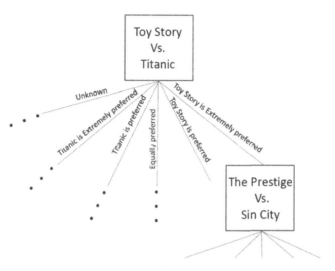

Fig. 16.6   An illustration of the pairwise decision tree.

Since each tree node is associated with a set of users, we can create a new user profile vector for each node by taking the mean of the vectors of the corresponding users. When a user decides to terminate the profile initialization, we generate her profile vector p_u based on the node she has reached on the tree. Then Equation (16.5) can be used to predict ratings. Using this vector we can generate a recommendation list by sorting the items according to Equation (16.5). We could also use Equation (16.5) without actually knowing the user bias b_u because the user bias does not affect the way the items are sorted. Sometime sorting the items is not sufficient and one is interested in the actual rating, for example, when it is necessary to calculate the RMSE evaluation measure. For predicting the user rating, we have to take it into account. But for that we need to know the user bias. To do this, we first reconstruct the user's supposed individual ratings $\tilde{r}_{u,i}$. We distinguish supposed ratings from original ones by using the tilde notation. Supposed ratings are pairwise responses that are converted to ratings using the right dominant eigenvector mapping procedure presented above.

In order to estimate b_u, we solve the least squares problem presented in Equation (16.6) by replacing $r_{u,i}$ with $\tilde{r}_{u,i}$. Note that in this case the parameters p_u, q_i, b_i and μ are fixed. Thus, we need to minimize an univariate function with respect to b_u over the domain $[-5, +5]$ (when ratings range from 1 to 5). Minimization is performed by the golden section search.

Bibliography

Aha D. W., Kibler D., and Albert M. K., Instancebased learning algorithms, *Machine Learning* 6(1):37–66, 1991.

A1-Sultan K. S., A tabu search approach to the clustering problem, *Pattern Recognition* 28:1443–1451, 1995.

Al-Sultan K. S., and Khan M. M., Computational experience on four algorithms for the hard clustering problem, *Pattern Recognition Letters* 17(3):295–308, 1996.

Ali K. M., and Pazzani M. J., Error reduction through learning multiple descriptions, *Machine Learning* 24(3):173–202, 1996.

Almuallim H., An efficient algorithm for optimal pruning of decision trees, *Artificial Intelligence* 83(2):347–362, 1996.

Almuallim H., and Dietterich T. G., Learning Boolean concepts in the presence of many irrelevant features, *Artificial Intelligence* 69(1–2):279–306, 1994.

Alsabti K., Ranka S., and Singh V., CLOUDS: A decision tree classifier for large datasets, *Conference on Knowledge Discovery and Data Mining (KDD-98)*, August 1998.

An A., and Wang Y., Comparisons of classification methods for screening potential compounds, *IEEE International Conference on Data Mining*, 2001.

Anand R., Methrotra K., Mohan C. K., and Ranka S., Efficient classification for multiclass problems using modular neural networks, *IEEE Trans Neural Networks* 6(1):117–125, 1995.

Anderson J. A., and Rosenfeld E., *Talking Nets: An Oral History of Neural Network Research*, Cambridge, MA: MIT Press, 2000.

Antwarg L., Rokach L., and Shapira B., Attribute-driven hidden markov model trees for intention prediction, *IEEE Transactions on Systems, Man, and Cybernetics, Part C* 42(6):1103–1119, 2012.

Ashenhurst R. L., The decomposition of switching functions, *Technical report, Bell Laboratories BL*-1(11), pp. 541–602, 1952.

Athanasopoulos D., *Probabilistic Theory*, Piraeus: Stamoulis, 1991.

Attneave F., *Applications of Information Theory to Psychology*, California: Holt, Rinehart and Winston, 1959.

Avnimelech R., and Intrator N., Boosted mixture of experts: An ensemble learning scheme, *Neural Computations* 11(2):483–497, 1999.

Baker E., and Jain A. K., On feature ordering in practice and some finite sample effects, *Proceedings of the Third International Joint Conference on Pattern Recognition*, pp. 45–49, San Diego, CA, 1976.

Bala J., Huang J., Vafaie H., De Jong K., and Wechsler H., Hybrid learning using genetic algorithms and decision trees for pattern classification, *IJCAI Conference*, 1995.

Banfield R., OpenDT, http://opendt.sourceforge.net/, 2005.

Banfield R. E., Hall L. O., Bowyer K. W., and Kegelmeyer W. P., A comparison of decision tree ensemble creation techniques, *IEEE Transactions on Pattern Analysis and Machine Intelligence*, 29(1):173–180, 2007.

Banfield J. D., and Raftery A. E., Model-based Gaussian and non-Gaussian clustering, *Biometrics* 49:803–821, 1993.

Bartlett P., and Shawe-Taylor J., Generalization performance of support vector machines and other pattern classifiers, In *Advances in Kernel Methods, Support Vector Learning*, B. Scholkopf, C. J. C. Burges, and A. J. Smola (eds.), Cambridge, USA: MIT Press, 1998.

Basak J., Online adaptive decision trees, *Neural Computations* 16(9):1959–1981, 2004.

Basak J., Online adaptive decision trees: Pattern classification and function approximation, *Neural Computations* 18(9):2062–2101, 2006.

Bauer E., and Kohavi R., An empirical comparison of voting classification algorithms: Bagging, boosting, and variants, *Machine Learning* 35:1–38, 1999.

Baxt W. G., Use of an artificial neural network for data analysis in clinical decision making: The diagnosis of acute coronary occlusion, *Neural Computation* 2(4):480–489, 1990.

Bay S., Nearest neighbor classification from multiple feature subsets, *Intelligent Data Analysis* 3(3):191–209, 1999.

Bellman R., *Adaptive Control Processes: A Guided Tour*, Princeton University Press, 1961.

BenBassat M., Myopic policies in sequential classification, *IEEE Trans. on Computing* 27(2):170–174, February, 1978.

Bennett K. P., and Demiriz A., and Maclin R., Exploiting unlabeled data in ensemble methods, *Proceedings of the Eighth ACM SIGKDD International Conference on Knowledge Discovery and Data Mining*, pp. 289–296, New York, NY, USA: ACM Press, 2002.

Bennett X., and Mangasarian O. L., Multicategory discrimination via linear programming, *Optimization Methods and Software* 3:29–39, 1994.

Bensusan H., and Kalousis A., Estimating the predictive accuracy of a classifier, *Proc. Proceedings of the 12th European Conference on Machine Learning*, pp. 25–36, 2001.

Bentley J. L., and Friedman J. H., Fast algorithms for constructing minimal spanning trees in coordinate spaces, *IEEE Transactions on Computers*, C-27(2):97–105, February, 1978.

Bernard M. E., Decision trees and diagrams, *Computing Surveys* 14(4):593–623, 1982.

Berry M., and Linoff G., *Mastering Data Mining*, John Wiley & Sons, 2000.

Bhargava H. K., Data mining by decomposition: Adaptive search for hypothesis generation, *INFORMS Journal on Computing* 11(3):239–247, 1999.

Biermann A. W., Faireld J., and Beres T., Signature table systems and learning, *IEEE Trans. Syst. Man Cybern.* 12(5):635-648, 1982.

Blockeel H., Raedt L. D., Ramon J., Top-down induction of clustering trees, ArXiv Computer Science e-prints, pp. 55–63, 1998.

Blum A. I., and Langley P., Selection of relevant features and examples in machine learning, *Artificial Intelligence*, 97:245–271, 1997.

Blum A., and Mitchell T., Combining labeled and unlabeled data with cotraining, *Proc. of the 11th Annual Conference on Computational Learning Theory*, pp. 92–100, 1998.

Bonner R., On some clustering techniques, *IBM Journal of Research and Development* 8:22–32, 1964.

Booker L., Goldberg D. E., and Holland J. H., Classifier systems and genetic algorithms, *Artificial Intelligence* 40(1–3):235–282, 1989.

Bou-Hamad I., Larocque D., and Ben-Ameur H., A review of survival trees, *Statistics Surveys* 5:44–71, 2011.

Brachman R., and Anand T., The process of knowledge discovery in databases, In *Advances in Knowledge Discovery and Data Mining*, pp. 37–58, AAAI/ MIT Press.

Bratko I., and Bohanec M., Trading accuracy for simplicity in decision trees, *Machine Learning* 15:223–250, 1994.

Brazdil P., Gama J., and Henery R., Characterizing the applicability of classification algorithms using meta level learning, In *Machine Learning: ECML-94*, F. Bergadano and L. de Raedt (eds.), LNAI No. 784, pp. 83–102, Springer-Verlag, 1994.

Breiman L., Bagging predictors, *Machine Learning* 24(2):123–140, 1996.

Breiman L., Random forests, *Machine Learning* 45:532, 2001.

Breiman L., Friedman J., Olshen R., and Stone C., *Classification and Regression Trees*, Wadsworth Int. Group, 1984.

Brodley C. E., Automatic selection of split criterion during tree growing based on node selection, *Proceedings of the Twelfth International Conference on Machine Learning*, pp. 73–80, Taho City, CA: Morgan Kaufmann, 1995.

Brodley C. E., and Utgoff P. E., Multivariate decision trees, *Machine Learning* 19:45–77, 1995.

Brown G., and Wyatt J. L., Negative correlation learning and the ambiguity family of ensemble methods, *Multiple Classifier Systems* 266–275, 2003.

Brown G., Wyatt J., Harris R., and Yao X., Diversity creation methods: A survey and categorisation, *Information Fusion* 6(1):5–20, 2005.

Bruzzone L., Cossu R., and Vernazza G., Detection of land-cover transitions by combining multidate classifiers, *Pattern Recognition Letters* 25(13):1491–1500, 2004.

Buchanan B. G., and Shortliffe E. H., *Rule Based Expert Systems*, pp. 272–292, Addison-Wesley, 1984.

Buhlmann P., and Yu B., Boosting with L_2 loss: Regression and classification, *Journal of the American Statistical Association* 98:324–338. 2003.

Buja A., and Lee Y. S., Data mining criteria for tree based regression and classification, *Proceedings of the 7th International Conference on Knowledge Discovery and Data Mining*, pp. 27–36, San Diego, USA, 2001.

Buntine W., A theory of learning classification rules, Doctoral Dissertation, School of Computing Science, University of Technology, Sydney, Australia, 1990.

Buntine W., Learning classification trees, *Statistics and Computing* 2:63–73, 1992.

Buntine W., Graphical models for discovering knowledge, In *Advances in Knowledge Discovery and Data Mining*, U. Fayyad, G. Piatetsky-Shapiro, P. Smyth, and R. Uthurusamy (eds.), pp. 59–82, AAAI/MIT Press, 1996.

Buntine W., Niblett T., A further comparison of splitting rules for decision-tree induction, *Machine Learning* 8:75–85, 1992.

Buczak A. L., and Ziarko W., Neural and rough set based data mining methods in engineering, *Handbook of Data Mining and Knowledge Discovery*, W. Klosgen and J. M. Zytkow (eds.), pp. 788–797, Oxford: Oxford University Press, 2002a.

Buczak A. L., and Ziarko W., Stages of the discovery process, *Handbook of Data Mining and Knowledge Discovery*, W. Klosgen and J. M. Zytkow (eds.), pp. 185–192, Oxford: Oxford University Press, 2002b.

Can F. Incremental clustering for dynamic information processing, *ACM Transactions on Information Systems*, No. 11, pp. 143–164, 1993.

Cantu-Paz E., and Kamath C., Inducing oblique decision trees with evolutionary algorithms, *IEEE Trans. on Evol. Computation* 7(1):54–68, 2003.

Cardie C., Using decision trees to improve cased-based learning, *Proceedings of the First International Conference on Knowledge Discovery and Data Mining*, AAAI Press, 1995.

Caruana R., Niculescu-Mizil A., Crew G., and Ksikes A., Ensemble selection from libraries of models, *Twenty-first International Conference on Machine Learning*, July 04–08, 2004, Banff, Alberta, Canada.

Carvalho D. R., and Freitas A. A., A hybrid decision-tree — genetic algorithm method for data mining, *Information Science* 163:13–35, 2004.

Catlett J., Mega induction: Machine learning on vary large databases, PhD, University of Sydney, 1991.

Chai B., Huang T., Zhuang X., Zhao Y., and Sklansky J., Piecewise-linear classifiers using binary tree structure and genetic algorithm, *Pattern Recognition* 29(11):1905–1917, 1996.

Chan P. K., and Stolfo S. J., Toward parallel and distributed learning by meta-learning, In *AAAI Workshop in Knowledge Discovery in Databases*, pp. 227–240, 1993.

Chan P. K., and Stolfo S. J., A comparative evaluation of voting and meta-learning on partitioned data, *Proc. 12th Intl. Conf. On Machine Learning ICML-95*, 1995.

Chan P. K., and Stolfo S. J., On the accuracy of meta-learning for scalable data mining, *Journal of Intelligent Information Systems* 8:5–28, 1997.

Charnes A., Cooper W. W., and Rhodes E., Measuring the efficiency of decision making units, *European Journal of Operational Research* 2(6):429–444, 1978.

Chawla N. V., Moore T. E., Hall L. O., Bowyer K. W., Springer C., and Kegelmeyer W. P., Distributed learning with bagging-like performance, *Pattern Recognition Letters* 24(1–3):455–471, 2002.

Chawla N. V., Hall L. O., Bowyer K. W., Kegelmeyer W. P., Learning ensembles from bites: A scalable and accurate approach, *The Journal of Machine Learning Research Archive* 5:421–451, 2004.

Chen K., Wang L., and Chi H., Methods of combining multiple classifiers with different features and their applications to text-independent speaker identification, *International Journal of Pattern Recognition and Artificial Intelligence* 11(3):417–445, 1997.

Cheeseman P., and Stutz J., Bayesian classification (AutoClass): Theory and results, *Advances in Knowledge Discovery and Data Mining* 153–180, 1996.

Cherkauer K. J., Human expert-level performance on a scientific image analysis task by a system using combined artificial neural networks, In *Working Notes, Integrating Multiple Learned Models for Improving and Scaling Machine Learning Algorithms Workshop, Thirteenth National Conference on Artificial Intelligence*. Portland, OR: AAAI Press, 1996.

Cherkauer K. J., and Shavlik J. W., Growing simpler decision trees to facilitate knowledge discovery, In *Proceedings of the Second International Conference on Knowledge Discovery and Data Mining*, Portland, OP: AAAI Press, 1996.

Chizi B., Maimon O., and Smilovici A., *On Dimensionality Reduction of High Dimensional Data Sets, Frontiers in Artificial Intelligence and Applications*, IOS press, pp. 230–236, 2002.

Christensen S. W., Sinclair I., and Reed P. A. S., Designing committees of models through deliberate weighting of data points, *The Journal of Machine Learning Research* 4(1):39–66, 2004.

Cios K. J., and Sztandera L. M., Continuous ID3 algorithm with fuzzy entropy measures, In *Proc. IEEE Internat. Con/i on Fuzz* Systems, pp. 469–476, 1992.

Clark P., and Niblett T., The CN2 rule induction algorithm, *Machine Learning* 3:261–284, 1989.

Clark P., and Boswell R., Rule induction with CN2: Some recent improvements, In *Proceedings of the European Working Session on Learning*, pp. 151–163, Pitman, 1991.

Clearwater S., Cheng T., Hirsh H., and Buchanan B., Incremental batch learning, In *Proceedings of the Sixth International Workshop on Machine Learning*, pp. 366–370, San Mateo CA: Morgan Kaufmann, 1989.

Clemen R., Combining forecasts: A review and annotated bibliography, *International Journal of Forecasting* 5:559–583, 1989

S. Cohen, Rokach L., and Maimon O., Decision tree instance space decomposition with grouped gain-ratio, *Information Science* 177(17):3592–3612, 2007.

Coppock D. S., Data modeling and mining: Why lift?, Published in DM Review online, June 2002.

Crawford S. L., Extensions to the CART algorithm, *International Journal of ManMachine Studies* 31(2):197–217, August, 1989.

Cunningham P., and Carney J., Diversity versus quality in classification ensembles based on feature selection, In: *Proc. ECML 2000, 11th European Conf. On Machine Learning*, R. L. de Mántaras, and E. Plaza (eds.), Barcelona, Spain, LNCS 1810, Springer, pp. 109-116, 2000.

Curtis H. A., *A New Approach to the Design of Switching Functions*, Van Nostrand: Princeton, 1962.

Dahan H., Cohen S., Rokach L., and Maimon O., *Proactive Data Mining with Decision Trees*, Springer, 2014.

Dhillon I., and Modha D., Concept decomposition for large sparse text data using clustering. *Machine Learning* 42:143–175, 2001.

Dempster A. P., Laird N. M., and Rubin D. B., Maximum likelihood from incomplete data using the EM algorithm, *Journal of the Royal Statistical Society* 39(B): 1977.

Derbeko P., El-Yaniv R., and Meir R., Variance optimized bagging, *European Conference on Machine Learning*, 2002.

Dietterich T. G., Approximate statistical tests for comparing supervised classification learning algorithms. *Neural Computation* 10(7):1895–1924, 1998.

Dietterich T. G., An experimental comparison of three methods for constructing ensembles of decision trees: Bagging, boosting and randomization, *Machine Learning* 40(2):139–157, 2000a.

Dietterich T., Ensemble methods in machine learning, In *First International Workshop on Multiple Classifier Systems*, J. Kittler, and F. Roll (eds.), Lecture Notes in Computer Science, pp. 1–15, Springer-Verlag, 2000b.

Dietterich T. G., and Bakiri G., Solving multiclass learning problems via error-correcting output codes, *Journal of Artificial Intelligence Research* 2:263–286, 1995.

Dietterich T. G., and Kong E. B., Machine learning bias, statistical bias, and statistical variance of decision tree algorithms, Technical Report, Oregon State University, 1995.

Dietterich T. G., and Michalski R. S., A comparative review of selected methods for learning from examples, *Machine Learning, an Artificial Intelligence Approach* 1:41–81, 1983.

Dietterich T. G., Kearns M., and Mansour Y., Applying the weak learning framework to understand and improve C4.5, In *Proceedings of the Thirteenth International Conference on Machine Learning*, pp. 96–104, San Francisco: Morgan Kaufmann, 1996.

Dimitriadou E., Weingessel A., and Hornik K., *A Cluster Ensembles Framework, Design and Application of Hybrid Intelligent Systems*, Amsterdam, The Netherlands: IOS Press, 2003.

Domingos P., Using partitioning to speed up specific-to-general rule induction, In *Proceedings of the AAAI-96 Workshop on Integrating Multiple Learned Models*, pp. 29–34, Portland, OR: AAAI Press, 1996.

Dominigos P., MetaCost: A general method for making classifiers cost sensitive. In *Proceedings of the Fifth International Conference on Knowledge Discovery and Data Mining*, pp. 155–164, ACM Press, 1999.

Domingos P., and Pazzani M., On the optimality of the naive bayes classifier under zero-one loss, *Machine Learning* 29(2):103–130, 1997.

Dror M., Shabtai A., Rokach L., and Elovici Y., OCCT: A one-class clustering tree for implementing one-to-many data linkage, *IEEE Transactions on Knowledge and Data Engineering*, 2014.

Dougherty J., Kohavi R, and Sahami M., Supervised and unsupervised discretization of continuous attributes, *Machine Learning: Proceedings of the twelfth International Conference*, Morgan Kaufman, pp. 194–202, 1995.

Duda R., and Hart P., *Pattern Classification and Scene Analysis*, New-York: Wiley, 1973.

Duda P. E. H., and Stork D. G., *Pattern Classification*, New York: Wiley, 2001.

Dunteman G. H., *Principal Components Analysis*, Sage Publications, 1989.

Džeroski S., and Ženko B., Is combining classifiers with stacking better than selecting the best one? *Machine Learning* 54(3):255–273, 2004.

Elder I., and Pregibon D., A statistical perspective on knowledge discovery in databases, In *Advances in Knowledge Discovery and Data Mining*, U. Fayyad, G. Piatetsky-Shapiro, P. Smyth, and R. Uthurusamy (eds.), pp. 83–113, Portland, OR: AAAI/MIT Press, 1996.

Esmeir S., and Markovitch S., Lookahead-basedalgorithms for anytime induction of decision trees, InICML'04, 257–264, 2004.

Esposito F., Malerba D., and Semeraro G., A comparative analysis of methods for pruning decision trees, *IEEE Transactions on Pattern Analysis and Machine Intelligence* 19(5):476–492, 1997.

Ester M., Kriegel H. P., Sander S., and Xu X., A density-based algorithm for discovering clusters in large spatial databases with noise, In *Proceedings of the 2nd International Conference on Knowledge Discovery and Data Mining (KDD-96)*, E. Simoudis, J. Han, and U. Fayyad, (eds.), pp. 226–231, Menlo Park, CA, AAAI Press, 1996.

Estivill-Castro V., and Yang J., A Fast and robust general purpose clustering algorithm, *Pacific Rim International Conference on Artificial Intelligence*, pp. 208–218, 2000.

Eyal A., Rokach L., Kalech M., Amir O., Chougule R., Vaidyanathan R., and Pattada K., Survival analysis of automobile components using mutually exclusive forests, *IEEE Transactions Systems, Man, and Cybernetics*, 2014.

Fayyad U., Grinstein G., and Wierse A., Information visualization in data mining and knowledge discovery, Morgan Kaufmann, 2001.

Fayyad U., and Irani K. B., The attribute selection problem in decision tree generation, In *Proceedings of Tenth National Conference on Artificial Intelligence*, pp. 104–110, Cambridge, MA: AAAI Press/MIT Press, 1992.

Fayyad U., Piatesky-Shapiro G., and Smyth P., from data mining to knowledge discovery: An overview, In *Advances in Knowledge Discovery and Data Mining*, U. Fayyad, G. Piatetsky-Shapiro, P. Smyth and R. Uthurusamy (eds.), pp. 1–30, Portland, OR: AAAI/MIT Press, 1996.

Feigenbaum E., Knowledge Processing — From File Servers to Knowledge Servers, In *Applications of Expert Systems*, J. R. Queinlan (ed.), Vol. 2, Chapter 1, pp. 3–11, Turing Institute Press, 1988.

Ferri C., Flach P., and Hernández-Orallo J., Learning decision trees using the area under the ROC curve. In *Proceedings of the 19th International Conference on Machine Learning*, C. Sammut and A. Hoffmann (ed.), pp. 139–146, Morgan Kaufmann, July 2002.

Fifield D. J., Distributed tree construction from large datasets, Bachelor's Honor Thesis, Australian National University, 1992.

Fisher D., Knowledge acquisition via incremental conceptual clustering, *Machine Learning* 2:139–172, 1987.

Fischer B., Decomposition of time series — comparing different methods in theory and practice, Eurostat Working Paper, 1995.

Fix E., and Hodges J. L., Discriminatory analysis. Nonparametric discrimination. Consistency properties, Technical Report 4, US Air Force School of Aviation Medicine, Randolph Field, TX, 1957.

Fortier J. J., and Solomon H. Clustering procedures, In *Proceedings of the Multivariate Analysis*, '66, P. R. Krishnaiah (ed.), pp. 493–506, 1996.

Fountain T. Dietterich T., and Sudyka B., Mining IC test data to optimize VLSI testing, *ACM SIGKDD Conference*, pp. 18–25, 2000.

Fraley C., and Raftery A. E., How many clusters? Which clustering method? Answers via model-based cluster analysis, Technical Report No. 329. Department of Statistics University of Washington, 1998.

Frank E., Hall M., Holmes G., Kirkby R., and Pfahringer B., WEKA — A machine learning workbench for data mining, In *The Data Mining and Knowledge Discovery Handbook*, O. Maimon, and L. Rokach (eds.), Springer, pp. 1305–1314, 2005.

Frawley W. J., Piatetsky-Shapiro G., and Matheus C. J., Knowledge discovery in databases: An overview, In *Knowledge Discovery in Databases*, G. Piatetsky-Shapiro, and W. J. Frawley (ed.), pp. 1–27, AAAI Press: Menlo Park, California, 1991.

Freitas A., Evolutionary algorithms for data mining, In *The Data Mining and Knowledge Discovery Handbook*, O. Maimon and L. Rokach (eds.), Springer, pp. 435–467, 2005.

Freitas X., and Lavington S. H., *Mining Very Large Databases With Parallel Processing*, Kluwer Academic Publishers, 1998.

Freund Y., and Schapire R. E., Experiments with a new boosting algorithm, In *Machine Learning: Proceedings of the Thirteenth International Conference*, pp. 325–332, 1996.

Friedman J. H., A recursive partitioning decision rule for nonparametric classifiers, *IEEE Trans. on Comp.* C26:404–408, 1977.

Friedman J. H., Multivariate adaptive regression splines, *The Annual of Statistics* 19:1–141, 1991.

Friedman J. H., Data mining and statistics: What is the connection? 1997a.

Friedman J. H., On bias, variance, 0/1 — loss and the curse of dimensionality, *Data Mining and Knowledge Discovery* 1(1):55–77, 1997b.

Friedman J. H., and Tukey J. W., A projection pursuit algorithm for exploratory data analysis, *IEEE Transactions on Computers* 23(9):881–889, 1973.

Friedman N., Geiger D., and Goldszmidt M., Bayesian network classifiers, *Machine Learning* 29(2–3):131–163, 1997.

Friedman J, Kohavi R., and Yun Y., Lazy decision trees, In *Proceedings of the Thirteenth National Conference on Artificial Intelligence*, pp. 717–724. Cambridge, MA: AAAI Press/MIT Press.

Fukunaga K., *Introduction to Statistical Pattern Recognition*, San Diego, CA: Academic, 1990.

Fürnkranz J., More efficient windowing, In *Proceeding of The 14th National Conference on Artificial Intelegence* (AAAI-97), pp. 509–514, Providence, RI: AAAI Press, 1997.

Gallinari P., Modular neural net systems, training of. In *The Handbook of Brain Theory and Neural Networks*, M. A. Arbib (ed.), Bradford Books/MIT Press, 1995.

Gama J., A linear-bayes classifier, In *Advances on Artificial Intelligence — SBIA2000*, C. Monard (ed.), LNAI 1952, pp. 269–279, Springer-Verlag, 2000.

Gams M., New measurements highlight the importance of redundant knowledge, In *European Working Session on Learning* , Montpeiller, France, Pitman, 1989.

Gago P., and Bentos C., A metric for selection of the most promising rules. In *Proceedings of the 2nd European Conference on The Pronciples of Data Mining and Knowledge Discovery (PKDD'98)*, 1998.

Gardner M., and Bieker J., Data mining solves tough semiconductor manufacturing problems, KDD:376–383, 2000.

Gehrke J., Ganti V., Ramakrishnan R., and Loh W., BOAT-optimistic decision tree construction. *SIGMOD Conference* pp. 169–180, 1999.

Gehrke J., Ramakrishnan R., and Ganti V., RainForest — A framework for fast decision tree construction of large datasets, *Data Mining and Knowledge Discovery* 4(2/3):127–162, 2000.

Gelfand S. B., Ravishankar C. S., and Delp E. J., An iterative growing and pruning algorithm for classification tree design. *IEEE Transaction on Pattern Analysis and Machine Intelligence* 13(2):163–174, 1991.

Geman S., Bienenstock E., and Doursat R., Neural networks and the bias/variance dilemma, *Neural Computation* 4:1–58, 1995.

George E., and Foster D., Calibration and empirical Bayes variable selection, *Biometrika* 87(4):731–747, 2000.

Gershman A., Meisels A., Luke K.-H., Rokach L., Schclar A., and Sturm A., A decision tree based recommender system, In *Proc. 10th International*

Conference on Innovative Internet Community Services (I2CS), Jubilee Edition 2010, June 3–5, Bangkok, Thailand, pp. 170–179, 2010.

Gilad-Bachrach R., Navot A., and Tisliby N., Margin based feature selection — theory and algorithms, *Proceeding of the 21'st International Conferenc on Machine Learning*, 2004.

Gillo M. W., MAID: A Honeywell 600 program for an automatised survey analysis, *Behavioral Science* 17:251–252, 1972.

Ginsberg J., Mohebbi M. H., Patel S., Rajan S., Brammer L., Smolinski M., and Brilliant L., Detecting influenza epidemics using search engine query data, *Nature* 457(7232):1012–1014, 2008.

Giraud-Carrier C., Vilalta R., and Brazdil R., Introduction to the special issue of on meta-learning, *Machine Learning* 54(3), 197–194, 2004.

Gluck M., and Corter J., Information, uncertainty, and the utility of categories, In *Proceedings of the Seventh Annual Conference of the Cognitive Science Society*, pp. 283–287, Irvine, California: Lawrence Erlbaum Associates, 1985.

Grossman R., Kasif S., Moore R., Rocke D., and Ullman J., Data mining research: Opportunities and challenges, Report of three NSF workshops on mining large, massive, and distributed data, 1999.

Guo Y., and Sutiwaraphun J., Knowledge probing in distributed data mining, In *Proc. 4h Int. Conf. Knowledge Discovery Data Mining* , pp. 61–69, 1998.

Guha S., Rastogi R., and Shim K., CURE: An efficient clustering algorithm for large databases, In *Proceedings of ACM SIGMOD International Conference on Management of Data*, pp. 73–84, New York, 1998.

Gunter S., and Bunke H., Feature selection algorithms for the generation of multiple classifier systems, *Pattern Recognition Letters* 25(11):1323–1336, 2004.

Guyon I., and Elisseeff A., An introduction to variable and feature selection, *Journal of Machine Learning Research* 3:1157–1182, 2003.

Hall M. Correlation-based feature selection for machine learning, University of Waikato, 1999.

Hampshire J. B., and Waibel A., The meta-Pi network — building distributed knowledge representations for robust multisource pattern-recognition, *Pattern Analyses and Machine Intelligence* 14(7):751–769, 1992.

Han J., and Kamber M. *Data Mining: Concepts and Techniques*, Morgan Kaufmann Publishers, 2001.

Hancock T. R., Jiang T., Li M., and Tromp J., Lower bounds on learning decision lists and trees, *Information and Computation* 126(2):114–122, 1996.

Hand D., Data mining — reaching beyond statistics, *Research in Official Stat.* 1(2):5–17, 1998.

Hansen J., Combining predictors. meta machine learning methods and bias/variance & ambiguity decompositions, PhD dissertation, Aurhus University, 2000.

Hansen L. K., and Salamon P., Neural network ensembles. *IEEE Transactions on Pattern Analysis and Machine Intelligence* 12(10):993–1001, 1990.

Hartigan J. A., Clustering Algorithms, John Wiley and Sons, 1975.

Huang Z., Extensions to the k-means algorithm for clustering large data sets with categorical values, *Data Mining and Knowledge Discovery* 2(3), 1998.

He D. W., Strege B., Tolle H., and Kusiak A., Decomposition in automatic generation of petri nets for manufacturing system control and scheduling, *International Journal of Production Research* 38(6):1437–1457, 2000.

He P., Chen L., and Xu X. H., Fast C4.5, *IEEE International Conference on Machine Learning and Cybernetics*, pp. 2841– 2846, 2007.

Hilderman R., and Hamilton H., Knowledge discovery and interestingness measures: A survey, In *Technical Report CS 99-04*, Department of Computer Science, University of Regina, 1999.

Ho T. K., The random subspace method for constructing decision forests, *IEEE Transactions on Pattern Analysis and Machine Intelligence* 20(8):832–844, 1998.

Holmes G., and Nevill-Manning C. G., Feature selection via the discovery of simple classification rules, In *Proceedings of the Symposium on Intelligent Data Analysis*, Baden-Baden, Germany, 1995.

Holmstrom L., Koistinen P., Laaksonen J., and Oja E., Neural and statistical classifiers — taxonomy and a case study, *IEEE Trans. on Neural Networks* 8:5–17, 1997.

Holte R. C., Very simple classification rules perform well on most commonly used datasets, *Machine Learning* 11:63–90, 1993.

Holte R. C., Acker L. E., and Porter B. W., Concept learning and the problem of small disjuncts. In *Proceedings of the 11th International Joint Conference on Artificial Intelligence*, pp. 813–818, 1989.

Hong S., Use of contextual information for feature ranking and discretization, *IEEE Transactions on Knowledge and Data Engineering* 9(5):718–730, 1997.

Hoppner F., Klawonn F., Kruse R., and Runkler T., *Fuzzy Cluster Analysis*, New York: Wiley, 2000.

Hothorn T., Hornik K., and Zeileis A., Unbiased recursive partitioning: A conditional inference framework, *Journal of Computational and Graphical Statistics* 15(3):651–674, 2006.

Hrycej T., *Modular Learning in Neural Networks*, New York: Wiley, 1992.

Hu X., Using rough sets theory and database operations to construct a good ensemble of classifiers for data mining applications, ICDM01, pp. 233–240, 2001.

Hubert L., and Arabie P., Comparing partitions, *Journal of Classification* 5:193–218, 1985.

Hulten G., Spencer L., and Domingos P., Mining time-changing data streams, In *Proceedings of the Seventh ACM SIGKDD International Conference on Knowledge Discovery and Data Mining*, pp. 97–106, 2001.

Hunter L., and Klein T. E., Finding relevant biomolecular features, *ISMB*: 190–197, 1993.

Hwang J., Lay S., and Lippman A., Nonparametric multivariate density estimation: A comparative study, *IEEE Transaction on Signal Processing* 42(10):2795–2810, 1994.

Hyafil L., and Rivest R. L., Constructing optimal binary decision trees is NP-complete, *Information Processing Letters* 5(1):15–17, 1976

Jacobs R. A., Jordan M. I., Nowlan S. J., and Hinton G. E. Adaptive mixtures of local experts, *Neural Computation* 3(1):79–87, 1991.

Jackson J., *A User's Guide to Principal Components*, New York: John Wiley and Sons, 1991.

Jang J., Structure determination in fuzzy modeling: A fuzzy CART approach, In *Proc. IEEE Conf. Fuzzy Systems*, pp. 480–485, 1994.

Janikow C. Z., Fuzzy decision trees: Issues and methods, *IEEE Transactions on Systems, Man, and Cybernetics* 28(1):1–14. 1998.

Jain A. K. Murty M. N., and Flynn P. J., Data clustering: A survey, *ACM Computing Surveys* 31(3):1999.

Jain A., and Zonker D., Feature selection: Evaluation, application, and small sample performance, *IEEE Trans. on Pattern Analysis and Machine Intelligence* 19:153–158, 1997.

Jenkins R., and Yuhas B. P., A simplified neural network solution through problem decomposition: The case of Truck backer-upper, *IEEE Transactions on Neural Networks* 4(4):718–722, 1993.

Jimenez L. O., and Landgrebe D. A., Supervised classification in high-dimensional space: Geometrical, statistical, and asymptotical properties of multivariate data, *IEEE Transaction on Systems Man, and Cybernetics — Part C: Applications and Reviews* 28:39–54, 1998.

Johansen T. A., and Foss B. A., A narmax model representation for adaptive control based on local model, *Modeling, Identification and Control* 13(1):25–39, 1992.

John G. H., Robust linear discriminant trees, In *Learning From Data: Artificial Intelligence and Statistics V*, D. Fisher and H. Lenz (eds.), Lecture Notes in Statistics, Chapter 36, pp. 375–385. New York: Springer-Verlag, 1996.

John G. H., Kohavi R., and Pfleger P., Irrelevant features and the subset selection problem, In *Machine Learning: Proceedings of the Eleventh International Conference*, San Mateo: Morgan Kaufmann, 1994.

John G. H., and Langley P., Estimating continuous distributions in Bayesian classifiers, In *Proceedings of the Eleventh Conference on Uncertainty in Artificial Intelligence*, pp. 338–345, San Mateo: Morgan Kaufmann, 1995.

Jordan M. I., and Jacobs R. A. Hierarchies of adaptive experts. In *Advances in Neural Information Processing Systems*, J. E. Moody, S. J. Hanson, and R. P. Lippmann (eds.), Vol. 4, pp. 985–992, Morgan Kaufmann Publishers, Inc., 1992.

Jordan M. I., and Jacobs R. A., Hierarchical mixtures of experts and the EM algorithm, *Neural Computation* 6:181–214, 1994.

Joshi V. M., On evaluating performance of classifiers for rare classes, *Second IEEE International Conference on Data Mining*, pp. 641–644, IEEE Computer Society Press, 2002.

Kamath C., and Cantu-Paz E., Creating ensembles of decision trees through sampling, Proceedings, 33-rd Symposium on the Interface of Computing Science and Statistics, Costa Mesa, CA, June 2001.

Kamath C., Cant-Paz E., and Littau D., Approximate splitting for ensembles of trees using histograms, In *Second SIAM International Conference on Data Mining* (SDM-2002), 2002.

Kanal L. N., Patterns in pattern recognition: 1968–1974. *IEEE Transactions on Information Theory* IT-20 6:697–722, 1974.

Kargupta H., and Chan P. (eds.), *Advances in Distributed and Parallel Knowledge Discovery*, pp. 185–210, Portland OR: AAAI/MIT Press, 2000.

Kaufman L., and Rousseeuw P. J., Clustering by means of medoids, In *Statistical Data Analysis, based on the L1 Norm*, Y. Dodge (ed.), pp. 405–416, Amsterdam: Elsevier/North Holland, 1987.

Kaufman L., and Rousseeuw P. J., *Finding Groups in Data*, New-York: Wiley, 1990.

Kass G. V., An exploratory technique for investigating large quantities of categorical data, *Applied Statistics* 29(2):119–127, 1980.

Kearns M., and Mansour Y., A fast, bottom-up decision tree pruning algorithm with near-optimal generalization, In *Machine Learning: Proceedings of the Fifteenth International Conference*, J. Shavlik (ed.), pp. 269–277, Morgan Kaufmann Publishers, Inc., 1998.

Kearns M., and Mansour Y., On the boosting ability of top-down decision tree learning algorithms. *Journal of Computer and Systems Sciences* 58(1):109–128, 1999.

Kenney J. F., and Keeping E. S., Moment-Generating and Characteristic Functions, Some Examples of Moment-Generating Functions, and Uniqueness Theorem for Characteristic Functions, x4.6 4.8, In *Mathematics of Statistics*, Pt. 2, 2nd edn. pp. 72–77, Princeton, NJ: Van Nostrand, 1951.

Kerber R., ChiMerge: Descretization of numeric attributes, In AAAI-92, *Proceedings Ninth National Conference on Artificial Intelligence*, pp. 123–128, AAAI Press/MIT Press, 1992.

Kim J. O., and Mueller C. W., *Factor Analysis: Statistical Methods and Practical Issues*, Sage Publications, 1978.

Kim D. J., Park Y. W., and Park D.-J., A novel validity index for determination of the optimal number of clusters, *IEICE Trans. Inf.* E84-D(2):281–285, 2001.

King B., Step-wise clustering procedures, *Journal of American Statistical Association* 69:86–101, 1967.

Kira K., and Rendell L. A., A practical approach to feature selection. In *Machine Learning: Proceedings of the Ninth International Conference*, 1992.

Klosgen W., and Zytkow J. M., KDD: The purpose, necessity and chalanges, In *Handbook of Data Mining and Knowledge Discovery*, W. Klosgen and J. M. Zytkow (eds.), pp. 1–9, Oxford: Oxford University Press, 2002.

Kohavi R., Bottom-up induction of oblivious read-once decision graphs, In *Proc. European Conference on Machine Learning*, F. Bergadano and L. De Raedt (eds.), pp. 154–169, Springer-Verlag, 1994.

Kohavi R., Scaling up the accuracy of naive-bayes classifiers: A decision-tree hybrid, In *Proceedings of the Second International Conference on Knowledge Discovery and Data Mining*, pp. 114–119, 1996.

Kohavi R., Becker B., and Sommerfield D., Improving simple Bayes, In *Proceedings of the European Conference on Machine Learning*, 1997.

Kohavi R., and John G., The wrapper approach, In *Feature Extraction, Construction and Selection: A Data Mining Perspective*, H. Liu and H. Motoda (eds.), Kluwer Academic Publishers, 1998.

Kohavi R., and Kunz C., Option decision trees with majority votes, In *Machine Learning: Proceedings of the Fourteenth International Conference*, D. Fisher (ed.), pp. 161–169, Morgan Kaufmann Publishers, Inc., 1997.

Kohavi R., and Provost F., Glossary of Terms, *Machine Learning* 30(2/3):271–274, 1998.

Kohavi R., and Quinlan J. R., Decision-tree discovery, In *Handbook of Data Mining and Knowledge Discovery*, W. Klosgen and J. M. Zytkow (eds.), Chapter 16.1.3, pp. 267–276, Oxford: Oxford University Press, 2002.

Kohavi R., and Sommerfield D., Targeting business users with decision table classifiers, In *Proceedings of the Fourth International Conference on Knowledge Discovery and Data Mining*, R. Agrawal, P. Stolorz and G. Piatetsky-Shapiro (eds.), pp. 249–253, Portland, OR: AAAI Press, 1998.

Kohavi R., and Wolpert D. H., Bias plus variance decomposition for zero-one loss functions, *Machine Learning: Proceedings of the 13th International Conference*, Morgan Kaufman, 1996.

Kolcz A., Chowdhury A., and Alspector J., Data duplication: An imbalance problem, In *Workshop on Learning from Imbalanced Data Sets* (ICML), 2003.

Kolen J. F., and Pollack J. B., Back propagation is sesitive to initial conditions, In *Advances in Neural Information Processing Systems*, Vol. 3, pp. 860–867, San Francisco, CA: Morgan Kaufmann, 1991.

Koller D., and Sahami M., Towards optimal feature selection, In *Machine Learning: Proceedings of the Thirteenth International Conference on machine Learning*, Morgan Kaufmann, 1996.

Kononenko I., Comparison of inductive and Naive Bayes learning approaches to automatic knowledge acquisition, In *Current Trends in Knowledge Acquisition*, B. Wielinga (ed.), Amsterdam, The Netherlands: IOS Press, 1990.

Kononenko I., SemiNaive Bayes classifier, In *Proceedings of the Sixth European Working Session on Learning*, pp. 206–219, Porto, Portugal: SpringerVerlag, 1991.

Krtowski M., An evolutionary algorithm for oblique decision tree induction, In *Proc. of ICAISC'04*, Springer, LNCS 3070, pp. 432–437, 2004.

Krtowski M., and Grze M., Global learning of decision trees by an evolutionary algorithm, In *Information Processing and Security Systems*, K. Saeed and J. Peja (eds.), Springer, pp. 401–410, 2005.

Krogh A., and Vedelsby J., Neural network ensembles, cross validation and active learning, *Advances in Neural Information Processing Systems* 7:231–238, 1995.

Kuhn H. W., The Hungarian method for the assignment problem, *Naval Research Logistics Quarterly* 2:83–97, 1955.

Kuncheva L. I., Diversity in multiple classifier systems (Editorial), *Information Fusion* 6(1):3–4, 2005.

Kuncheva L., and Whitaker C., Measures of diversity in classifier ensembles and their relationship with ensemble accuracy, *Machine Learning*: 181–207, 2003.

Kusiak A., Decomposition in data mining: An industrial case study, *IEEE Transactions on Electronics Packaging Manufacturing* 23(4):345–353, 2000.

Kusiak A., Rough set theory: A data mining tool for semiconductor manufacturing, *IEEE Transactions on Electronics Packaging Manufacturing* 24(1):44–50, 2001a.

Kusiak A., Feature transformation methods in data mining, *IEEE Transactions on Elctronics Packaging Manufacturing* 24(3):214–221, 2001b.

Kusiak A., and Kurasek C., Data mining of printed-circuit board defects, *IEEE Transactions on Robotics and Automation* 17(2):191–196, 2001.

Kusiak A., E. Szczerbicki, and K. Park, A novel approach to decomposition of design specifications and search for solutions, *International Journal of Production Research* 29(7):1391–1406, 1991.

Langdon W. B., Barrett S. J., and Buxton B. F., Combining decision trees and neural networks for drug discovery, In *Genetic Programming, Proceedings of the 5th European Conference*, EuroGP 2002, Kinsale, Ireland, pp. 60–70, 2002.

Langley P., Selection of relevant features in machine learning, In *Proceedings of the AAAI Fall Symposium on Relevance*, pp. 140–144, Portland, OR: AAAI Press, 1994.

Langley P., and Sage S., Oblivious decision trees and abstract cases, In *Working Notes of the AAAI-94 Workshop on Case-Based Reasoning*, pp. 113–117, Seattle, WA: AAAI Press, 1994a.

Langley P., and Sage S., Induction of selective Bayesian classifiers, In *Proceedings of the Tenth Conference on Uncertainty in Artificial Intelligence*, pp. 399–406. Seattle, WA: Morgan Kaufmann, 1994b.

Larsen B., and Aone C., Fast and effective text mining using linear-time document clustering, In *Proceedings of the 5th ACM SIGKDD*, pp. 16–22, San Diego, CA, 1999.

Lee S., Noisy Replication in skewed binary classification, *Computational Statistics and Data Analysis*, 34, 2000.

Leigh W., Purvis R., and Ragusa J. M., Forecasting the NYSE composite index with technical analysis, pattern recognizer, neural networks, and genetic algorithm: A case study in romantic decision support, *Decision Support Systems* 32(4):361–377, 2002.

Lewis D., and Catlett J., Heterogeneous uncertainty sampling for supervised learning, In *Machine Learning: Proceedings of the Eleventh Annual Conference*, pp. 148–156, New Brunswick, New Jersey: Morgan Kaufmann, 1994.

Lewis D., and Gale W., Training text classifiers by uncertainty sampling, In *Seventeenth Annual International ACM SIGIR Conference on Research and Development in Information Retrieval*, pp. 3–12, 1994.

Li X., and Dubes R. C., Tree classifier design with a Permutation statistic, *Pattern Recognition* 19:229–235, 1986.

Liao Y., and Moody J., Constructing heterogeneous committees via input feature grouping, In *Advances in Neural Information Processing Systems*, S. A. Solla, T. K. Leen and K.-R. Muller (eds.), Vol.12, MIT Press, 2000.

Liaw A., and Wiener M., Classification and regression by random forest, *R news* 2(3):18–22, 2002.

Lim X., Loh W. Y., and Shih X., A comparison of prediction accuracy, complexity, and training time of thirty-three old and new classification algorithms, *Machine Learning* 40:203–228, 2000.

Lin Y. K., and Fu K., Automatic classification of cervical cells using a binary tree classifier, *Pattern Recognition* 16(1):69–80, 1983.

Ling C. X., Sheng V. S., and Yang Q., Test strategies for cost-sensitive decision trees, *IEEE Transactions on Knowledge and Data Engineering* 18(8):1055–1067, 2006.

Liu H., Hsu W., and Chen S., Using general impressions to analyze discovered classification rules, In *Proceedings of the Third International Conference on Knowledge Discovery and Data Mining (KDD'97)*, Newport Beach, California, 1997.

Liu H., Mandvikar A., and Mody J., An empirical study of building compact ensembles, *WAIM*:622–627, 2004.

Liu H., and Motoda H., *Feature Selection for Knowledge Discovery and Data Mining*, Kluwer Academic Publishers, 1998.

Liu H., and Setiono R., A probabilistic approach to feature selection: A filter solution, In *Machine Learning: Proceedings of the Thirteenth International Conference on Machine Learning*, Morgan Kaufmann, 1996.

Liu Y., Generate different neural networks by negative correlation learning, *ICNC* (1):149–156, 2005.

Loh W. Y., and Shih X., Split selection methods for classification trees, *Statistica Sinica* 7:815–840, 1997.

Loh W. Y., and Shih X., Families of splitting criteria for classification trees, *Statistics and Computing* 9:309–315, 1999.

Loh W. Y., and Vanichsetakul N., Tree-structured classification via generalized discriminant Analysis, *Journal of the American Statistical Association* 83:715–728, 1988.

Long C., Bi-decomposition of function sets using multi-valued logic, Eng. Doc. Dissertation, Technischen Universitat Bergakademie Freiberg, 2003.

Lopez de Mantras R., A distance-based attribute selection measure for decision tree induction, *Machine Learning* 6:81–92, 1991.

Lu B. L., and Ito M., Task decomposition and module combination based on class relations: A modular neural network for pattern classification, *IEEE Trans. on Neural Networks* 10(5):1244–1256, 1999.

Lu H., Setiono R., and Liu H., Effective data mining using neural networks, *IEEE Transactions on Knowledge and Data Engineering* 8(6):957–961, 1996.

Luba T., Decomposition of multiple-valued functions, In *Intl. Symposium on Multiple-Valued Logic*, Bloomigton, Indiana, pp. 256–261, 1995.

Lubinsky D., Algorithmic speedups in growing classification trees by using an additive split criterion, *Lecture Notes in Statistics* 89:435–444, 1993.

Maher P. E., and Clair D. C, Uncertain reasoning in an ID3 machine learning framework, In *Proc. 2nd IEEE Int. Conf. Fuzzy Systems*, 1993, p. 712.

Maimon O., and Rokach L., Data mining by attribute decomposition with semiconductors manufacturing case study, In *Data Mining for Design and*

Manufacturing: Methods and Applications, D. Braha (ed.), pp. 311–336, Kluwer Academic Publishers, 2001.

Maimon O., and Rokach L., Improving supervised learning by feature decomposition, *Proceedings of the Second International Symposium on Foundations of Information and Knowledge Systems*, Lecture Notes in Computer Science, pp. 178–196, Springer, 2002.

Maimon O., and Rokach L., Ensemble of decision trees for mining manufacturing data sets, *Machine Engineering* 4(1–2): 2004.

Maimon O., and Rokach L., *Decomposition Methodology for Knowledge Discovery and Data Mining: Theory and Applications*, Singapore: World Scientific Publishing, 2005.

Mallows C. L., Some comments on Cp, *Technometrics* 15:661–676, 1973.

Mangiameli P., West D., and Rampal R., Model selection for medical diagnosis decision support systems, *Decision Support Systems* 36(3):247–259, 2004.

Mansour Y., and McAllester D., Generalization bounds for decision trees, In *Proceedings of the 13th Annual Conference on Computer Learning Theory*, pp. 69–80, San Francisco: Morgan Kaufmann, 2000.

Marcotorchino J. F., and Michaud P., *Optimisation en Analyse Ordinale des Donns*, Masson, Paris.

Margineantu D., and Dietterich T., Pruning adaptive boosting, In *Proc. Fourteenth Intl. Conf. Machine Learning*, pp. 211–218, 1997.

Margineantu D., Methods for cost-sensitive learning, Doctoral Dissertation, Oregon State University, 2001.

Martin J. K., An exact probability metric for decision tree splitting and stopping. An exact probability metric for decision tree splitting and stopping, *Machine Learning* 28(2–3):257–291, 1997.

Mehta M., Rissanen J., and Agrawal R., MDL-based decision tree pruning, *KDD*: 216–221, 1995.

Mehta M., Agrawal R., and Rissanen J., SLIQ: A fast scalable classifier for data mining, In *Proc. If the fifth Int'l Conference on Extending Database Technology* (EDBT), Avignon, France, March 1996.

Melville P., and Mooney R. J., Constructing diverse classifier ensembles using artificial training examples, IJCAI 2003: 505–512.

Meretakis D., and Wthrich B., Extending Naive bayes classifiers using long itemsets, In *Proceedings of the Fifth International Conference on Knowledge Discovery and Data Mining*, pp. 165–174, San Diego, USA, 1999.

Merkwirth C., Mauser H., Schulz-Gasch T., Roche O., Stahl M., and Lengauer T., Ensemble methods for classification in cheminformatics, *Journal of Chemical Information and Modeling* 44(6):1971–1978, 2004.

Merz C. J., Using correspondence analysis to combine classifier, *Machine Learning* 36(1–2):33–58, 1999.

Merz C. J., and Murphy P. M., *UCI Repository of Machine Learning Databases*, Irvine, CA: University of California, Department of Information and Computer Science, 1998.

Michalski R. S., A theory and methodology of inductive learning, *Artificial Intelligence* 20:111–161, 1983.

Michalski R. S., Understanding the nature of learning: Issues and research directions, In *Machine Learning: An Artificial Intelligence Approach*, R. Michalski, J. Carbonnel and T. Mitchell (eds.), Paolo Alto, CA: Kaufmann, pp. 3–25, 1986.

Michalski R. S., and Tecuci G., *Machine Learning, A Multistrategy Approach*, Paolo Alto, CA: J. Morgan Kaufmann, 1994.

Michie D., Problem decomposition and the learning of skills, In *Proceedings of the European Conference on Machine Learning*, pp. 17–31, Springer-Verlag, 1995.

Michie D., Spiegelhalter D. J., and Taylor C .C., *Machine Learning, Neural and Statistical Classification*, Prentice Hall, 1994.

Mingers J., An empirical comparison of pruning methods for decision tree induction, *Machine Learning* 4(2):227–243, 1989.

Minsky M., Logical vs. Analogical or Symbolic vs. Connectionist or Neat vs. Scruffy, In *Artificial Intelligence at MIT, Expanding Frontiers*, Patrick H. Winston (ed.), Vol. 1, MIT Press, 1990. Reprinted in AI Magazine, 1991.

Mishra S. K., and Raghavan V. V., An empirical study of the performance of heuristic methods for clustering, In *Pattern Recognition in Practice*, E. S. Gelsema and L. N. Kanal (eds.), 425–436, 1994.

Mitchell T., *Machine Learning*, McGraw-Hill, 1997.

Mitchell T., The need for biases in learning generalizations, Technical Report CBM-TR-117, Rutgers University, Department of Computer Science, New Brunswick, NJ, 1980.

Moody J., and Darken C., Fast learning in networks of locally tuned units, *Neural Computations* 1(2):281–294, 1989.

Moore S. A., Daddario D. M., Kurinskas J. and Weiss G. M., Are decision trees always greener on the open (source) side of the fence?, *Proceedings of DMIN*, pp. 185–188, 2009.

Morgan J. N., and Messenger R. C., THAID: A sequential search program for the analysis of nominal scale dependent variables, Technical report, Institute for Social Research, Univ. of Michigan, Ann Arbor, MI, 1973.

Muller W., and Wysotzki F., Automatic construction of decision trees for classification, *Annals of Operations Research* 52:231–247, 1994.

Murphy O. J., and McCraw R. L., Designing storage efficient decision trees, *IEEE-TC* 40(3):315–320, 1991.

Murtagh F., A survey of recent advances in hierarchical clustering algorithms which use cluster centers, *The Computer Journal* 26:354–359, 1984.

Murthy S. K., Automatic construction of decision trees from data: A multi-disciplinary survey, *Data Mining and Knowledge Discovery* 2(4):345–389, 1998.

Murthy S. K., Kasif S., and Salzberg S., A system for induction of oblique decision trees, *Journal of Artificial Intelligence Research* 2:1–33, August 1994.

Murthy S., and Salzberg S., Lookahead and pathology in decision tree induction, In *Proceedings of the 14th International Joint Conference on Artificial Intelligence*, C. S. Mellish (ed.), pp. 1025–1031, Paolo Alto, CA: Morgan Kaufmann, 1995.

Naumov G. E., NP-completeness of problems of construction of optimal decision trees, *Soviet Physics: Doklady* 36(4):270–271, 1991.

Neal R., Probabilistic inference using Markov Chain Monte Carlo methods, Tech. Rep. CRG-TR-93-1, Department of Computer Science, University of Toronto, Toronto, CA, 1993.

Ng R., and Han J., Very large data bases, In *Proceedings of the 20th International Conference on Very Large Data Bases*, VLDB94, Santiago, Chile, Sept., VLDB Endowment, Berkeley, CA, 144–155, 1994.

Niblett T., Constructing decision trees in noisy domains, In *Proceedings of the Second European Working Session on Learning*, pp. 67–78, 1987.

Niblett T., and Bratko I., *Learning Decision Rules in Noisy Domains, Proc. Expert Systems* 86, Cambridge: Cambridge University Press, 1986.

Nowlan S. J., and Hinton G. E., Evaluation of adaptive mixtures of competing experts, In *Advances in Neural Information Processing Systems*, R. P. Lippmann, J. E. Moody, and D. S. Touretzky (eds.), Vol. 3, pp. 774–780, Paolo Alto, CA: Morgan Kaufmann Publishers Inc., 1991.

Nunez M., Economic induction: A case study, In *Proceeding of the Third European Working Session on Learning*, D. Sleeman (ed.), London: Pitman Publishing, 1988.

Nunez M., The use of Background knowledge in decision tree induction, *Machine Learning* 6(12.1):231–250.

Oates T., and Jensen D., Large datasets lead to overly complex models: An explanation and a solution, *KDD*:294–298, 1998.

Ohno-Machado L., and Musen M. A., Modular neural networks for medical prognosis: Quantifying the benefits of combining neural networks for survival prediction, *Connection Science* 9(1):71–86, 1997.

Olaru C., and Wehenkel L., A complete fuzzy decision tree technique, *Fuzzy Sets and Systems* 138(2):221–254, 2003.

Oliveira L. S., Sabourin R., Bortolozzi F., and Suen C. Y., A methodology for feature selection using multi-objective genetic algorithms for handwritten digit string recognition, *International Journal of Pattern Recognition and Artificial Intelligence* 17(6):903–930, 2003.

Opitz D., Feature selection for ensembles, In *Proc. 16th National Conf. on Artificial Intelligence*, AAAI, pp. 379–384, 1999.

Opitz D., and Maclin R., Popular ensemble methods: An empirical study, *Journal of Artificial Research* 11:169–198, 1999.

Opitz D., and Shavlik J., Generating accurate and diverse members of a neuralnetwork ensemble. In *Advances in Neural Information Processing Systems*, D. S. Touretzky, M. C. Mozer, and M. E. Hasselmo (eds.), Vol. 8, pp. 535–541, The MIT Press, 1996.

Pagallo G., and Huassler D., Boolean feature discovery in empirical learning, *Machine Learning* 5(1):71–99, 1990.

Panda B., Herbach J. S., Basu S., and Bayardo R. J., Planet: Massively parallel learning of tree ensembles with mapreduce, *Proceedings of the VLDB Endowment* 2(2):1426–1437, 2009.

Pang S., Kim D., and Bang S. Y., Membership authentication in the dynamic group by face classification using SVM ensemble, *Pattern Recognition Letters* 24:215–225, 2003.

Park C., and Cho S., Evolutionary computation for optimal ensemble classifier in lymphoma cancer classification, In *Foundations of Intelligent Systems, 14th International Symposium, ISMIS 2003*, N. Zhong, Z. W. Ras, S. Tsumoto, E. Suzuki (eds.), Maebashi City, Japan, October 28–31, Proceedings. Lecture Notes in Computer Science, pp. 521–530, 2003.

Parmanto B., Munro P. W., and Doyle H. R., Improving committee diagnosis with resampling techinques, In *Advances in Neural Information Processing Systems*, D. S. Touretzky, M. C. Mozer, and M. E. Hesselmo (eds.), Vol. 8, pp. 882–888, Cambridge, MA: MIT Press, 1996.

Pazzani M., Merz C., Murphy P., Ali K., Hume T., and Brunk C., Reducing Misclassification Costs, In *Proc. 11th International Conference on Machine Learning*, 217–225, Paolo Alto, CA: Morgan Kaufmann, 1994.

Pearl J., *Probabilistic Reasoning in Intelligent Systems: Networks of Plausible Inference*, Paolo Alto, CA: Morgan-Kaufmann, 1988.

Peng F., Jacobs R. A., and Tanner M. A., Bayesian inference in mixtures-of-experts and hierarchical mixtures-of-experts models with an application to speech recognition, *Journal of the American Statistical Association* **91**:953–960, 1996.

Peng Y., Intelligent condition monitoring using fuzzy inductive learning, *Journal of Intelligent Manufacturing* 15(3):373–380, 2004.

Perkowski M. A., A survey of literature on function decomposition, Technical report, GSRP Wright Laboratories, Ohio OH, 1995.

Perkowski M. A., Luba T., Grygiel S., Kolsteren M., Lisanke R., Iliev N., Burkey P., Burns M., Malvi R., Stanley C., Wang Z., Wu H., Yang F., Zhou S., and Zhang J. S., Unified approach to functional decompositions of switching functions, Technical report, Warsaw University of Technology and Eindhoven University of Technology, 1995.

Perkowski M., Jozwiak L., and Mohamed S., New approach to learning noisy Boolean functions, In *Proceedings of the Second International Conference on Computational Intelligence and Multimedia Applications*, pp. 693–706, World Scientific, Australia, 1998.

Perner P., Improving the accuracy of decision tree induction by feature pre-selection, *Applied Artificial Intelligence* 15(8):747–760, 2001.

Pfahringer B., Controlling constructive induction in CiPF, In *Proceedings of the seventh European Conference on Machine Learning*, F. Bergadano and L. De Raedt (eds.), pp. 242–256, Springer-Verlag, 1994.

Pfahringer B., Compression-based feature subset selection, In *Proceeding of the IJCAI- 95 Workshop on Data Engineering for Inductive Learning*, pp. 109–119, 1995.

Pfahringer B., Bensusan H., and Giraud-Carrier C., Tell me who can learn you and i can tell you who you are: Landmarking various learning algorithms, In *Proc. of the Seventeenth International Conference on Machine Learning* (ICML2000), pp. 743–750, 2000.

Piatetsky-Shapiro G., *Discovery Analysis and Presentation of Strong Rules*, Knowledge Discovery in Databases, Portland, OR: AAAI/MIT Press, 1991.

Poggio T., and Girosi F., Networks for approximation and learning, *Proc. IEER*, 78(9):1481–1496, 1990.

Polikar R., Ensemble based systems in decision making, *IEEE Circuits and Systems Magazine* 6(3):21–45, 2006.

Pratt L. Y., Mostow J., and Kamm C. A., Direct transfer of learned information among neural networks, In *Proceedings of the Ninth National Conference on Artificial Intelligence*, Anaheim, CA, pp. 584–589, 1991.

Prodromidis A. L., Stolfo S. J., and Chan P. K., Effective and efficient pruning of metaclassifiers in a distributed data mining system, Technical report CUCS-017-99, Columbia Univ., 1999.

Provan G. M., and Singh M., Learning Bayesian networks using feature selection, In *Learning from Data, Lecture Notes in Statistics*, D. Fisher and H. Lenz (eds.), pp. 291–300. New York: Springer-Verlag, 1996.

Provost F., Goal-Directed inductive learning: Trading off accuracy for reduced error cost, AAAI Spring Symposium on Goal-Driven Learning, 1994.

Provost F., and Fawcett T., Analysis and visualization of Classifier Performance Comparison under Imprecise Class and Cost Distribution, In *Proceedings of KDD-97*, pp. 43–48, AAAI Press, 1997.

Provost F., and Fawcett T., The case against accuracy estimation for comparing induction algorithms, In *Proc. 15th Intl. Conf. On Machine Learning*, pp. 445–453, Madison, WI, 1998.

Provost F., and Fawcett T., Robust {C}lassification for {I}mprecise {E}nvironments, *Machine Learning* 42(3):203–231, 2001.

Provost F. J., and Kolluri V., A survey of methods for scaling up inductive learning algorithms, *Proc. 3rd International Conference on Knowledge Discovery and Data Mining*, 1997.

Provost F., Jensen D., and Oates T., Efficient progressive sampling, In *Proceedings of the Fifth International Conference on Knowledge Discovery and Data Mining*, pp. 23–32, 1999.

Quinlan J. R., Learning efficient classification procedures and their application to chess endgames, *Machine Learning: An AI Approach*, R. Michalski, J. Carbonell, and T. Mitchel (eds.), Los Altos, CA: Morgan Kaufman, 1983.

Quinlan J. R., Induction of decision trees, *Machine Learning* 1:81–106, 1986.

Quinlan J. R., Simplifying decision trees, *International Journal of Man-Machine Studies* 27:221–234, 1987.

Quinlan J. R., Decision trees and multivalued attributes, In *Machine Intelligence*, J. Richards (ed.), Vol. 11, pp. 305–318, Oxford, England: Oxford Univ. Press, 1988.

Quinlan J. R., Unknown attribute values in induction, In *Proceedings of the Sixth International Machine Learning Workshop Cornell*, A. Segre (ed.), New York: Morgan Kaufmann, 1989.

Quinlan J. R., *C4.5: Programs for Machine Learning*, Los Altos: Morgan Kaufmann, 1993.

Quinlan J. R., Bagging, Boosting, and C4.5, In *Proceedings of the Thirteenth National Conference on Artificial Intelligence*, pp. 725–730, 1996.

Quinlan J. R., and Rivest R. L., Inferring decision trees using the minimum description length principle, *Information and Computation* 80:227–248, 1989.

Ragavan H., and Rendell L., Look ahead feature construction for learning hard concepts, In *Proceedings of the Tenth International Machine Learning Conference*, pp. 252–259, Los Altos: Morgan Kaufman, 1993.

Rahman A. F. R., and Fairhurst M. C., A new hybrid approach in combining multiple experts to recognize handwritten numerals, *Pattern Recognition Letters* 18:781–790, 1997.

Ramamurti V., and Ghosh J., Structurally adaptive modular networks for non-stationary environments, *IEEE Transactions on Neural Networks* 10(1):152–160, 1999.

Rand W. M., Objective criteria for the evaluation of clustering methods, *Journal of the American Statistical Association*, 66:846–850, 1971.

Rao R., Gordon D., and Spears W., For every generalization action, is there really an equal or opposite reaction? Analysis of conservation law, In *Proc. of the Twelfth International Conference on Machine Learning*, pp. 471–479, Los Altos: Morgan Kaufmann, 1995.

Rastogi R., and Shim K., PUBLIC: A decision tree classifier that integrates building and pruning, *Data Mining and Knowledge Discovery* 4(4):315–344, 2000.

Ratsch G., Onoda T., and Muller K. R., Soft margins for Adaboost, *Machine Learning* 42(3):287–320, 2001.

Ray S., and Turi R. H., Determination of number of clusters in K-means clustering and application in color image segmentation, Monash University, 1999.

R'enyi A., *Probability Theory*, Amsterdam: North-Holland, 1970.

Ridgeway G., Madigan D., Richardson T., and O'Kane J., Interpretable boosted naive bayes classification, In *Proceedings of the Fourth International Conference on Knowledge Discovery and Data Mining*, pp. 101–104, 1998.

Rissanen J., *Stochastic Complexity and Statistical Inquiry*, Singapore: World Scientific, 1989.

Rodriguez J. J., Kuncheva L. I., and Alonso C. J., Rotation forest: A new classifier ensemble method, *IEEE Transactions on Pattern Analysis and Machine Intelligence* 28(10):1619–1630, 2006.

Rokach L., and Kisilevich S., Initial profile generation in recommender systems using pairwise comparison, *IEEE Transactions on Systems, Man, and Cybernetics, Part C: Applications and Reviews* 42(6):1854–1859, 2012.

Rokach L., Chizi B., and Maimon O., A methodology for improving the performance of non-ranker feature selection filters, *International Journal of Pattern Recognition and Artificial Intelligence* 2007.

Rokach L., and Maimon O., Theory and application of attribute decomposition, In *Proceedings of the First IEEE International Conference on Data Mining, IEEE Computer Society Press*, pp. 473–480, 2001.

Rokach L., and Maimon O., Top down induction of decision trees classifiers: A survey, *IEEE SMC Transactions Part C.* 35(3):2005a.

Rokach L., and Maimon O., Feature set decomposition for decision trees, *Journal of Intelligent Data Analysis* 9(2):131–158, 2005b.

Rokach L., Naamani L., and Shmilovici A., Pessimistic cost-sensitive active learning of decision trees for profit maximizing targeting campaigns, *Data Mining and Knowledge Discovery* 17(2):283–316, 2008.

Ronco E., Gollee H., and Gawthrop P. J., Modular neural network and self-decomposition, CSC Research Report CSC-96012, Centre for Systems and Control, University of Glasgow, 1996.

Rosen B. E., Ensemble learning using decorrelated neural networks, *Connection Science* 8(3):373–384, 1996.

Rounds E., A combined non-parametric approach to feature selection and binary decision tree design, *Pattern Recognition* 12:313–317, 1980.

Rudin C., Daubechies I., and Schapire R. E., The dynamics of Adaboost: Cyclic behavior and convergence of margins, *Journal of Machine Learning Research* 5:1557–1595, 2004.

Rumelhart D., Hinton G., and Williams R., Learning internal representations through error propagation, In *Parallel Distributed Processing: Explorations in the Microstructure of Cognition*, Vol. 1, D. Rumelhart, and J. McClelland (eds.), pp. 25–40, Cambridge, MA: MIT Press, 1986.

Saaty X., The analytic hierarchy process: A 1993 overview, *Central European Journal for Operations Research and Economics* 2(2):119–137, 1993.

Safavin S. R., and Landgrebe D., A survey of decision tree classifier methodology, *IEEE Trans. on Systems, Man and Cybernetics* 21(3):660–674, 1991.

Sakar A., and Mammone R. J., Growing and pruning neural tree networks, *IEEE Trans. on Computers* 42:291–299, 1993.

Salzberg S. L., On comparing classifiers: Pitfalls to avoid and a recommended approach, *Data Mining and Knowledge Discovery* 1:312–327, 1997.

Samuel A., Some studies in machine learning using the game of checkers II: Recent progress, *IBM J. Res. Develop.* 11:601–617, 1967.

Saar-Tsechansky M., and Provost F., Decision-centric active learning of binary-outcome models, *Information System Research* 18(1):422, 2007.

Schaffer C., When does overfitting decrease prediction accuracy in induced decision trees and rule sets? In *Proceedings of the European Working Session on Learning* (EWSL-91), pp. 192–205, Berlin, 1991.

Schaffer C., Selecting a classification method by cross-validation, *Machine Learning* 13(1):135–143, 1993.

Schaffer J., A conservation law for generalization performance, In *Proceedings of the 11th International Conference on Machine Learning*, pp. 259–265, 1993.

Schapire R. E., *The strength of Week Learnability, Machine learning* 5(2):197–227, 1990.

Schmitt M., On the complexity of computing and learning with multiplicative neural networks, *Neural Computation* 14(2):241–301, 2002.

Schlimmer J. C., Efficiently inducing determinations: A complete and systematic search algorithm that uses optimal pruning, In *Proceedings of the 1993 International Conference on Machine Learning*, pp. 284–290, San Mateo, CA: Morgan Kaufmann, 1993.

Seewald A. K., and Fürnkranz J., Grading classifiers, Austrian Research Institute for Artificial Intelligence, 2001.

Selim S. Z., and Ismail M. A., K-means-type algorithms: A generalized convergence theorem and characterization of local optimality, In *IEEE Transactions on Pattern Analysis and Machine Learning*, Vol. PAMI-6, No. 1, January, 1984.

Selim S. Z., and Al-Sultan K., A simulated annealing algorithm for the clustering problem, *Pattern Recognition* 24(10):1003–1008, 1991.

Selfridge O. G. Pandemonium: A paradigm for learning, In *Mechanization of Thought Processes: Proceedings of a Symposium Held at the National Physical Laboratory*, November, pp. 513–526, London: H.M.S.O., 1958.

Servedio R., On learning monotone DNF under product distributions, *Information and Computation* 193, pp. 57–74, 2004.

Sethi K., and Yoo J. H., Design of multicategory, multifeature split decision trees using perceptron learning, *Pattern Recognition* 27(7):939–947, 1994.

Shapiro A. D., and Niblett T., Automatic induction of classification rules for a chess endgame, In *Advances in Computer Chess 3*, M. R. B. Clarke (ed.), pp. 73–92, Oxford, Pergamon, 1982.

Shapiro A. D., *Structured Induction in Expert Systems*, Turing Institute Press in association with Addison-Wesley Publishing Company, 1987.

Sharkey A., On combining artificial neural nets, *Connection Science* 8:299–313, 1996.

Sharkey A., Multi-net iystems, In *Combining Artificial Neural Networks: Ensemble and Modular Multi-Net Systems*, A. Sharkey (ed.), pp. 1–30, Springer-Verlag, 1999.

Shafer J. C., Agrawal R., and Mehta M., SPRINT: A Scalable Parallel Classifier for Data Mining, In *Proc. 22nd Int. Conf. Very Large Databases*, T. M. Vijayaraman, A. P. Buchmann, C. Mohan, and N. L. Sarda (eds.), pp. 544–555, San Mateo, CA: Morgan Kaufmann, 1996.

Shilen S., Multiple binary tree classifiers, *Pattern Recognition* 23(7):757–763, 1990.

Shilen S., Nonparametric classification using matched binary decision trees, *Pattern Recognition Letters* 13:83–87, 1992.

Sklansky J., and Wassel G. N., *Pattern Classifiers and Trainable Machines*, New York: SpringerVerlag, 1981.

Skurichina M., and Duin R. P. W., Bagging, boosting and the random subspace method for linear classifiers, *Pattern Analysis and Applications* 5(2):121–135, 2002.

Smyth P., and Goodman R., *Rule Induction using Information Theory*, Knowledge Discovery in Databases, Portland, OR: AAAI/MIT Press.

Sneath P., and Sokal R. *Numerical Taxonomy*, San Francisco, CA: W.H. Freeman Co., 1973.

Snedecor G., and Cochran W., *Statistical Methods*, Ames, IA: Owa State University Press, 1989.

Sohn S. Y., and Choi H., Ensemble based on data envelopment analysis, ECML Meta Learning Workshop, Sep. 4, 2001.

van Someren M., Torres C., and Verdenius F., A systematic description of greedy optimisation algorithms for cost sensitive generalization, In *Advance in Intelligent Data Analysis* (IDA-97), X. Liu, P. Cohen, and M. Berthold (eds.), LNCS 1280, pp. 247–257, 1997.

Sonquist J. A., Baker E. L., and Morgan J. N., Searching for structure, Institute for Social Research, Univ. of Michigan, Ann Arbor, MI, 1971.

Spirtes P., Glymour C., and Scheines R., *Causation, Prediction, and Search*, Springer Verlag, 1993.

Steuer R. E., *Multiple Criteria Optimization: Theory, Computation and Application*, New York: John Wiley, 1986.

Strehl A., and Ghosh J., Clustering guidance and quality evaluation using relationship-based visualization, In *Proceedings of Intelligent Engineering Systems Through Artificial Neural Networks*, 5–8 November St. Louis, Missouri, USA, pp. 483–488, 2000.

Strehl A., Ghosh J., and Mooney R., Impact of similarity measures on web-page clustering, In *Proc. AAAI Workshop on AI for Web Search*, pp. 58–64, 2000.

Tadepalli P., and Russell S., Learning from examples and membership queries with structured determinations, *Machine Learning* 32(3):245–295, 1998.

Tan A. C., Gilbert D., and Deville Y., Multi-class protein fold classification using a new ensemble machine learning approach. *Genome Informatics* 14:206–217, 2003.

Tani T., and Sakoda M., Fuzzy modeling by ID3 algorithm and its application to prediction of heater outlet temperature, In *Proc. IEEE Internat. Conf. on Fuzzy Systems*, March 1992, pp. 923–930.

Taylor P. C., and Silverman B. W., Block diagrams and splitting criteria for classification trees, *Statistics and Computing* 3(4):147–161, 1993.

Therneau T. M., and Atkinson E. J., An introduction to recursive partitioning using the RPART routines, Technical Report 61, Section of Biostatistics, Mayo Clinic, Rochester, 1997.

Tibshirani R., Walther G., and Hastie T., Estimating the number of clusters in a dataset via the gap statistic, Technical Report 208, Dept. of Statistics, Stanford University, 2000.

Towell G., and Shavlik J., Knowledge-based artificial neural networks, *Artificial Intelligence* 70:119–165, 1994.

Tresp V., and Taniguchi M., Combining estimators using non-constant weighting functions, In *Advances in Neural Information Processing Systems*, G. Tesauro, D. Touretzky, and T. Leen (eds.), Vol. 7, pp. 419–426, The MIT Press, 1995.

Tsallis C., Possible generalization of Boltzmann–Gibbs statistics, *J. Stat. Phys.* 52:479–487, 1988.

Tsymbal A., and Puuronen S., Ensemble feature selection with the simple bayesian classification in medical diagnostics, In *Proc. 15th IEEE Symp. on Computer-Based Medical Systems CBMS2002*, Maribor, Slovenia, pp. 225–230, IEEE CS Press, 2002.

Tsymbal A., Puuronen S., and D. Patterson, Feature selection for ensembles of simple Bayesian classifiers, In *Foundations of Intelligent Systems*: ISMIS2002, LNAI, Vol. 2366, pp. 592–600, Springer, 2002.

Tsymbal A., Pechenizkiy M., and Cunningham P., Diversity in search strategies for ensemble feature selection, *Information Fusion* 6(1):83–98, 2005.

Tukey J. W., *Exploratory Data Analysis*, Reading, Mass: Addison-Wesley, 1977.

Tumer K., and Ghosh J., Error correlation and error reduction in ensemble classifiers, *Connection Science, Special Issue on Combining Artificial Neural Networks: Ensemble Approaches* 8(3–4):385–404, 1996.

Tumer K., and Ghosh J., Linear and order statistics combiners for pattern classification, In *Combining Articial Neural Nets*, A. Sharkey (ed.), pp. 127–162, Springer-Verlag, 1999.

Tumer K., and Ghosh J., Robust order statistics based ensembles for distributed data mining, In *Advances in Distributed and Parallel Knowledge Discovery*, H. Kargupta, and P. Chan (eds.), pp. 185–210, AAAI/MIT Press, 2000.

Turney P., Cost-sensitive classification: Empirical evaluation of hybrid genetic decision tree induction algorithm, *Journal of Artificial Intelligence Research* 2:369–409, 1995.

Turney P., Types of cost in inductive concept learning, Workshop on Cost Sensitive Learning at the 17th ICML, Stanford, CA, 2000.

Tuv E., and Torkkola K., Feature filtering with ensembles using artificial contrasts, In *Proceedings of the SIAM 2005 Int. Workshop on Feature Selection for Data Mining*, Newport Beach, CA, pp. 69–71, 2005.

Tyron R. C., and Bailey D. E., *Cluster Analysis*, McGraw-Hill, 1970.

Urquhart R., Graph-theoretical clustering, based on limited neighborhood sets, *Pattern Recognition* 15:173–187, 1982.

Utgoff P. E., Perceptron trees: A case study in hybrid concept representations, *Connection Science* 1(4):377–391, 1989a.

Utgoff P. E., Incremental induction of decision trees, *Machine Learning* 4:161–186, 1989b.

Utgoff P. E., Decision tree induction based on efficient tree restructuring, *Machine Learning* 29(1):5–44, 1997.

Utgoff P. E., and Clouse J. A., A Kolmogorov–Smirnoff metric for decision tree induction, Technical Report 96-3, University of Massachusetts, Department of Computer Science, Amherst, MA, 1996.

Vafaie H., and De Jong K., Genetic algorithms as a tool for restructuring feature space representations, In *Proceedings of the International Conference on Tools with A. I.* IEEE Computer Society Press, 1995.

Valiant L. G., A theory of the learnable, *Communications of the ACM* 1134–1142, 1984.

Van Rijsbergen C. J., *Information Retrieval*, Butterworth, 1979.

Van Zant P., *Microchip Fabrication: A Practical Guide to Semiconductor Processing*, New York: McGraw-Hill, 1997.

Vapnik V. N., *The Nature of Statistical Learning Theory*, New York: Springer-Verlag, 1995.

Veyssieres M. P., and Plant R. E., Identification of vegetation state-and-transition domains in California's hardwood rangelands, University of California, 1998.

Wallace C. S., MML inference of predictive trees, graphs and nets, In *Computational Learning and Probabilistic Reasoning*, A. Gammerman (ed.), pp. 43–66, New York: Wiley, 1996.

Wallace C. S., and Dowe D. L., Intrinsic classification by mml — the snob program, In *Proceedings of the 7th Australian Joint Conference on Artificial Intelligence*, pp. 37–44, 1994.

Wallace C. S., and Patrick J., Coding decision trees, *Machine Learning* 11:7–22, 1993.

Walsh P., Cunningham P., Rothenberg S., O'Doherty S., Hoey H., and Healy R., An artificial neural network ensemble to predict disposition and length of stay in children presenting with bronchiolitis, *European Journal of Emergency Medicine* 11(5):259–264, 2004.

Wan W., and Perkowski M. A., A new approach to the decomposition of incompletely specified functions based on graph-coloring and local transformations and its application to FPGAmapping, In *Proc. of the IEEE EURO-DAC '92*, pp. 230–235, 1992.

Wang W., Jones P., and Partridge D., Diversity between neural networks and decision trees for building multiple classifier systems, In *Proc. Int. Workshop on Multiple Classifier Systems* (LNCS 1857), Springer, Calgiari, Italy, pp. 240–249, 2000.

Wang X., and Yu Q., Estimate the number of clusters in web documents via gap statistic, May 2001.

Ward J. H., Hierarchical grouping to optimize an objective function, *Journal of the American Statistical Association* 58:236–244, 1963.

Warshall S., A theorem on Boolean matrices, *Journal of the ACM* 9:11–12, 1962.

Webb G., MultiBoosting: A technique for combining boosting and wagging, *Machine Learning* 40(2):159–196, 2000.

Webb G., and Zheng Z., Multistrategy ensemble learning: Reducing error by combining ensemble learning techniques, *IEEE Transactions on Knowledge and Data Engineering* 16(8):980–991, 2004.

Weigend A. S., Mangeas M., and Srivastava A. N., Nonlinear gated experts for time-series — discovering regimes and avoiding overfitting, *International Journal of Neural Systems* 6(5):373–399, 1995.

Widmer G., and Kubat M., Learning in the presence of concept drift and hidden contexts, *Machine Learning* 23(1):69–101, 1996.

Witten I. H., Frank E., and Hall M. A., *Data Mining: Practical Machine Learning Tools and Techniques*, Elsevier, 2011.

Wolf L., and Shashua A., Feature selection for unsupervised and supervised inference: The emergence of sparsity in a weight-based approach, *Journal of Machine Learning Research* 6:1855–1887, 2005.

Wolpert D. H., *Stacked Generalization, Neural Networks*, Vol. 5, pp. 241–259, Pergamon Press, 1992.

Wolpert D. H., The relationship between PAC, the statistical physics framework, the Bayesian framework, and the VC framework, In *The Mathematics of Generalization, The SFI Studies in the Sciences of Complexity*, D. H. Wolpert, (ed.), pp. 117–214, AddisonWesley, 1995.

Wolpert D. H., The lack of a priori distinctions between learning algorithms, *Neural Computation* 8:1341–1390, 1996.

Woods K., Kegelmeyer W., and Bowyer K., Combination of multiple classifiers using local accuracy estimates, *IEEE Transactions on Pattern Analysis and Machine Intelligence* 19:405–410, 1997.

Wyse N., Dubes R., and Jain A. K., A critical evaluation of intrinsic dimensionality algorithms, In *Pattern Recognition in Practice*, E. S. Gelsema and L. N. Kanal (eds.), pp. 415–425, Amsterdam: North-Holland, 1980.

Yin W., Simmhan Y., and Prasanna V. K., Scalable regression tree learning on hadoop using openplanet, In *Proceedings of Third International Workshop on MapReduce and its Applications Date*, pp. 57–64, 2012.

Yuan Y., and Shaw M., Induction of fuzzy decision trees, *Fuzzy Sets and Systems* 69(1995):125–139.

Zahn C. T., Graph-theoretical methods for detecting and describing gestalt clusters, *IEEE trans. Comput.* C-20(Apr.):68–86, 1971.

Zaki M. J., Ho C. T., and Agrawal R., Scalable parallel classification for data mining on shared-memory multiprocessors, In *Proc. IEEE Int. Conf. Data Eng., Sydney, Australia*, WKDD99, pp. 198–205, 1999.

Zaki M. J., and Ho C. T., (eds.), *Large-Scale Parallel Data Mining*, New York: Springer-Verlag, 2000.

Zantema H., and Bodlaender H. L., Finding small equivalent decision trees is hard, *International Journal of Foundations of Computer Science* 11(2):343–354, 2000.

Zadrozny B., and Elkan C., Learning and making decisions when costs and probabilities are both unknown, In *Proceedings of the Seventh International Conference on Knowledge Discovery and Data Mining* (KDD'01), 2001.

Zeileis A., Hothorn T., and Hornik K., Model-based recursive partitioning, *Journal of Computational and Graphical Statistics* 17(2):492–514, 2008.

Zeira G., Maimon O., Last M., and Rokach L., *Change Detection in Classification Models of Data Mining, Data Mining in Time Series Databases*, Singapore: World Scientific Publishing, 2003.

Zenobi G., and Cunningham P. Using diversity in preparing ensembles of classifiers based on different feature subsets to minimize generalization error, In *Proceedings of the European Conference on Machine Learning*, 2001.

Zhou Z., and Chen C., Hybrid decision tree, *Knowledge-Based Systems* 15:515–528, 2002.

Zhou Z., and Jiang Y., NeC4.5: Neural Ensemble Based C4.5, *IEEE Transactions on Knowledge and Data Engineering* 16(6):770–773, Jun., 2004.

Zhou Z. H., and Tang W., Selective ensemble of decision trees, In *Rough Sets, Fuzzy Sets, Data Mining, and Granular Computing, 9th International Conference, RSFDGrC*, G. Wang, Q. Liu, Y. Yao, and A. Skowron (eds.), Chongqing, China, Proceedings. Lecture Notes in Computer Science 2639, pp. 476–483, 2003.

Zhou Z. H., Wu J., and Tang W., Ensembling neural networks: Many could be better than all, *Artificial Intelligence* 137:239–263, 2002.

Zimmermann H. J., *Fuzzy Set Theory and its Applications*, Springer, 4th edn., 2005.

Zupan B., Bohanec M., Demsar J., and Bratko I., Feature transformation by function decomposition, *IEEE Intelligent Systems & Their Applications* 13:38–43, 1998.

Zupan B., Bratko I., Bohanec M., and Demsar J., Induction of concept hierarchies from noisy data, In *Proceedings of the Seventeenth International Conference on Machine Learning* (ICML-2000), San Francisco, CA, pp. 1199–1206, 2000.

Index